LABOR
AND COAL

by

ANNA ROCHESTER

INTERNATIONAL PUBLISHERS
NEW YORK

LABOR AND INDUSTRY SERIES

LABOR AND TEXTILES
    By Robert W. Dunn and Jack Hardy
LABOR AND COAL
    By Anna Rochester
LABOR AND LUMBER
    By Charlotte Todes
LABOR AND AUTOMOBILES
    By Robert W. Dunn
LABOR AND SILK
    By Grace Hutchins

Other volumes in this series are planned
on *Steel, Transportation, Construction,
Clothing, Leather and Shoes, Food* and
Tobacco.

CONTENTS

5

CONTENTS

ILLUSTRATIONS

PREFACE TO LABOR AND INDUSTRY SERIES

THIS is one volume in a series of industrial studies being prepared by the Labor Research Association, an organization devoted to the gathering and interpretation of economic material for the labor movement.

The aim of this series is to present a picture of the development of the important American industries in relation to the workers employed in them. Other books dealing with American industries have been written from the viewpoint of the employer, the personnel manager, and the technical expert. But they have all been interested in perpetuating the present system of exploitation and in piling up more profits for powerful corporations.

The present series studies American industries from the worker's viewpoint. What is the trend of production in a given industry? What are the wages, hours, and conditions of employment, and how do these compare with those in other industries? What is the extent of unemployment and what are the prospects of keeping their jobs for those workers still employed? What profits are the companies making, and how are they often concealing them? What mergers are being carried through as the employing class attempts to tighten its control? How are the corporations associated to protect their interests and oppose those of labor? To what extent are the workers already organized in company unions, in the American Federation of Labor, in the new Left Wing unions? What are the prospects for effective unionization? What is the real purpose of the "welfare" and "industrial relations" propaganda of the employers? What can the workers in the industries of the United States look forward to under the present economic system? These are some of the questions this series seeks to answer.

These books describe not only the hardships and grievances of the workers in a given industry. They analyze the class conflicts arising between those who uphold the capitalist system of production and distribution and the workers who are organizing for revolutionary change. Those who seek to put an end to the rule of the employing class will find in these volumes not only graphic pictures of living and working conditions, but an interpretation of economic struggle and suggested programs of action to meet the offensives of the corporations.

To the militant workers who, in the face of overwhelming obstacles, are carrying on the fight against the strongly organized forces of the capitalist class these books are dedicated.

LABOR RESEARCH ASSOCIATION.

PREFACE

AT least 850,000 workers have been permanently frozen out of the coal mining industry in Great Britain, Germany, and the United States in recent years. Some 4,000,000 men, women, and children—or more than the whole population of such a city as Chicago—have been deprived of their livelihood by the changes in coal.

For the workers this is one basic fact which makes coal mining the most important industry in the world. But coal is of primary importance for other reasons.

Coal mining in these greatest coal-producing countries still employs more workers than any other industry except transportation or agriculture: about 900,000 in Great Britain; about 650,000 in the United States; about 570,000 in Germany. France, Belgium and Holland together have nearly half a million. Considerably more than a million are scattered through the other countries in which coal is mined. Roughly we may estimate the total number of coal mine workers in the entire world as over 3,500,000. But year by year these figures will be reduced. More and more coal miners will swell the numbers of the unemployed, for the mechanization of mining and the sharpness of competition for the limited markets for coal are still in their early stages.

To-day the world has a surfeit of coal. The scramble for coal markets is a dangerous element in the international situation. "Coal and politics are inflammable." The passing of the world's need for British coal and British steel is at once a cause and a result of capitalist Britain's decay. The war and the Treaty of Versailles introduced fresh elements in the conflicts of the great coal-producing countries. In the United States coal operators, also facing an overexpanded industry, are talking of increased exports of coal as one factor in the solution of their problem. In so far as they succeed in building up substantial exports, American coal will become an added source of friction between American and British interests.

But in spite of the over-capacity of existing coal mines and the masses of unemployed miners, coal is still of basic importance in modern industry. Even with the increasing use of oil and of water-power, coal remains the most important fuel. Electric power depends chiefly on coal. The steel industry depends on coal and on coke derived from coal. Coal is still the chief railroad fuel. Many of the chemicals used in industry—and in war—are derived from coal. Coal miners are strategically placed. If they were united, class-conscious, and internationally organized, they could take the lead in militant action for the working class. With other workers they could block the plans for imperialist war.

This book analyzes the coal situation in the United States as it affects the mine workers. It takes up such questions as these:

How is the coal problem here different from the coal problem in Great Britain and in Germany?

What is the economic situation of the industry?

What is happening to the miners,—to those thrown out of the industry as well as to those who are still employed?

How can they not only resist the attacks of the operators, but secure the full value that they, as workers, are creating and advance the interests of the whole working class?

CHAPTER I

WHAT IS THE MATTER WITH COAL?

A MINER's son asked his mother, "Why don't you light the fire? It's so cold."

"Because we have no coal. Your father is out of work, and we have no money to buy coal."

"But why is he out of work, Mother?"

"Because there's too much coal."

Like every industry in a profit system, coal mining was developed without a plan. When the market was good and prices were rising many men would open new coal mines. They did not need much capital, for before the days of machine mining, the miners' wages were far and away the largest item in the cost of coal. Loading directly from the tipple into cars or barges for immediate shipment has meant a quick financial return on the output of the mine.

Even in the pre-war years when the demand for coal followed closely the curves of industrial growth, coal operators played exciting games of profit and loss. But pickings were good for the lucky ones. New mines usually outnumbered those that were abandoned and, except after financial panics, each year saw more coal produced and sold than the year before. When times were hard, owners and miners would look hopefully to the upward swing of the business cycle to relieve their difficulties.

"Overdevelopment" or "overexpansion" of coal mining, which is glibly stated as the cause of the present crisis in coal, was chronic in the United States long before the war. Nothing shows this more clearly than the records of part-

11

time operation published by the United States Bureau of
Mines. From 1890 to 1914, the average number of days
that coal mines in the United States were operated during
any year ranged from 178 to 238. In the best years the
average never rose so high as four-fifths of full time. On
the whole, mines were in operation slightly more than two-
thirds of the working year.

This means that even in the pre-war days, coal mines were
drawing into the industry more men than they could steadily
employ. Some hard-boiled open-shoppers blame the unions
for all their difficulties and try to claim that irregularity in
operation has been chiefly due to coal strikes. But other
figures published by the United States Bureau of Mines give
the total of more than 800,000,000 man-days of mine idleness from 1900 to 1913 and assign 11 per cent to strikes and
lockouts and 89 per cent to "no market, car shortage, and
similar difficulties."

This irregularity was much more marked in the United
States than in other coal countries, partly because American
coal reserves were more abundant and more easily tapped than
those in western Europe. It was easier here than elsewhere
to get into the game. Also, industrial life in general was
more flexible than in Great Britain and Germany. The
operator who failed in coal here had a better chance of
elbowing into some other industry than coal operators who
failed in older countries. Rapid expansion of industry in the
United States meant a rising demand. Both the high rate of
increase and the volume of new coal needed in the United
States from year to year encouraged speculative expansion
of coal mining.

For the world as a whole, just as for the United States,
the actual output of coal was rising before the war in fairly
direct ratio to general industrial growth. Iron and steel,
railroads, manufacturing, shipping—all were dependent on
coal. World output of coal rose from 516,000,000 tons in

1890, with the United States producing 28 per cent of the total, to 1,342,000,000 tons in 1913, with the United States producing 39 per cent of this much larger total.

The United States absorbed practically all of its own increasing output. Quite different was the situation in Great Britain and Germany, where a steadily increasing share of the tonnage went into export trade. By 1913, exports were carrying off one-third of the British output and about one-seventh of the German. Meantime French, Belgian, and Russian mines and mines in Japan, India, China, Australia and South Africa were pushing forward.

The stage was already set for future trouble, but the war greatly hastened the crisis.

THE WAR BOOM

For the post-war years the most important fact about coal during the war was the intense speeding-up of this expansion of coal in all non-European countries.

After a general slump in coal production in 1914 and 1915, world output pushed up again until in 1917 it overtopped by 14,000,000 tons the high 1913 level. It was almost as high in 1918 and again in 1920. While British, German, French and Belgian coal mines were unable to approach their 1913 output, the United States increased production from 570,000,000 tons in 1913 to 678,000,000 tons in 1918. Other continents were mining more coal also, and by 1920 the output of Asia, Oceania, and Africa had risen to about 95,-000,000 tons, or more than 8 per cent of that year's total; by 1928 it had risen to over 104,000,000 tons.[1] This is still a small share in the world's output, but the fact of their steady increase is important.

In the United States, feverish wartime activity in iron, steel, munitions and shipping was absorbing most of the increased output of American coal. Exports, as before, went chiefly to Canada, and the net export tonnage rose only from

23,213,000 tons in 1913 to 28,376,000 tons in 1917. Even in 1920, the peak year for export coal, when the brief post-war boom had brought demand for more coal across the ocean than British and European mines could yet supply, exports and foreign bunkers took considerably less than 10 per cent of the coal mined in this country.

It is easy now to forget how great the surplus capacity in American mines was before the war. According to figures published by the United States Bureau of Mines, if the mines that were open in 1913 had operated steadily throughout the year with the machinery then in use and the number of men then employed, they could have produced more than 600,000,000 tons of bituminous coal, or, roughly, about 125,000,000 tons more than they actually did produce in 1913. Anthracite mines also had an excess capacity of some 15,-000,000 tons. This means that with planned production, cutting out excessive seasonal variations, the mines of 1913 could have supplied all the tonnage produced in the peak year, 1918, and still have had a margin of at least 25,000,-000 tons capacity to spare.

But there never has been and never could be planned production under capitalism. Instead the war years brought sudden booms and coal car shortages, with a scramble by consumers to pile up coal for coming weeks; then consumers were caught with large stocks and a cloud of general depression. Both 1918 and 1920 saw four extraordinary months with bituminous coal output pushed to a daily average of more than 2,000,000 tons, while in other months of the same years daily output dropped 25 or 30 per cent below the peak. New mines were brought into operation at the rate of over a thousand a year while some 200 a year were abandoned. Many old mines were equipped with new machinery which greatly increased their capacity. But the irregularities in demand, the variations in grades of coal and in location of mine fields, and acute shortage of coal cars in the busiest weeks, meant at times actual shortage of coal in spite of a rapidly increasing surplus capacity in the mines.

War Profits in the United States

High prices brought high profits to hundreds of coal companies. Their fattest years were 1917, when the market was booming and the speed-up of inflated mine capacity was only beginning, and 1920 when a much greater irregularity of operation was balanced by months of extraordinary prices. In 1918, in spite of price regulation, operators' profits were also far above the average. The United States Coal Commission published in 1925 a mass of material on the subject of war profits in coal mining.

On soft coal companies the clearest summary in their report is given by the income tax returns for the five years, 1917 to 1921, for a group of 1,234 corporations.

BITUMINOUS COAL MINING COMPANIES

	Number of companies reporting		Ratio of net income to invested capital	
			Before Federal tax	After Federal tax
	Net income	Deficit	Per cent	Per cent
1917	1,149	85	26.5	17.3
1918	1,106	128	16.0	8.9
1919	817	417	6.3	5.0
1920	1,152	82	25.1	17.4
1921	503	731	2.6	1.6

In the three boom years, at least 90 per cent of these companies reported a net income. This averaged from 16 to 26 per cent of invested capital, before payment of Federal taxes, and after payment of Federal taxes a clear return averaging from 9 per cent to 17 per cent. The boom was broken by a slump in 1919 and in 1921, and the figures show how much more seriously the profits were affected in the later year.

Anthracite companies had been more profitable than bituminous companies before the war. How the railroad coal companies fared from 1913 to 1922 is summed up in part by the following statements in the Report of the United States Coal Commission:

The surplus of these six companies * rose from $8,700,000 in 1912 to $53,000,000 in 1919. In other words it increased more than five-fold in seven years. In 1920 it decreased slightly, chiefly because of the payment by the Lehigh Valley out of its surplus of a dividend of 134 per cent. In 1921 the combined surplus fell to $37,000,000, chiefly because of the payment out of surplus of another dividend of 227 per cent, this time by the Lehigh and Wilkes-Barre. Other large dividends were paid during the year, notably $2,050,000 by the Hillside, equivalent to 205 per cent on its small capital stock, and $6,850,000 by the Pennsylvania Coal Company, on its capital of $5,000,000.

The Pennsylvania and Hillside companies again, during the strike year, 1922, paid dividends of 168 per cent and 190 per cent, respectively. At the end of the year, 1922, the surplus of the six companies was nearly three times as great as it had been in 1912.

The Delaware, Lackawanna and Western R. R. Co. coal properties were not included in this summary because they were transferred to the Glen Alden company in 1921. But the commission says: "Were the company included, the profits of the industry would appear larger."

The United States Coal Commission made no comparison of war profits in coal with war profits of other industries, but from the gross totals given in the *Income Tax Statistics,* published by the United States Internal Revenue Office, it is clear that coal mining companies (including

---

* Pennsylvania Coal Co., Hillside Coal and Iron Co., Lehigh Valley Coal Co., Coxe Bros. and Co., Inc., Lehigh and Wilkes-Barre Coal Co., Hudson Coal Co. Lehigh Coal and Navigation Company is not included because its income is derived chiefly from transportation, etc. Its earned surplus rose from $1,655,000 in 1912 to $7,467,000 in 1922. For Philadelphia and Reading Coal and Iron Co., see page 244.

bituminous, anthracite, and coke producing) fared exceedingly well during the war and ranked close after shipbuilding, steel, chemicals, oil refining and textiles in their wartime "prosperity."

Continued Expansion

Wartime inflation of prices and profits were drawing into the soft-coal industry more operators, more mines, and more miners. It was widening the unstable speculative fringe. By 1920, there were 6,277 bituminous operators. These did not include the nearly 6,000 owners of wagon mines and "country banks" which produce a few tons a day for local sale and contribute less than one per cent of the total output. But the 6,277 commercial operators did include 2,349 with a yearly output of less than 10,000 tons apiece. At the other extreme were 80 companies, each producing more than 1,000,000 tons and together producing more than one-third of the total.

For the mine workers the war boom brought at first steadier employment than they had ever known. In 1917 and 1918 coal mines in the United States operated on the average 251 and 258 days, but in 1920, with practically the same production, the average of mine operation was only 230 days. Then the depression of 1921 pulled the year's average down to 173 days, the lowest point it had ever reached.

Yet the chaos and madness of expansion continued. The depression of 1921 slowed up the pace and temporarily reduced the number of active mines. But operators still assumed that when industry revived it would bring in a new period of rapidly rising demand for coal, so more old mines were fitted with improved equipment, more new mines were opened, and more and more workers were drawn into coal mining after 1921.

The real turning point in the bituminous industry was

reached in 1923. That year, and not 1920, was the peak year for the number of mines in operation and the average number of miners employed in the United States. During the ten years from 1913 to 1923, the number of bituminous and lignite mines (exclusive of wagon mines and "country banks") had risen from 5,776 to 9,331. Total bituminous mine capacity had risen from around 600,000,000 tons a year to well over 900,000,000 tons a year. Some 133,-000 additional workers had been lured into the industry.

YEARLY COAL PRODUCTION IN THE UNITED STATES (NET TONS)

	Bituminous	Anthracite
1911-1915 average	440,000,000	89,200,000
1916-1920 average	533,800,000	92,700,000
1921-1925 average	481,400,000	77,600,000
1926-1929 average	531,700,000	79,100,000

But in 1923, with capacity to double the pre-war output, the bituminous mines of the United States produced barely 20 per cent more coal than in 1913. Only once again—in 1926, the year of the great British coal strike—has the yearly tonnage risen so far above the 1913 level. Jagged irregularity of production has been characteristic of the post-war period, and the few years of high output —1920, 1923, and 1926—stand out as peaks towering above their neighbors. Never since 1921 and 1922 has the output fallen below the 1913 figure,* and never has it risen to the 1918 peak. Grouping the years, high and low together, we find that the average from 1926 to 1929 was 21 per cent above the average from 1911 to 1915 and 11 per cent above the pre-war peak, 1913.

Anthracite production has been falling below the pre-war level, but the loss in anthracite tonnage has been less than the gain in bituminous output. Demand for coal has not kept pace with the growth in population and industrial activity. The American coal industry, with a surplus ca-

* Preliminary figures for nine months of 1930 indicate an output slightly less than the 1913 output.

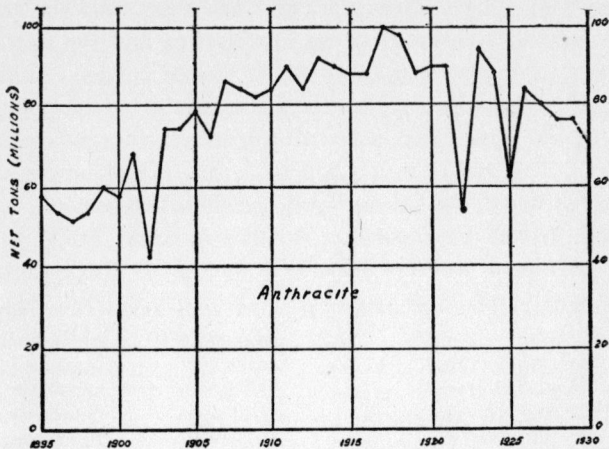

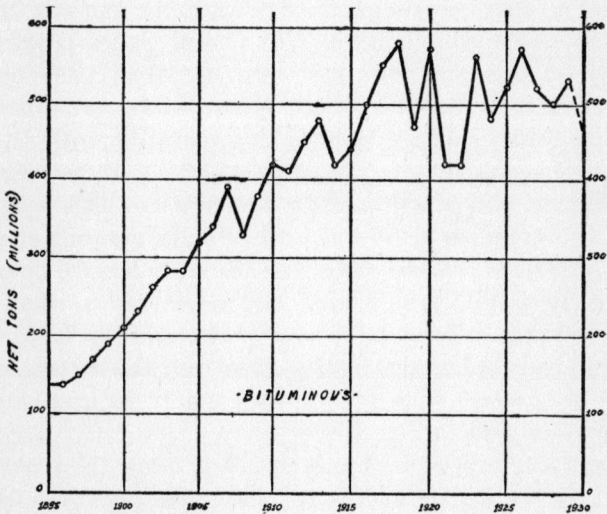

COAL PRODUCTION IN THE UNITED STATES, 1895-1930
(The 1930 figure is a preliminary estimate)

pacity which would have been excessively burdensome even in years of rapidly rising consumption of coal, has faced a practically arrested demand.

Similar situations are found in other countries. World output in coal tonnage has risen somewhat in recent years, not only above the world output of 1913 but above the slightly higher output of 1917. But this foreign tonnage includes a larger amount of lignite than was mined in pre-war years.

In tons the world output of 1928 was about 8 per cent above 1913. In units of heat value it was only 4 per cent above 1913.

WHAT CHECKED THE DEMAND FOR COAL?

Oil and water power have been the most spectacular but by no means the only elements in checking the expected increase in the use of coal. Quite as important are the technical advances in the use of machinery and fuel.

More Energy from Every Ton

Just as machines have been improved and speeded since the war so that they produce more than formerly per worker employed, so machines are producing more per horsepower of energy used. Roughly, but unmistakably, this appears in the fact that from 1919 to 1927 the horsepower installed in American factories and mills increased by 32 per cent while the value added by manufacture increased by 55 per cent. (The "value added" is corrected for changes in wholesale prices.[2]) Along with this mechanical progress has gone the other great technical advance which reduces the amount of fuel required to create each unit of energy.

The story of increasing fuel efficiency goes back to the days when Watt studied the atmospheric engine which burned 30 pounds of coal per horsepower-hour and evolved his steam engine, burning 10 pounds of coal per horsepower-hour. Engineers have worked along on the problem of reducing the fuel needed for each unit of heat or mechanical power, but never from the days of Watt to the World War was their progress, in any ten years, so rapid as it has been since the war.

How great the waste of energy has been appears in *The Case of Bituminous Coal,* by Walton Hamilton and Helen Wright. They give an estimate by the director of the United States Geological Survey, which showed for 1920 the average distribution of each net ton of coal after it reached the tipple.

Of each 2,000 pounds of bituminous coal:

110 pounds were converted into usable mechanical energy.
120 pounds were consumed in transportation of coal.
 18 pounds were lost on the way to the boiler room.
809 pounds represented waste in firing.
942 pounds were lost in exhaust steam and friction.

Fuel efficiency has increased in general with the steady replacement of many small boilers by fewer large boilers which, of course, accompanies the shift of production to larger industrial plants, the increasing use of electric power from central station power houses, and the replacement of small power houses by huge super-power generating stations.

The most striking decrease in fuel consumption per unit of energy is reported by electric utilities in the United States. In 1919 they used on the average 3.2 pounds of coal for each kilowatt-hour, but in 1928 only 1.76 pounds, a decrease of 45 per cent. An expert of the Bureau of Mines points out:

In electric power generation, the average efficiency has not reached its limit. . . . A number of plants are down to 1 pound per kilowatt-hour, and the Columbia Gas and Electric station at Cincinnati has touched a record of 0.85 pound.

Steam locomotive fuel gives a familiar illustration of saving in coal. In 1917 freight locomotives of Class I railroads used 176 pounds of coal per thousand gross-ton miles; in 1929 they used only 121 pounds, a decrease of 31 per cent. Individual locomotives are making records far beyond these averages. Also there is a distinct trend toward saving of railroad coal by electrification. Recent developments in this field include oil-electric locomotives, gas-electric motor-cars for branch services, and high power engines using a distillate fuel in place of gasoline.

Fuel economy in power plants and locomotives is of special importance since railroads and electric utilities together consume more than one-third of the total soft coal used in the United States. According to a press report in June, 1928, E. C. Mahan, then president of the National Coal Association, estimated that the amount of coal used by these two groups would then have been 227,000,000 tons larger but for the increased efficiency in combustion and the development of other sources of power during the last ten years.

The amount of coking coal needed for the making of each gross ton of pig iron was reduced by 15 per cent between 1918 and 1928. At the same time, the by-product coke oven, which is crowding out the old beehive oven, has been saving heat values through the recovery of gas, tar, light oils, and breeze.

Fuel engineers have worked also on the technique of stoking. One firm which had examined hundreds of factory boiler plants reported that "by proper engineering supervision" their thermal efficiency had been raised from an average of 58 per cent to an average of 70 per cent. This meant a saving of 17 per cent in amount of coal required without any change in existing equipment.

The limit to such saving of coal, quite apart from the substitution of other sources of energy, is not yet in sight. After the Second International Bituminous Coal Conference (of technicians) held at Pittsburgh in November, 1928, the following comment appeared in *Coal Age,* chief trade paper of the operators:

. . . The reductions in unit consumption through increasing combustion efficiency have not run their course. Indeed, in the background lurk possibilities of the employment of new boiler mediums, such as di-phenyl and di-phenyl oxide (coal tar products), which would make present reductions in unit consumption seem picayune.

Substitutes for Coal

The 26,000,000 automobiles and motor trucks and buses on the roads of the United States have played an important part in checking the increased use of coal. Railroads reported, for example, that they carried 400,000,000 fewer passengers in 1927 than in 1920.

Oil has become the fuel for all the great navies of the world and for a steadily increasing share of all shipping. Before the war the merchant tonnage using fuel oil was 3 per cent of the world total. In July, 1928, it was 38 per cent of the world total.[3] But the permanent importance of this can easily be overestimated. High prices for oil and low prices for coal could bring a situation where most merchant shipping would return to the use of coal. Successful use of pulverized coal for marine engines has brought the possibility of shifting from oil to coal and back again to oil with less change in equipment than was formerly necessary.

Oil is an important competitor of coal as a fuel for heating. In the United States this affects especially the anthracite trade, since domestic fuel takes more than half the anthracite and only about one-eighth of the bituminous coal used in the United States. So the coal interests feed out propaganda on the safety of coal and the treacherousness of oil while the oil companies boost the simplicity and cleanliness of an oil-fed boiler.

The future of oil is uncertain. At the present rate of exploitation, the known reserves of oil would be exhausted long before the reserves of coal. Already, in Germany, the Dye Trust is making synthetic gasoline from coal by the Bergius Method, and Standard Oil of New Jersey has thought it worth while to acquire the rights to use this process in the United States. The New York *Times* (February 23, 1929) reported from England the successful production of aviation gasoline from coal. Ultimately, no doubt, coal will come into greater demand both as a fuel in itself and as a source for oil. But oil interests are still going strong in their great game of boring new wells and pushing up production, and optimists declare there is no danger of a world shortage of oil for three or four generations. The ultimate scarcity of natural oil will not solve the immediate problem of coal.

Natural gas is an increasingly important rival of coal. Units of energy derived from it in the United States had more than doubled in the ten years from 1919 to 1929.

Water power, which, one hundred and fifty years ago, was the chief source of mechanical energy flared again to a picturesque importance in the American mind with the harnessing of Niagara Falls some thirty years ago. Since then the building of other giant-power hydro-electric stations and the discussion on the control of power from the St. Lawrence, Muscle Shoals, and Boulder Dam have kept the development of water power alive in the news. But public utilities—the chief direct users of water power—still depend on coal for more than half their total power. Of the future, F. G. Tryon of the United States Bureau of Mines says:

The possibilities of water power are limited. It is, indeed, growing faster than coal at present, but it appears unlikely that water power will take over more than a minor part of the total energy burden, and every advance in fuel economy further limits the water-power sites that can economically be developed.

Just how much do oil, natural gas and water power already amount to as competitors of coal? To answer this question we turn again to the annual volume on Coal, published by the United States Bureau of Mines. Here we find the various fuels and sources of power translated into a common measure, the British thermal unit, familiarly known as B.t.u.

DISTRIBUTION OF ENERGY BY SOURCE OF POWER, UNITED STATES
(In trillions of British thermal units)

	1913	1925	1929
Estimated total	17,831	22,827	26,471
Water power	588	1,290	1,929
Natural gas	626	1,278	2,000
Oil	1,593	4,953	6,510
Coal	15,025	15,306	16,032

In 1913, coal contributed 84 per cent of the total thermal units in the United States; in 1929 its share had fallen to 61 per cent. Oil and natural gas had risen from 12 per cent of the total in 1913 to 32 per cent in 1929. Water power had increased from 3.3 per cent to 7 per cent. But meantime, the total use of energy had risen so that although coal's share in this total had fallen, the actual amount of energy derived from coal was above the 1913 level.

THE PRESENT CRISIS

Coal miners were facing special hardships before these post-war changes in fuel and source of power had shaped themselves. Symptoms of crisis had appeared in the coal industry immediately with the collapse of the war boom.

In the United States, even while the number of miners was increasing, unemployment of coal miners began to take on alarming proportions. During the feverish market of 1920, with extraordinary exports, record prices and weeks of coal shortage, bituminous mines were active on the average only 220 days. When the feverish market collapsed and the general industrial stagnation of 1921 set in, American soft-coal miners faced the shortest working year they had ever had. Increases in union wage scales could not cover more than 150 days of idleness.

Abroad the miners' immediate problem in 1919 and 1920 was how to make ends meet on wage rates far below the cost of living. Operators were pushing to restore to the pre-war level the coal output which had slumped in all the European fighting countries, and had fallen farthest in Germany, France, and Belgium. The number of miners at work rose steadily in 1919 and 1920. But wages had not risen to match the fall in their purchasing power and the short boom of 1920 brought a sharp contrast between the high profits of European coal operators and the low pay of their workers.

In Great Britain

British miners were the hardest hit in 1921, when coal prices collapsed and British industry was idle. By November nearly 160,000 British coal miners were unemployed. In Germany and France, on the other hand, the slow upward climb in the output of steel and coal and in the number of miners employed was not interrupted by the crisis which brought cold furnaces, idle mines, and idle workers in Great Britain and the United States.

British coal seemed to recover in the following years. American miners were on strike in 1922 and special exports of British coal were shipped to North America. The Miners' Federation of Great Britain, although affiliated with the United Mine Workers of America, through the International Miners' Federation, did nothing to discourage this scabbing by British miners against their fellow workers across the ocean. British heavy industry and coal exports had another spurt of activity when production stopped in the Ruhr district in 1923. Then British industry slowed down again. British coal met fresh competition from German and Polish coal, and prices began a steady and disastrous fall. By 1925, over 125,000 British miners were unemployed.

The operators demanded a longer working day and reduction of wages. Miners were already down to the so-called standard minimum, but the operators formally insisted that there could be no national wage agreement and no minimum basic wage while, in the same statement, they claimed that 13 per cent of the proceeds from the coal should be credited to profits "irrespective of what the resultant wages proved to be." [4]

The miners were ready to resist, but the wage cut was postponed from August, 1925, to May, 1926, by last-minute measures. The government, hoping that they might somehow pass on to the workers, without a fight, the burden of British industrial decline, promised a subsidy to the coal operators while a royal commission was appointed to investigate and smooth over the conflict. The commission, in the spring of 1926, made a series of futile recommendations. It urged the operators to make a fresh national wage agreement and told the miners that lower wages or a longer day was inevitable.

The great mine strike that began on May 1, 1926, lasted for eight months. At first other British workers backed up the miners' demands by a general strike but the officials of the British Trades Union Congress were startled by their own audacity and called off this effective demonstration of solidarity. They left the miners without the only support which could have brought victory in the most crucial struggle of post-war Britain. The national unions affiliated with the International Miners' Federation sent contributions to the strike fund but the total from all other countries was less than the $5,000,000 given by the workers of the Soviet Union. Left Wing groups in Germany, France, and elsewhere pressed for strike action by miners and transport workers to aid the British miners, but the old line union officials coöperated with employers to speed up production and supply coal for the British markets.

The British miners stood out heroically only to be finally starved into submission. They lost their national agreement with the operators. Hours were lengthened, wages were cut. Since 1926 wages have gone further down and the number of miners at work has continued to dwindle. By the end of 1929 over 300,000 men had been eliminated from the industry.

The Coal Mines Bill of the Labor Government (1930) attempts to strengthen the position of British coal operators against their competitors in the export market. It proposes combines and cartels to prevent price cutting in the British market. It encourages increased investment of private capital for mechanizing and cheapening production. These schemes are planned to benefit the operators; they carry a threat of still greater mass unemployment, wage-cutting and speed-up for the workers.

In Germany

Germany lost under the Treaty of Versailles territory in which one-fourth of the German tonnage had been mined before the war. France was given a long-term control of the Saar district, while reparation deliveries of coal were required from mines still in German territory to France, Belgium, Luxemburg, and Italy. Poland, industrially undeveloped, was presented with German coal territory in Upper Silesia and thus invited to join in the competition for export trade.

These treaty provisions, instead of permanently crippling German industry, stimulated the development of German coal. During the war, German technicians had been working out new uses for lignite, or sub-bituminous coal, and the output of lignite had been pushed above the pre-war level. With the loss of rich bituminous fields, the intensive exploitation of Germany's lignite resources became even more important.

When the French came in, the Ruhr coal owners, with the approval of the German government, stopped production of coal. Their miners were left to starve on small special allowances which trailed far behind the collapsing currency, while the powerful companies of the German coal syndicate were sweeping off their old funded debts and reorganizing for the drive to rationalize the mines. It has been claimed that even during 1923 they were beginning to reconstruct their mines, using workers paid by the government's subsidy for the special allowances. However that may be, the fact remains that since 1923 an increase in machine mining and increasing output of coal with a steady reduction in the number of miners have been the outstanding facts in the German coal industry.

Decline in employment was interrupted only in the fall and winter of 1926-27 when German miners were digging coal for the British market and for European industries which were especially active because of the British strike. The crisis in German coal has been primarily a workers' crisis. The operators feel the pressure of low prices as German, Polish, and British producers bid fiercely against one another. But the German companies are few, powerful, and closely organized. Thus far they have succeeded in passing on most of the burden to the workers.

More than one-third of the coal miners employed in 1922—the year with the largest numbers enrolled in the German coal industry—now have no place in the mines. In the Ruhr district alone the total number of insured workers in coal mining had fallen by July, 1930, from an average of 545,000 to about 330,000. In the German lignite fields more than 90,000 men had been crowded out in the drive for rationalization.

Sharper Competition Ahead

The total output of German mines is still slightly below the output of all the mines which were in Germany before the war. But for the general European coal situation it is more important to note that mines in the five countries— Germany, France, Poland, Belgium and Netherlands—produced in 1928 nearly 40,000,000 tons more than in 1913, while the output of British coal fell by over 50,000,000 tons. (For this comparison nine tons of lignite are reckoned as two tons of coal.) Competition between British coal and continental coal will be increasingly sharp as further mechanization pushes up the capacity of the mines. Unless the miners of all countries unite for aggressive, militant resistance, the lowest prices, the lowest wages, and the longest days will pull down the standards everywhere. More tens of thousands of miners will be thrown out of work.

British and continental coal have competed since the war, with results disastrous to the miners, much as the competition of non-union West Virginia and Kentucky coal has helped to bring disaster to the miners of the northern fields in the United States. British workers were better paid before the war than the German and the French. Post-war years have brought a steady increase in total European mine capacity without a corresponding increase in markets for coal. Sharp price competition has pulled the better paid districts down to the lowest levels.

But the comparison must not be pushed too far. The British coal industry has in addition to all its other difficulties the high costs peculiar to very old mines, with deep shafts and thin seams. The German coal industry is burdened with heavy taxation and with sharp competition from Britain and Poland but, unlike the coal industry in any other important coal country, it is one of the most closely knit capitalist syndicates in the world.

In no soft coal field in the United States is there a syndicate comparable to the German. And no field here offers as yet so high a proportion of worn-out, high-cost workings as there are in Great Britain. There has been no Treaty of Versailles and no Dawes Plan artificially stimulating over-development in the United States.

THE UNDERLYING STRUGGLE

In spite of differences peculiar to each country and each industry, the underlying process of capitalist development is everywhere the same: chaotic over-expansion of the capacity to produce; a struggle for markets; price-cutting; reduction of labor costs; technical improvements displacing workers and constantly increasing the capacity to produce; renewed struggle for markets; further price-cutting and sharper competition with capitalists combining in stronger groups and squeezing out the small producers; more technical improvements; more capacity to produce; aggressive attack on workers' organizations to prevent resistance as unemployment increases; more price-cutting; more debasing of workers' standards; more machinery; more capacity to produce—this is the typical round of capitalist industry.

Every capitalist industry is headed toward mass unemployment and ultimately a condition of long drawn out crisis when swollen capacity to produce and saturated markets reduce the profits of the capitalist class. The world-wide economic crisis of 1929-1930 reflects such a situation in many industries besides coal. But the coal industry had reached the crisis stage, even in the United States, long before the general "prosperity" had collapsed. What special conditions had been peculiar to coal?

1. Speculative irregularities in the market and relatively small necessary capital had brought acute overdevelopment

of capacity in coal mining while technical and financial organizations were comparatively backward.

2. Arrested demand for coal hit the overdeveloped industry in Great Britain and the bituminous fields of the United States before the mine owners had built up their defenses with mergers and large combinations.

3. While attempting to adjust to an average demand far below the top peak of war boom production, the coal industry has suffered from great irregularities in demand. For three reasons these have been sharper since the war than they used to be: The substitutes for coal tend, on the whole, to replace the steadier market and to increase the proportionate share of coal output which is especially affected by seasonal and general industrial variations. General industrial activity has been more uncertain from year to year since the war. And the fact that struggles of the miners to resist attacks on their unions and working conditions have not been fought on the international scale has led to spurts of false prosperity in other countries while each national struggle was on.

4. The crisis of arrested demand in an overexpanded industry hit coal before the modern technique of mining had been brought into general use. Competing operators resort to mechanization as a weapon with which to fight one another, but every new mining machine that is installed further increases the capacity of the mines. It increases the difficulties of operators with small capital and backward equipment. It throws more miners out of work. The coal industry in Germany and the United States—and to a less degree in Great Britain—is making an extraordinarily rapid transition from handicraft to complicated machinery. By itself the very speed of the change would sharpen the fight between large and small units of capital and would involve a crisis of unemployment for the miners. But coming, as it does, in an industry where producing capacity had already far out-

stripped an arrested demand rationalization becomes itself one of the major factors in the present disaster.

Coal miners, thrown from their jobs by the hundreds of thousands, go out into a world where other industries are also mechanizing and rationalizing with a relentless drive. The miners are simply the largest single group among the increasing millions who are unemployed.

These jobless masses and the workers who are still able to cling to their vanishing jobs face an increasingly hostile employing class. As the conflict grows sharper among great units of capital and operating groups fight for their own survival, they will try to pass on to the workers the cost of their battles. They have been perfecting the machinery of state and corrupting the union leaders in their determination to prevent resistance from the working class.

From this sketch of the great trends in coal, let us turn now to fill in the picture of coal in the United States. In spite of the crisis a good many investors are making money out of coal. And in spite of the hostile drives of the employing class and the corruption of reactionary union officials, the coal miners are preparing for fresh struggles to protect themselves.

CHAPTER II

PROFITS, INTEREST, AND ROYALTIES

In spite of the present crisis in coal, thousands of coal-mining investors are still drawing a return on their money. In the competitive struggle of capitalism, companies in an industry normally range from those at one extreme, making high profits, to those at the other extreme, on the verge of bankruptcy or already operating in receivership. The American coal industry, overtaken by permanent crisis before it had reached the stage of trusts and centralized financial control, clearly shows these sharp variations. Relatively few companies are reporting profits, many are approaching bankruptcy, while the great mass of operators hover between these two extremes.

But "profits" in the strict capitalist sense of the word greatly understate the amounts which the capitalist class draws from an industry. And it is peculiarly true in coal that the "profits" of coal mining companies in the United States give no adequate picture of the financial strength of the forces lined up against the coal miners.

How some investors are making money in coal, through "profits" and otherwise, is shown in this chapter.

Fixed Charges

Various "fixed charges," so-called, must be met from the operating margin of a company before the reckoning of profits. A company operating no business except the mining of coal must meet its fixed charges from the difference between its income from the sale of coal (sales realization) and the cost of its operations, or it cannot survive indefinitely.

34

And unless this operating margin is great enough to cover fixed charges and leave a balance to spare, the company is making no profit.

These fixed charges, which are not reckoned as profits, consist chiefly of amounts which sooner or later go back into the pockets of the capitalist class. Countless companies are thus making a financial return to certain investors even though they have no profits from which to pay dividends to their stockholders. Also these charges are by no means so fixed as the financial world pretends that they are. It is here that figures are often juggled to conceal the true condition of a company.

Certain fixed charges are of special importance in analyzing the condition of a coal company, or in considering the income which coal mining returns to the capitalist class: royalties and rents, depletion and depreciation, and interest on bank loans, mortgages and bonds.

Royalties and Rents

Mining companies operating under lease must pay so much a ton as royalty to the owner of the land. If the mine shaft and equipment are also leased, the operating company must pay rent in addition to royalty on the tonnage mined. Coal operators in the United States paid in 1919 more than $34,-000,000 in royalties and rents, according to the Census of Mines and Quarries. Pennsylvania alone showed royalties of about $6,000,000 on bituminous coal and nearly $12,000,000 on anthracite. West Virginia ran ahead of Pennsylvania in the tonnage of bituminous on which royalties were paid. With a slightly lower average rate per ton, the West Virginia royalties also totaled about $6,000,000.

Just about one-third of the anthracite and slightly over one-third of the bituminous coal mined in 1919 was taken from lands leased and not owned by the operator. The royalty payment varies considerably in amount, but the census showed for 1919 an average of 44 cents a ton on anthracite and 12 cents a ton on bituminous coal. These averages apply only to the tonnage mined under lease.

How these royalties are divided—how much goes directly into the pockets of individual landowners and how much goes into the treasury of landowning corporations—the census does not show. The United States Coal Commission in 1923 gathered a mass of material on royalties but analyzed only that relating to anthracite.

So far as bituminous coal is concerned we do know, however, that great land companies, subsidiary to the Norfolk and Western Railway and the Chesapeake and Ohio Railway, take toll in the form of royalties on much of the tonnage mined in southern West Virginia. Thus the Pocahontas Coal and Coke Company (of the Norfolk and Western) owns 300,000 acres including some lands over the line in Virginia and receives well over a million and a half in royalties each year. This company and the Crozer Land Association (dominated by Philadelphia financial interests) between them drew royalties from 95 per cent of the twenty million tons shipped from the Pocahontas field in 1920. The Western Pocahontas Corporation (of the Chesapeake and Ohio) owns over 30,000 acres in southern West Virginia.[1]

Individuals also draw royalties on large coal properties. For example, it came out during the Senate hearings on coal in the spring of 1928 that one Judge Lazelle (who had decided against the union in a case involving the United Mine Workers and a Paisley company) was receiving an income of 20 cents a ton, with a minimum of $60,000 a year guaranteed to himself and his family from their personal holdings in coal lands leased to Paisley in northern West Virginia.[2]

One of the important landowners in the anthracite is the Girard Estate, a charitable trust in Philadelphia. In 1914 the trustees drafted fifteen-year contracts providing that companies operating under lease with this estate should no longer pay a flat rate per ton but instead a sliding scale royalty, related to the price of anthracite. With the tremendous increase in prices during the war, the royalties received by the Girard Estate had risen to an average of $1.27 a ton on the 2,983,723 tons mined in 1921 from its lands in Schuylkill County. One operator told the United States Coal Commission that in 1921 he had paid another estate an average royalty of $1.50 a ton. Anthracite prices have been even higher since 1921 and sliding scale royalties have continued to furnish a royal income to certain coal-land owners. When the former contracts of the Girard Estate expired, *Coal Age* announced (June, 1929), that the royalty was reduced from $1.36 to *only* 70 cents a ton.

Royalties on anthracite are paid chiefly by the so-called "independent" operators. At least 70 per cent of their output is mined from land which they lease, while among the "railroad" companies the great bulk of the output comes from lands which they own.[3]

Depletion and Depreciation

The operating company which owns the coal its miners are taking out of the ground carries a depletion reserve. Owners and investors in coal companies not only expect to receive an income year by year from their invested capital but, finally when the coal reserves of the company are exhausted, they can legally expect, under capitalism, to get back at least the full amount of the principal itself. So the company sets aside each year an amount credited to depletion reserve and thus builds up a fund which, in theory, is related to the value of the coal lands and the reduction in value due to the removal of coal.

Depreciation reserves are set aside in the same way for the replacement of buildings, machinery, and equipment. A moderate, fairly estimated depreciation reserve is a reasonable charge. But depletion reserves, like royalties and rents which go into the pockets of individuals and private corporations, are not socially necessary and would cease to exist with the passing of capitalism. Depletion and depreciation are frequently lumped together in the published reports of the coal companies. Both funds are "fixed charges" taken out from the companies' earnings before "profits" are computed.

Depletion is supposed to represent, as we have said, that share of the total value of the company's coal reserves which the year's output has destroyed. But what value shall the company put on its total coal reserves? The United States Coal Commission report describes four ways of estimating value of reserves and after discussing the difficulties and defects in each method arrives at no solution of this capitalist problem. In actual practice the policy, both as to total value and the writing off of depletion, varies widely.

Pittsburgh Coal Company, for example, carries its "coal lands, etc." (apart from "plants and equipment") at a book value of about $107,000,000. Consolidation Coal Company with coal reserves at least as large as the reserves of Pittsburgh Coal Company and probably larger, carries "coal lands and other real estate" (as distinct from "mining plants, equipment, etc.") at a book value of only about $40,000,000. These two companies write off approximately the same amount of depreciation year by year, but very different sums for depletion. Pittsburgh Coal, with a production of 13,378,-304 tons in 1929, charged off $1,437,500 for depletion, while Consolidation Coal, the same year, reported 13,657,000 tons mined from its lands and charged off only $336,962 for depletion.

The years of war profits and heavy Federal taxes saw a general writing up of valuations and a marked increase in the amounts set aside for depletion reserves, since a high value set on capital assets and the charging off of a correspondingly high depletion reserve make "profits" look small and reduce the amount of Federal income tax. On the other hand, setting a low valuation on reserves helps to keep down the local taxes levied on coal lands.

But taxes are not the whole story. If the company wants to increase its stock or float a bond issue, it must have a presentable property value. So it frequently happens that values of coal reserves have been overstated to serve as bait for stockholders or as mortgage security for bonds.

Interest

Most companies use borrowed money representing at least two different kinds of loans. The interest which must be paid on all loans is reckoned either as a fixed charge or an operating expense, and although much of it goes directly into the pockets of investors it is quite distinct from the "profits" from which dividends are paid to stockholders. The wage-earner, however, who must work for his income, knows that the capitalist distinction between interest and profits is far less important than the basic difference between wages paid for his labor and any kind of return on invested capital.

Cash advances for payment of wages and other immediate expenses are commonly borrowed from commercial banks. Such cash loans of "working capital" are usually secured only by the general credit of the company and granted in amounts small in relation to its total assets. How much the company owes at the close of the year for the repayment of such loans is usually shown on its published balance sheet, but this may or may not be typical of the average amount borrowed from banks throughout the year. Companies seldom report in the summaries available to the public how much interest they have paid on bank loans in the course of the year; sometimes it is lumped with other operating expenses, sometimes it is lumped with other interest as a "fixed charge."

The lending of working capital is one of the chief functions of commercial banks and a source of great profit to the owners of bank stocks. Coal operators in 1919, a bad coal year, paid in wages, salaries and other expenses, upwards of $1,300,000,000, or, on the average, some $25,000,000 a week. Much of this current expenditure was met by short-term loans from commercial banks, but just how much it is impossible to estimate.*

More important is the so-called "funded debt," represented by mortgages and by bonds sold to investors through investment bankers and brokers. The bonds of a coal-mining company are usually secured by a mortgage on the property, with an agreement also to set aside some definite amount for each ton of coal taken out of the property as a special so-called "sinking fund" distinct from other depletion reserves. Bond interest and such "sinking fund" reserves must be met or the bondholders get together and demand reorganization of the company, foreclosure of the mortgage or bankruptcy proceedings. So, even in a depressed industry, like coal, countless companies which pay no dividends to their stockholders, are still paying regularly the interest on mortgages and outstanding bonds. This interest goes directly into the pockets of the capitalist class. Besides that, every time a new bond issue is floated the investment bankers who help the company reach individual investors take a tidy commission for themselves.

Over one-fifth of the total investment in coal mining and in undeveloped coal reserves is represented by mortgages

* Capital stock returns in United States Internal Revenue Office report on Statistics of Income for 1925, showed for 3,793 coal mining companies (including coke producers and peat) a total of $194,500,000 notes payable, as reported in balance sheets filed for fiscal year 1925-1926.

and bonded indebtedness.[4]   In 1926 the total interest paid
by 3,679 coal-mining companies on notes, mortgages, and
bonds was close to $40,000,000. This item had steadily in-
creased since 1922 when, for a larger number of companies, it was $32,400,000.[5] This figure somewhat under-
states the real total for the industry since it does not include
companies producing coal solely for use in their own steel
mills or other plants. Neither does it include the small percentage of coal from mines owned by individuals and partnerships.

A very few companies—notably Island Creek Coal Company and Westmoreland Coal Company—are operating with
no funded debt whatever. Their whole balance remaining
after depletion, depreciation, and taxes, is available for
profits. At the other extreme are the operating companies
burdened with interest on bonds which are secured by undeveloped coal reserves held for operation in some far-
distant future. More common than either are the companies carrying a funded debt secured by an inflated valuation of their operating properties and meeting an interest
charge which left a "satisfactory" profit in the good years
but drains off all or more than all of the operating margin
when coal prices are low and production highly irregular.

The thirst for interest and profits on inflated capital
values has been one important factor in the drive for reducing operating costs at the expense of the mine workers.

Undeveloped Coal Reserves

While the companies owning huge undeveloped coal reserves are comparatively few, they are of great importance
in the general situation. They are strategically placed for the
future. Their efforts to cover, from the returns on coal
mined and sold year by year, the cost of carrying coal reserves good for 100 or 200 years to come places such an
unfair burden on their operating margin that it called forth

criticism from such conservative bodies as the Federal Trade Commission and the United States Coal Commission.

Excess coal reserves were defined by the Federal Trade Commission (1922) as "reserves in excess of the quantities necessary to supply the respective mines for their normal life on the scale of their present production. In many instances reserves are sufficient to last the companies at their present scale for 100 years and sometimes much longer. In the main they consist of undeveloped lands that cannot be mined from the present shafts or with the other present mining improvements or equipment." [6] The United States Coal Commission set coal reserves for 40 years to come as the approximate maximum that a company should expect to carry from its current operating margin.

Six of the 32 anthracite companies whose books were examined by the Coal Commission (1924) had reserves—either owned or held under long-term lease—which at the current rate of production would last more than 100 years. Ten others among these 32 companies owned or controlled coal reserves good for less than 100 but more than 40 years. The outstanding example of companies with excessive reserves of coal lands is, of course, the Philadelphia and Reading Coal and Iron Company, which owns about one-third of the unmined anthracite in Pennsylvania and at the average post-war rate of production would be mining coal from its present coal beds in the year 2,150, with reserves still good for a more distant future.

Few of the several thousand bituminous coal companies have such huge reserves and the Coal Commission report gives no information on this point. But we know from financial statements that the largest owner of bituminous coal reserves is the United States Steel Corporation with its 800,-000 acres of coal lands, including some 63,000 acres controlled under long-term lease. Consolidation Coal Company,

Elk Horn Coal Corporation, Pittsburgh Coal Company, and Peabody Coal Company are among those reporting reserve tonnage or coal acreage good for 100 years or more at their present rate of production, while several companies report smaller coal reserves which would last well beyond forty years.

Some Companies That Pay No Dividends

How strong financially a company may be, even when it is paying no dividends, will be most clearly shown, perhaps, by a glance at the figures for three leading coal producers, one in the anthracite and two bituminous companies.

Hudson Coal Company

The Hudson Coal Company, third largest anthracite producer, was manipulated in 1927 in a way which illustrates perfectly how fixed charges can vary and how a money-making corporation can show a loss instead of a profit. Up to 1926 it was paying about $1,200,000 a year in dividends to the Delaware and Hudson Company on its $17,748,250 of stock, all owned by the D. and H. The coal company had no funded debt and was writing off depletion at about $200,000 a year. In 1927, the valuation of the "coal lands, real estate and equipment" was raised from about $13,000,-000 to over $60,000,000, so that a $35,000,000 bond issue might be floated to raise cash for the Delaware and Hudson Company to buy stock in other railroads. This has entirely changed the balance in the coal company's income account.

The total income in 1928 was some $880,000 less than in 1926 but this does not account for the shift from a $2,192,-217 "profit" to a $1,416,458 "loss." Depletion was written off in 1928 at $1,483,054 instead of $214,346. The new bond issue brought the interest item up from $277,550 to

HUDSON COAL COMPANY INCOME ACCOUNT[7]

	1928	1926
Operating Income	$1,704,083	$2,081,370
Other Income	425,948	932,743
Total Income	2,130,031	3,014,113
Fixed charges reported:		
Depletion	1,483,054	214,346
Interest	2,063,435	277,550
Federal taxes	....	330,000
Total Charges	3,546,489	821,896
Loss	1,416,458	....
Profit	....	2,192,217
Dividends	....	1,215,427
Added to surplus	....	976,790

over $2,000,000. In the earlier year, fixed charges of about $800,000 were deducted from an income of $3,000,000. But in 1928 the higher interest and depletion had raised the fixed charges to over $3,500,000, or half a million more than the income of 1926 and nearly $1,500,000 more than the income of 1928. So the company, with a total income of over $2,000,000, now reports a "loss" instead of a "profit." But note that in spite of the "loss" the coal company turned back to the capitalist class in interest in 1928 a larger sum than it had paid in dividends in 1926. For 1929, the company reported a total income of $4,128,124, and a net profit of $651,224, but paid no dividends.

This is not the whole story. While the coal company was pleading hard times and putting through various economy measures which earned the bitterest resentment from its more than 20,000 mine workers, the Delaware and Hudson Company was reaping high profits from the capital raised through the bond issue of its coal subsidiary. After a few months it sold to the Pennsylvania Railroad the stock in the Lehigh Valley and Wabash Railroads, clearing more than $20,000,000 in the deal. Then it began lending some $50,000,000 in the call-money market which supplies the daily credit for stock speculation, and the *New York Times,* in analyzing the annual report of the Delaware and Hudson Company in April, 1929, pointed out that "call rates stiffened in 1928 and recently reached a high level of 20 per cent." So while the Hudson Coal Company was showing a "loss" of $1,400,000, the parent Delaware and Hudson Company—largely through the use of capital raised by the coal company bonds—increased its income and "earned" in 1928 over $6,300,000 net, or more than $12 a share.*

Pittsburgh Coal Company

During the fat war years and the boom of 1923, Pittsburgh Coal Company made large profits in the strict capitalist sense of the word. Besides paying regular dividends the company allowed profits to accumulate in a surplus which at the end of 1923 stood at over $33,000,000. Since 1925 no dividends have been declared and surplus from accumulated profits has been reduced to *only* $8,000,000. The company was well able to go through a period of "loss" while it was breaking the union and not only to meet its "fixed charges" but to report that "in the past four years $12,000,-000 have been invested in mines, electrical and mechanical equipment, cleaning plants and rehabilitation of mining towns." [8]

But the "net loss" which the company reported in each of the four years from 1925 through 1928, and which in 1926 amounted to over $2,000,000 does not mean that the company was making no income from its operations. Operating expenses reported for these four years evidently include the outlay for technical improvements—averaging, as we have just noted, about $3,000,000 a year. In spite of this special

* For a similar analysis of Philadelphia and Reading Coal and Iron Company see page 244.

expenditure, the "net revenue," after operating expenses were subtracted from gross receipts, was as much as $3,-119,000 even in the company's "poorest" year, 1926. In 1928, the net revenue was over $5,500,000. This income, however, has been too small since 1925 to cover the taxes on coal reserves good for a century to come, high charges for depletion and depreciation, and interest on funded debt. So the company claimed for 1928 a "net loss" of $493,871.

Fixed charges were further increased in January, 1929, when a new $20,000,000 bond issue added over a million dollars a year to the interest payments on funded debt. Meantime wage cuts and speed-up were bringing "satisfactory" results. In spite of the increase in fixed charges and the low prices for coal, the company reported a net profit of $15,592 in 1929.

Consolidation Coal Company

Consolidation Coal Company has been in a similar situation, declaring no dividends since 1926 and no dividends on common stock since 1924. But except in 1924, the first year of the anti-union drive, the company's total income—operating margin plus other income—has been sufficient to cover more than two millions of taxes, from one and a half to two millions of depletion and depreciation, and about $1,750,000 of interest on bonds, etc., and guaranteed dividends on the stock of a subsidiary company. The company has made heavy expenditures for improvements, amounting in 1929 to $2,600,000. These improvements have evidently been included in operating expenses.

PROFITS IN RECENT YEARS

Are there then no profits in coal? Since the collapse of the war boom have no companies had a net income for dividends after meeting their fixed charges? For clearly, however much the capitalist class may draw off from the coal industry in royalties and rents, depletion reserves, and interest on mortgages, bonds, and bank loans, the stockholders who are the owners of coal-mining companies will expect also to have a current income from their investment.

Most of the big anthracite companies and a small minority of bituminous companies have had clear profits throughout the recent years of crisis and chronic depression in coal.

Anthracite

Glen Alden Coal Company was reorganized in 1921 to take over the coal-mining properties of the Delaware, Lackawanna and Western Railroad. The stock was offered to stockholders of the railroad at $5 a share. Those who bought at this price and have held on to their Glen Alden stock have had a rich return on their investment. Dividends of $10 a share (or 200 per cent a year on this five-dollar share) were paid each year from 1926 to 1929. For two years before that they had been $7 a year, or 140 per cent, on the original payment. Since the exposure of Glen Alden's juggled valuations and special accounts by the United States Coal Commission in 1925, the company has been reticent about its affairs and publishes no balance sheet. But from the number of shares reported as outstanding it is clear that a total of $46,759,720 was paid out in dividends during the four years, 1926 to 1929. In addition, the company has paid some $2,340,000 yearly interest on outstanding bonds and sets aside each year $1,500,000 as sinking fund for retiring the principal of the bonds.

Lehigh and Wilkes-Barre Coal Company sold its collieries and coal reserves to the Glen Alden Coal Company in September, 1929. Lehigh and Wilkes-Barre was originally a mining subsidiary of the Central Railroad of New Jersey. Since 1923 it has been controlled by the Lehigh and Wilkes-Barre Corporation, a Morgan holding company created to carry out the "segregation" of the mining company from the railroad. Dividends of the holding company have been paid regularly and the rate on common stock has been rising from year to year. In 1929, they totaled $24 a share. The first quarter of 1930 brought a dividend of $8, indicating an annual payment of $32 a share. The Lehigh and Wilkes-Barre Coal Company paid preferred stock dividends at 7 per cent to the end of 1929, but no dividend on common stock after June, 1928. The minority owner who did not happen also to own a share in the holding corporation was frozen out from the fattest profits. But he need not be pitied! If he had been a stockholder since January 1, 1924, he had received the 200 per cent stock dividend of March, 1924. This had given him a share of preferred stock and an extra share of common stock for each share he owned before. Then he had received during four and a half years cash dividends totaling $131.58, or 267 per cent, for each $50 par share of his original holding.

Lehigh Valley Coal Company, under the plan for segregation from the Lehigh Valley Railroad approved in 1923, started its new independent existence with a heavy funded debt and yet through 1928 it paid dividends averaging $3,000,000 a year. In 1927, the dividend was 5½ per cent on the par value of the stock. During 1928, a new holding company, the Lehigh Valley Coal Corporation, was created by J. P. Morgan and Company to combine the Lehigh Valley Coal Company and the Lehigh Valley Coal Sales Company. This holding company reported in 1929 a profit of nearly $500,000 after payment of all charges, including dividends on six per cent preferred stock.

The Pittston Company was formed in January, 1930, to operate the anthracite properties owned by the Erie Railroad subsidiaries, Pennsylvania Coal Company and Hillside Coal and Iron Company. These companies had been producing from five to six million tons of anthracite. Dividends coming to the railroad from these anthracite companies and from its smaller bituminous properties during the years 1924 to 1928 have ranged from $3,000,000 to $5,600,000 a year except during 1925 when they fell to $2,550,000. The stocks of the coal companies have par value of $7,500,000, which means a dividend return of 34 per cent in the poorest and of nearly 75 per cent in the best of recent years. No wonder that in its analysis of the Erie Railroad, the Standard Statistics Company says, "Coal properties are valuable and earnings from this source have been highly important in preserving the company's financial status." [9]

Lehigh Coal and Navigation Company has been the other important "railroad" company among the anthracite operators. Its dividends of 8 to 10 per cent a year were in large part derived from its Lehigh and New England Railroad, from valuable leases to the Central Railroad of New Jersey, and profitable investments in power companies. The operating margin from its coal mines has twice since 1923 been too low to cover the fixed charges for taxes, depletion, and depreciation, but it has never in recent years been less than 60 cents for each ton of anthracite mined from the company's property. This is a clear margin after the company has included as an operating cost the sinking fund payments which are charged against a considerable share of its output at the rate of 5 cents a ton. And in spite of "loss" in 1925 and 1928, the coal operations brought the company a net profit of $1,974,867 during five years after 1923, or an average of nearly $400,000 a year. In 1930 its coal properties were "segregated" and turned over to the Lehigh Navigation Coal Company.

Little or no information is at hand as to recent profits of the so-called "independent" operators in the anthracite. Most of these companies are closely owned and do not publish their balance sheets. Up to 1922, twelve independents studied by the United States Coal Commission were as a group making a net profit year by year after all fixed charges had been met. Since then anthracite prices have wavered considerably, but in spite of a general downward trend they have remained on the whole higher than they had ever been before 1923. Production has been far below the high points of the war years, but whether these "hard times" in the anthracite have really destroyed the profits of the "independent" operators it is impossible to state.

Bituminous

Island Creek Coal Company is the most spectacular money maker among the bituminous mining companies. "Located in the non-union West Virginia area and normally disposing of virtually its entire output on an annual contract basis, it is probably the most strongly entrenched of the larger soft-coal producers." [10]   Its mines are favored with naturally low production costs, and the company has no funded debt, so the fixed charges are relatively small. With an output ranging in recent years from five and a half million to seven and a half million tons, the company has made a clear profit of nearly $3,000,000 a year, with still higher profits during the 1927 strike in the northern coal fields. For the six years, 1924 to 1929, profits totaled $17,261,721. Dividends on common stock were $12 a share in 1924 and 1925; in 1926 they went up to $17 a share. In 1927 the company declared a 400 per cent stock dividend, multiplying by five each stockholder's number of shares, and paid cash dividends giving him $21 on each of his original shares. In 1929 the dividend rate was $4 a share, which meant for the old stockholder who had held on to his stock $20 on each original share. The holder of common stock who went in on the original organization of the company and stayed in had received from 1912 up to the end of 1929 cash dividends totaling $190.50 for each share, an average return for the eighteen years of about 25 per cent a year on his original investment.

The Northwestern Improvement Company, a Northern Pacific Railway subsidiary, operates among other properties the big Rosebud strip mine in Montana. Here the output per worker in 1928 had been speeded up to an average of nearly 50 tons a day. This Rosebud coal was said to be costing in 1926 only 88 cents a ton to mine and load on cars for shipment. The Northern Pacific Railway uses most of the 2,000,000 tons produced in a "normal year" by all the mines of the Northwestern Improvement Company. Since the railroad claimed in 1926 that it paid on the average $3.16 a ton for its locomotive coal, it is not surprising that the mining subsidiary made in 1926 a net profit of more than $1,250,000 from its Montana properties alone. In 1929, a regular dividend of $992,000 and an extra cash dividend of $3,500,000 were paid to the railroad by this subsidiary. Unfortunately, the total profits of the Northwestern Improvement Company are not reported.[11]

Union Pacific Coal Company, subsidiary of the Union Pacific Railway, is the largest operator in Wyoming and has mines in other western coal fields also. It has carried through technical improvements which give Wyoming the lead among all the coal states in the percentage of its total output coming from mines equipped with mechanical loaders. From it the railroad drew dividends of $1,750,000, or 35 per cent of the par value of the coal company stock, in each of the three years from 1925 to 1927.*

No exhaustive study of the several thousand mining companies in the United States could be undertaken except by a government body. But when the Federal Trade Commission in 1922 and the United States Coal Commission in 1925 reported on war boom profits in bituminous mining, the

* Other mining companies for which dividend payments or profits have been reported more or less regularly since the collapse of the bituminous market in 1923 are listed on page 245.

secrets of the individual companies were carefully guarded from public knowledge.

Apart from the vast extent of the material to be covered, there would be other difficulties in attempting more than such a short and rather haphazard list as we have assembled. For the mining operations of many important producers of commercial coal no data on profits or loss are available. Such companies as Rockefeller's Colorado Fuel and Iron Company and the M. A. Hanna Company of Cleveland with its subsidiaries, publish financial statements in which the mining and sale of coal cannot be disentangled from other operations.

Companies which are closely owned and do not attempt to draw in outside investors rarely, if ever, choose to publish financial statements. The Koppers group of companies, for example, which Andrew Mellon admitted to be his chief coal-mining interest, had given no information until one subsidiary, not engaged in the mining of coal, published certain figures when it floated a bond issue early in 1929. The big anti-union Berwind companies (Berwind-White Coal Mining Company, in Pennsylvania, and New River and Pocahontas Consolidated Coal Company, in West Virginia) give no information on profits or dividends. In 1929 the Berwind-White company received a refund of $545,962 on Federal taxes.

Holding companies are a favorite device for concealing profits and evading taxation. Several have been organized in recent years, apparently as a screen to cover the true condition of one or another mining company. The operating company can then, under the guise of fixed charges, make a tidy return to the holding company and through the holding company pay dividends to stockholders, while it claims "losses" and insists on the necessity for wage-cutting.

For all companies whose chief business is the mining of coal or the making of coke we have certain important totals in the Federal income tax returns from corporations. Here we learn that since 1923 less than two-fifths of these companies have shown a net profit. The lowest point thus far was reached in 1924 when three companies out of four claimed a net deficit, after payment of fixed charges, including interest. With that year began the first maneuvers in the anti-union drive in northern fields and more systematic efforts to improve technique and concentrate production. So in 1927, in spite of falling prices for coal, the number and the percentage of companies reporting a net income were considerably greater than in 1924. But still the 1,087 companies that reported a profit in 1927 were only 35 per cent of all the companies classified as engaged in coal mining, including the making of coke.

How many coal companies paid dividends, the Internal Revenue Office does not show in its published reports. But during the four years, 1924 to 1927 inclusive, stockholders in coal-mining companies received a total of $220,774,000 in dividends, including $14,850,000 paid not in cash but in increased holdings of stock.[12] Unfortunately no similar total is yet available for later years.

FINANCIAL OUTLOOK FOR THE INDUSTRY

Clearly, even in years of depression, some are making money in coal mining. During each of these four years the industry paid, on the average, at least $59,000,000 in dividends, at least $37,000,000 in interest, and roughly some $34,000,000 in rent and royalties. This gives a yearly total of at least $130,000,000 taken from the products of labor and paid to investors, apart from the depletion and depreciation reserves set aside to protect their capital. And these figures are incomplete. They do not include companies producing coal for use in their own steel mills and plants. Neither do they include individuals and partnerships engaged in coal mining. They cannot therefore be related to tonnage produced. They merely illustrate that even in years of crisis many millions are drawn off from the industry by the capitalist class.

Now "the bituminous coal-mining industry is definitely on the upgrade," according to the National Coal Association. A tone of optimism was carefully cultivated at the 1929 annual meeting. Harry L. Gandy, the executive secretary, gave a special report on the subject, based on Federal income tax returns and on figures privately supplied by 339 companies to the Market Research Institute of the Association.

But in spite of official optimism, and the millions that coal companies do succeed in returning to investors, there is still over-expansion and surplus capacity. More capital is invested in coal mining than can possibly bring a "satisfactory" return to the capitalist class. The desperate scramble for markets and cost-cutting continues. The slow upward financial trend is based on measures which fall with fearful impact upon the mine workers and it holds no promise of anything like permanent stability.

The drive for profits is bringing drastic cutting of wage rates, cutting of labor costs by technical changes to reduce the number of workers, and an increasing concentration of operation. For many companies the installing of new equipment is the only hope of survival, but technical changes lie beyond the reach of those without large surplus reserves, or a balance sheet and a steady market that make the company attractive to bankers as the basis for fresh investment. So strong companies grow stronger and weak companies go under, while financiers more and more supersede the old-time operators as the controlling power.

Meanwhile the technical improvements which seem to solve the problem for certain companies are preparing fresh problems for the industry as a whole and ultimately for the strong companies themselves. New machinery increases mine capacity. And the stronger companies, ruthlessly expanding at the expense of the weaker, are headed towards a day when their large modernized mines will alone be able to produce more coal than is needed. Then more serious crises of competition and irregularity will develop. For it is one of the basic inconsistencies of capitalism that in an overdeveloped, overcapitalized industry, victory in the fight for financial survival goes to those companies which are further increasing productive capacity and capital investment and thereby leading the way to new crises and still sharper conflict.

For the workers, all this means increasing exploitation and intensified struggle. It has already brought wage cuts and unemployment. But before we turn to see in detail the immediate situation of the workers, we must look a little more closely at this trend toward concentration of production and concentration of control. These are of vital importance in the workers' struggle to protect their standards. For as the miners organize their forces for fresh resistance they find themselves face to face with the most powerful financial forces that dominate American industry.

CHAPTER III

MINES AND OPERATORS GROW FEWER

WHEN the Consolidation Coal Company announced in May, 1928, that it was permanently closing ten high-cost mines and dismissing 2,500 workers, it merely drew the attention of the capitalist newspapers and their readers to a process with which mine workers have long been familiar from their own experience. For in recent years, Consolidation Coal has reduced the number of its operating mines from 80 to 32, without any decrease in output. Pittsburgh Coal has been pursuing the same policy, and concentrating production in its most efficient mines. These companies and other big corporations have been deliberately following within their own groups of mines a general trend apparent in the industry as a whole. Tens of thousands of miners have been thrown out of work since 1923 by the closing of some three thousand mines, chiefly the smaller operations.

The number of operating companies and private operators has been decreasing. Most of the 1,750 mines that closed down immediately at the end of 1923 were ventures owned by individuals or small companies who had sailed into the industry on the high prices of boom years and were left stranded and bankrupt when the market receded. Such "snowbirds" or "fly-by-nights" had flocked into the industry in unprecedented numbers from 1917 to 1923. Since 1923, although we have no exact figures on failures in the coal industry, it is commonly believed that the number has continued to be high. Also, an uncounted number of operators and companies have dropped out because their properties have been bought by larger or stronger companies. No spectacular mergers have been carried through but the records of many big coal companies show a steady extension of their holdings. They have been reorganizing and concentrating production and yet, on the whole, relatively few of the nearly 3,300 mines squeezed out of the industry since the collapse of the boom in 1923 were closed as part of a deliberate program of rationalization.

LARGE MINES REPLACING SMALL

Small mines as a rule have higher production costs than large mines for each ton of coal produced. In a period like the recent years of sharp competition and price-cutting, this is the primary economic fact that has been steadily driving the small mines out of business.

Of course there are exceptions. Some small mines are highly favored in their natural conditions, or their owners have access to a steady market and are able to hold their own by maintaining exceptional regularity of operation. Some large mines are unskillfully planned and badly managed, or seriously handicapped by natural difficulties which have not been overcome. These exceptions in both groups account for the fact that there are still some 3,900 mines in the United States each producing less than 50,000 tons a year. But in 1929 they contributed less than 8 per cent of the total output, and since 1923 and 1924 their share in the total has steadily fallen.

Only in the larger mines, on the whole, is it worth while to install the expensive modern equipment with which each company that can afford the investment is trying to reduce its costs and standardize its coal. And only the larger companies can, on the whole, find the capital for this equipment. Improved technical equipment further increases the daily capacity of the large mine. Having invested more capital in the mine, the company is driven to seek greater steadiness in operation. For when wages are the chief expense it can let the mine lie idle part of every week. What matter to investors if the miners and their families go hungry? But when interest and other capital costs are increased, the balance sheet is far more seriously affected by irregular production. Capital charges must be met, and directors worry more over idle equipment than over idle men.

So large mines are tending to become larger in daily capacity, and with increased steadiness of operation their annual output is further increased. The trend is plainly shown in the coal reports from the United States Bureau of Mines. The years 1925 and 1929 give a fair basis for comparison as the output of bituminous coal was only slightly less in 1925 than in 1929. In the latter year, more than one-fourth of the output came from mines producing each more than half a million tons, and about two-thirds of the output came from mines producing more than 200,000 tons. While the average output and the number of large mines had increased markedly in the four years, 1,200 of the smaller mines had dropped out of the industry.

BITUMINOUS MINES

| | 1925 | | 1929 | |
Class of mine	Number of mines	Per cent of output	Number of mines	Per cent of output
1A (more than 500,000 tons)	145	20.9	209	29.6
1B (200,000 to 500,000 tons)	569	32.8	618	35.6
2 (100,000 to 200,000 tons)	833	22.7	660	17.9
3 (50,000 to 100,000 tons)	891	12.4	668	9.1
4 (10,000 to 50,000 tons)	1,969	9.4	1,361	6.3
5 (less than 10,000 tons)	2,737	1.8	2,541	1.5
	7,144	100.0	6,057	100.0

Within nearly every important coal state the same thing has happened. Whether production has been decreasing as in Indiana and Ohio, or increasing as in Kentucky and West Virginia, the number of mines in operation has fallen and the biggest mines are contributing a growing share in the output of the state. What disaster this has brought to the miners we shall see in detail in later chapters.

In the Pennsylvania anthracite fields production has always been more concentrated than in bituminous mining. Many new breakers were built during the war boom until in 1919 as many as 259 were in operation. But the following years saw a steady decline in the number of active breakers, interrupted only by the boom of 1923. One in eight had ceased operation by 1928, and further reduction looms in the near future. The new gigantic, completely electrified breakers under construction by Philadelphia and Reading Coal and Iron will, for example, replace most of the company's older breakers and will almost certainly lead to the shutdown of other less modern plants in the anthracite.

Many washeries were built during the war for the preparation of old coal taken from the piles of culm surrounding the mines, and the dredging of coal from river bottoms in the anthracite was also developed. Of the 158 washeries and dredges operating in 1919, more than half had been given up in 1928.

TALK OF MERGERS

Coal operators and bankers have had much to say since 1923 on the need for price agreements and consolidation of bituminous mining interests, and various proposals for district mergers have been put forward during these years of depression. The most ambitious merger plan was worked out in 1928 by a committee representing Consolidation Coal, Pocahontas Fuel, New River Company, Island Creek Coal, and other important commercial producers in southern West Virginia. A $200,000,000 corporation with an annual output of some 55,000,000 tons was proposed, but after several months of negotiation the plan was dropped because several companies refused to accept the valuation placed on their properties by the committee's engineers.

Several much smaller local combinations have been effected since 1923, but in none of the principal soft coal fields is there as yet any single corporation or group of related companies which so dominates the market as to restrict competition and regulate prices. Operating companies are united in their anti-union policies, but in relation to the coal market they are still in sharp competition with one another.

Large Companies Growing Larger

The size of the competing units has, however, been steadily growing. Most of the bigger bituminous companies have been little by little increasing their holdings and consolidating their interests. Northern companies have been reaching out for properties in the southern fields. Old Ben Coal Corporation of Illinois, the Youghiogheny and Ohio Coal Company, Paisley's Valley Camp Coal Company, the newly expanded Truax-Traer Coal Company and others too numerous to mention are now operating subsidiaries in West Virginia or Kentucky.

The recent growth of Peabody Coal Company and of the coal interests of the Mellon family illustrate what many other groups have been doing on a smaller scale.

Peabody-Insull

Peabody Coal Company—a leading producer in Illinois—was reorganized in May, 1928, shortly after Samuel Insull bought control, and subsidiary companies previously acquired in Illinois and Kentucky were brought into closer relation with the parent company. Shortly afterwards, Peabody Coal purchased the Saline County Coal Company, adding five big mines to its Illinois properties. It acquired controlling interest in three other companies which had mines in eastern Kentucky, West Virginia, Illinois and Oklahoma.[1] Peabody Coal also operates the Bellwood Coal Company, with a mine in Fayette County, W. Va., and the mine of

Donk Bros. Coal and Coke in Illinois. It has for some years operated the nine Pennsylvania soft-coal mines owned by the Erie Railroad.

Peabody Coal has a close working relationship with the United States Distributing Corporation. This corporation has a sales subsidiary which handles in the eastern market the Erie coal mined by Peabody in Pennsylvania, while Peabody handles in the Chicago market the Wyoming coal produced by another United States Distributing subsidiary, the Sheridan Wyoming Coal Mining Company. H. T. Peters of New York is, incidentally, a director in Peabody Coal, Erie coal subsidiaries, and Sheridan-Wyoming Coal.

But this is not the whole story. The Insull family, which dominates Peabody Coal, is interested in four other small mining companies in Oklahoma.[2] And one of the Insull utilities owns part interest in the important Kingston-Pocahontas Coal Company in southern West Virginia.

Mellon

The Mellon interests which dominate Pittsburgh Coal Company have extended their coal properties in recent years chiefly through the Koppers Company, a holding company organized in 1927. The Koppers group now includes several coal mining companies in West Virginia, Kentucky and Pennsylvania.[3] The Koppers Company and W. J. Rainey, Inc., which owns ten mines in western Pennsylvania, acquired jointly in 1929 the Alan Wood Iron and Steel Company. And early in that year, Pittsburgh Coal Company announced that it had arrived at a close working agreement with the Koppers companies. During 1929 the Koppers Company acquired a considerable interest in the Massachusetts Gas Companies whose coal subsidiaries produce nearly 5,000,000 tons a year in West Virginia.

Mellon influence in coal extends beyond the properties of Pittsburgh Coal and the Koppers companies. R. B. Mellon is a director of the Pennsylvania Railroad which controls the Norfolk and Western Railway, owner (through a subsidiary company) of immense coal properties in West Virginia. He is also on the board of Indian Creek Coal and Coke, one of the Zimmerman companies in Somerset County, Pennsylvania. And the Mellon family is interested in Crucible Steel Co. and Pittsburgh Plate Glass Co.

Henry C. McEldowney, president of one of the Mellon banks (Union Trust Co. of Pittsburgh) is a director of Pittsburgh Steel Co. Two leading directors of the Koppers companies are on the boards of Republic Iron and Steel Co. and Harbison-Walker Refractories Co. These five corporations produce coal primarily for their own use.

The coal mining connections of other men who are directors of Mellon companies carry the Mellon influence indirectly to a wider circle. To give just one example: Howard N. Eavenson, a director of Pittsburgh Coal Co., is president of Comago Smokeless Fuel Company, with four mines in Raleigh County, West Virginia, and of Clover Splint Coal Co., Inc., which owns one big mine in eastern Kentucky.

Loosely Related Groups

Groups of companies tied together as subsidiaries of a parent corporation or coöperating under acknowledged working agreements are only one phase of the trend toward concentration. Perhaps more characteristic of the bituminous coal industry at present in the United States are the many connections among apparently independent and competing companies.

Great numbers of the smaller companies fall into definite groups marked by actual identity of ownership or of dominant financial interest.

Hillman of Pittsburgh, Warner of Cleveland, Justus Collins in West Virginia, Miller in Illinois, Mahan in Tennessee, —these are only a few among many names familiar to the

mine workers as operators or important stockholders, each
with active interest in several apparently unrelated companies. It is impossible here to give an exhaustive list of
such operators, or even to describe the connections of the
few we have named.

Like the bigger corporations, northern operators of this
type have been extending their holdings in southern coal
fields, but they have done it chiefly through personal investment in additional companies. Perhaps the safety of a
scattered interest through a number of companies whose
business fortunes can go up and down without involving one
another in possible losses seems to outweigh the advantages
and economies of a single company with subsidiaries. Also
when the investor or operator who serves as connecting link
holds only a strong minority interest he may find his efforts
at closer combination balked by disagreements about valuation of properties.

Rockefeller

The Rockefeller coal interests constitute a group of this
loosely tied-together type, with connections so extensive and
so important that they should be briefly described. Four
bituminous coal companies, apparently independent of one
another, are clearly in the Rockefeller group. Directors of
these companies have other coal connections through which
the Rockefeller influence extends out indirectly over a still
wider circle.

(1) *Consolidation Coal Company.* John D. Rockefeller,
Jr., told the Senate sub-committee which investigated the
coal industry in the early months of 1928, that he held 72
per cent of the preferred stock and 28 per cent of the common stock of this corporation. He does not personally sit
on the board of directors, but we note the presence of
Raymond B. Fosdick, one of Rockefeller's personal counsel,
Arthur Woods, who is commonly known as a Rockefeller

man, and Walter C. Teagle, president of Standard Oil Co. of New Jersey.

The chairman of Consolidation Coal Co. is Robert C. Hill, who was vice-president and is still a director of the Madeira-Hill Company, a close corporation with fourteen coal mining subsidiaries operating in the anthracite, in Pennsylvania bituminous, and in Maryland and West Virginia.

C. W. Watson, who was for many years president of Consolidation Coal Co., was also chairman of Elk Horn Coal Corporation, a large Kentucky company which owns a minority block of Consolidation Coal Company stock.

(2) *Colorado Fuel and Iron Company.* This bitterly anti-union company, with the Ludlow massacre in 1914 on its record, is also a Rockefeller interest. J. F. Welborn, the president in 1914, is now chairman of the board of directors. Rockefeller is represented on the board by Thomas M. Debevoise and Arthur Woods.

(3) *Davis Coal and Coke Company* operates the coal properties owned by the Western Maryland Railway. Harry P. Fish, secretary to John D. Rockefeller, is a director of Davis Coal and Coke.

(4) *Clinchfield Coal Company,* operating in Virginia, includes among its directors Henry E. Cooper, who was a director and vice-president of Rockefeller's Equitable Trust Company before its merger with Chase National Bank, and had been for several years "personal representative of John D. Rockefeller." C. E. Bockus, chairman and president of Clinchfield Coal, is also a director of the Pacific Coast Company, of which a subsidiary is the leading coal producer in the state of Washington. Another director of Pacific Coast Company, H. B. Clark, was a director of Equitable Trust Company and is now on the board of the Chase National Bank. F. S. Landstreet, a director of Clinchfield Coal, is chairman of Pennsylvania Coal and Coke Company. This is tied up with the New York Central Railroad through the

Central's subsidiary, Clearfield Bituminous Company. The New York Central, in turn, includes among its directors Bertram Cutler, "personal representative of John D. Rockefeller." *

(5) *Anthracite.* Hudson Coal Company is owned by the Delaware and Hudson Company which has five directors in common with the Chase National Bank. Theodore Pratt, long an important figure in Standard Oil Co. of New York, is also on the Delaware and Hudson board.

(6) *Consumer-owned mines.* Among the important corporations owning "captive" mines there are several in which the Rockefeller interests are strongly represented on the board of directors,—notably, Bethlehem Steel, Anaconda Copper, American Smelting and Refining, and Union Pacific and Illinois Central railroads, besides the New York Central Railroad, already mentioned.

These various companies related to Rockefeller interests are largely represented among the 1929-1930 officials of the National Coal Association. Thus, the president of the N. C. A. is C. E. Bockus of Clinchfield Coal Corporation and Pacific Coast Company. Two vice-presidents are J. F. Welborn of Colorado Fuel and Iron Co., and J. W. Searles, president of Pennsylvania Coal and Coke Corp. The directors include also George J. Anderson, president of Consolidation Coal Co., A. B. Stewart, president of Davis Coal and Coke Co., L. C. Madeira, III, of Madeira-Hill Company, and Walter Barnum, president of Pacific Coast Co.

Cross-Directorships

Many companies and groups of companies are loosely connected by a network of cross-directors. For example, Pittsburgh Terminal is the largest company in the Taplin group,

---

* Morgan interests are also strong in New York Central. In many companies dominated by one of these two leading financial groups, the other "interest" is now also represented on the board. For Morgan connections in coal, see below, page 70.

which includes Standard Island Creek Coal Company, Powhatan Mining Company, and Pursglove Mining Company and ties in with the large Atwater group in West Virginia. Pittsburgh Terminal is also linked with Paine, Webber and Company of Boston and through them with West Virginia-Pittsburgh Coal and the large New River Company in West Virginia. A Paine-Webber representative sits on the board of the new Pittston Company in the anthracite. F. E. Taplin is also a director of Logan County Coal Corporation which, through another director, C. S. Newhall, is linked with a Philadelphia bank and other anthracite mining interests.

Pittsburgh Terminal Coal has had a vice-president in common with Landstreet Downey and Red Bird Pocahontas, two small companies in West Virginia, and these in turn are loosely linked with Island Creek Coal Company. Another director links Pittsburgh Terminal with still another group of small companies in Ohio, western Pennsylvania and West Virginia.[4]

Companies having one director in common may or may not represent an identical financial interest. When the common director is partner or agent of an investment house which floated the securities of the several companies, or of a bank which has extended considerable credit, the relation of the several companies to the bank or the investment house may be much closer than their relation to one another. But this loose grouping is often preliminary to financial reorganization and consolidation.

So the loose network of cross-directorships, which is much more far-reaching and more tangled than these few illustrations can convey to the reader, is one important phase of the progress of capitalist industry away from the competition of several thousand unrelated units and toward the mergers which will precede the fight for monopoly control.

CAPTIVE MINES AND CONCENTRATION

While large coal companies are growing larger and successful operators are reaching out for new properties and this loose network of cross-directorships is gradually being woven out of the tangled chaos of the bituminous industry, a considerable amount of soft coal has been withdrawn from the *commercial* coal industry entirely. Many large consumers of coal have become large producers of coal. And since these same big consumers include some of the most powerful corporations in the country, their development of consumer-owned or "captive" mines has shifted thousands of mine workers from the domain of the coal operator to the domain most closely controlled by the financial overlords of American industry.

Steel plants, railroads, public utilities, and coke producers together use nearly three-fifths of the yearly output of bituminous coal in the United States. They are still the largest purchasers of coal, but they are now mining more than one-third of the coal they use and more than one-fifth of the total output. Other industries also own captive mines. Ford, for example, has large coal operations in Kentucky and West Virginia. Metal-mining corporations have large coal holdings in the West. But the four groups first mentioned produce more than 90 per cent of the consumer-owned coal.

In the Pittsburgh district where coal and steel have been developed side by side some two-thirds of the coal is said to come from captive mines. In Alabama the coal mines of a United States Steel subsidiary and of Sloss-Sheffield Steel and Iron, and in Utah the coal produced by copper, smelting and steel companies, bring the consumer-owned output above 40 per cent of the totals for these states. The latest Federal figures on captive mines refer to the year 1926. Since then Insull has taken over Peabody Coal and the Mellon coke and utility interests have been developing captive mines. Such changes have certainly raised somewhat the relatively low percentage of consumer-owned output in Illinois, Kentucky and West Virginia.

Part of the coal produced in captive mines finds its way into the commercial market, but corporations and coal fields vary greatly on this point. United States Steel, the largest bituminous producer in the country, mines coal almost entirely for its own use. Colorado Fuel and Iron sells more than half of its coal output, Peabody Coal, under Insull management, provides fuel for Insull utilities and coke plants and at the same time operates a large and profitable wholesale business. Taking the country as a whole, consumer owners use from 80 to 90 per cent of the coal they produce. Most of them are far more concerned in securing for themselves a cheap and dependable supply of special grades of coal than they are in finding a stable commercial market.

The growth of captive mines tends to increase the irregularities and difficulties of the commercial coal producers, for captive mines are producing coal to meet a demand that is, on the whole, steadier than the demand on which the commercial producer must depend.

But while captive mines tend to sharpen the competition in the commercial coal industry, they are at the same time an important phase of the movement toward concentration of control. For rails, utilities and steels are all dominated by a relatively small number of financiers and we have already noted how some of these financial leaders are active also in commercial bituminous mining. Many other links and cross-directorships between captive and commercial operations could be traced.

To the miners, this ownership of mines by railroads, steel corporations and other great companies means that their struggle requires a close alliance between coal miners, railroad, steel, metal and auto workers.

THE ANTHRACITE MONOPOLY

While the bituminous industry is moving slowly and irregularly toward trust combination and centralized financial control, the anthracite industry had many years ago arrived at the monopoly stage. Anthracite reserves are concentrated in the mountains of eastern Pennsylvania and this made it easy for the small group of closely interrelated anthracite-carrying railroads and their mining subsidiaries to develop in the mining of anthracite one of the earliest monopoly combinations in modern American industry. Before the war the railroad coal companies had acquired 90 per cent of the unmined anthracite reserves. They were producing about three-fourths of the annual output and through long-term sales agreements and carrying contracts controlling more than half the remainder.[5]

Since 1920 the chief mining subsidiaries have been "segregated" from the railroad companies, and theoretically the courts have destroyed the anthracite monopoly. The business of mining anthracite is now distinct from the business of carrying anthracite as freight, and mining companies and railroad companies are compelled to make their separate drives for profit instead of lumping their operations as formerly.

Theoretically, the mining companies are unrelated to the railroads and unrelated to one another, but Morgan and Morgan banks, and to a less degree the Rockefeller interests, controlled and still control the anthracite railroads, and directly or indirectly they still control the segregated mining companies. Glen Alden Coal Co. was reorganized to take over the Lackawanna Railroad's coal properties before the Supreme Court fixed the terms of segregation and the stock was issued to stockholders in the railroad company.

The big anthracite companies still work together in a price-fixing combination. The few big companies still have long-term sales agreements and directors in common with many of the so-called "independent" producers. Most of them are tied together by cross-directors. All of them are tied to a small group of New York and Philadelphia banks. Glen Alden's purchase of Lehigh and Wilkes-Barre properties and the organization of the Pittston Company are fresh steps toward more concentrated management in actual operation and sales.

MORGAN LINKS BETWEEN ANTHRACITE AND BITUMINOUS

Rockefeller links between anthracite and bituminous mining we have already referred to. Many anthracite operators, both among the "independents" and among the directors of the big companies directly controlled by the House of Morgan, are actively interested also in bituminous coal mining.

For example, a group of directors of Lehigh Coal and Navigation Company are also directors of Westmoreland Coal Company and of Virginia Coal and Iron with its subsidiaries. Several directors link Morgan anthracite companies with West Virginia Coal and Coke, recently reorganized under the guidance of the Morgan-Baker First National Bank of New York. These directors include J. L. Kemmerer whose bituminous interests are scattered from West Virginia to Wyoming and Colorado.

Richard F. Grant of Lehigh Valley Coal Corporation and Michael Gallagher of the new Pittston Company and the Erie coal subsidiaries are directors of the M. A. Hanna Company, while the Hanna Company, although mainly interested in bituminous coal, itself owns and operates the Susquehanna Collieries in the anthracite. The Pittston Company, controlled by the Van Sweringen brothers, who operate within the Morgan sphere of influence, has acquired controlling interest in the United States Distributing Corporation whose connections with Peabody Coal Company were noted above.

J. P. Morgan and Company have other direct and indirect connections with bituminous coal. Through the leading steel companies; through railroads and utilities and other corporations owning captive mines; through the coal properties owned by Morgan or the Van Sweringen railroads and leased to others for operation, the influence of Morgan has penetrated every coal field. Morgan and Rockefeller interests overlap far more than formerly, and we find F. W. Shibley, a vice-president of Morgan's Bankers Trust Company of New York, sitting on the board of the Consolidation Coal.

Distinctively within the Morgan sphere of influence are the large mining interests of the Berwind companies, operating in Pennsylvania and West Virginia. E. J. Berwind and Charles E. Dunlap, an important official in the Berwind companies, are both directors of Morgan's Guaranty Trust Company of New York. Harry A. Berwind is a director of the Pennsylvania Company for Insurance on Lives and Granting Annuities,—a Morgan bank in Philadelphia.[6]

This Morgan bank in Philadelphia—the Pennsylvania Company—is tied through its directors to many coal companies. The list of these connections illustrates how, through Morgan banks, the financial power of the House of Morgan reaches out indirectly beyond the corporations in which partners of the Morgan firm are themselves directors.

MINING COMPANIES HAVING ONE OR MORE DIRECTORS IN COMMON WITH THE PENNSYLVANIA COMPANY FOR INSURANCE ON LIVES AND GRANTING ANNUITIES

Anthracite

Lehigh Coal and Navigation Company, and subsidiaries.

Philadelphia and Reading Coal and Iron.

Lehigh Valley Coal Sales Company, subsidiary of Lehigh Valley Coal Corporation.

Hazle Brook Coal Company.

Shamokin Coal Company.

South Penn Collieries Company.

Bituminous

Berwind-White Coal Mining Company (Penn. and W. Va.).
Jamison Coal and Coke (Penn. and W. Va.).
Bertha Consumers' Company (Penn., W. Va., and Ky.).
Old Ben Coal Corporation (Ill. and W. Va.).
Logan County Coal Corporation (W. Va.).
Westmoreland Coal Company (Penn. and W. Va.).
Virginia Coal and Iron Company (Va. and W. Va.).
Monroe Coal Mining Company (Penn.).
Richland Coal Company (W. Va.).
Pocahontas Coal and Coke (land-owning subsidiary of Norfolk
    and Western Railway in W. Va. and Va.).
Crozer Land Association (another important land-owning
    company in the Pocahontas field, W. Va.).
Crozer Coal and Coke (W. Va.).
Upland Coal and Coke (W. Va.).
Page Coal and Coke (W. Va.).

It is a truism that company failures and receiverships are the financier's opportunity. In the anthracite this was illustrated years ago when the House of Morgan "saved" the Reading Railroad—and secured control. No such spectacular move has yet been made by the Morgan interests in bituminous mining. But smaller failures can also be turned to good account. For example:

The Pennsylvania Company, acting as agent for mortgagee and bondholders, of the Consolidated Connellsville Coke Company, in February, 1929, bought up at a receiver's sale for $150,500 the company's coal and coke properties "valued a few years ago at more than a million dollars." The *New York Times* (February 18, 1929) tells how one Fred Mercer of Pittsburgh who "represented wage claimants and persons holding liens against the property," was trying to bid against the bank. But he could not go above $150,000 so the bank was an easy winner!

Finance Capitalism Developing in Coal

The biggest financial interests are already involved in coal. They link anthracite and bituminous. They link captive and commercial mines. They have monopoly control in the anthracite. They have begun to penetrate the bituminous industry. But bituminous mining is most unevenly developed. Much of the production is still dominated by genuine coal operators and not by the dictates of financiers; but their number is dwindling and their position is most insecure. The companies controlled by financial interests are spreading and the old-time operator is dropping into place as the salaried agent of a board that knows little about coal mining and a good deal about the Wall Street game.

These coal companies of financiers are still scattered and highly competitive. The trend toward concentration is genuine and fairly rapid, but the process has not yet gone far enough to give any group a dominating control in bituminous. And as the competing companies grow fewer and bigger, the competition will grow sharper. Mergers, trusts, a dominating monopoly, will not be arrived at without a struggle even sharper than the chaotic competition of the present. This is true partly because the financial giants are perpetually fighting among themselves for power; partly because the strong companies who turn to technical improvements and concentration of production for their immediate salvation are thereby increasing capacity in an overdeveloped industry and laying the foundation for future crises.

Some capitalist leaders are looking beyond competition in the bituminous industry and hoping to achieve effective combinations to "save" it. But district mergers—even those sponsored by the strongest companies—have fallen through. (Even weak companies cling to inflated valuations and do not yet see that if their present is bad their future will be worse.) Rumor has it that the House of Morgan will soon take a hand in some big consolidation of bituminous interests.

Meantime, J. A. Paisley of Cleveland, notoriously anti-union president of the Valley Camp Coal Co., has proposed a two-billion-dollar holding corporation which would "acquire by issuance of stock active coal lands in competitive states and in turn lease certain of these lands to reliable companies at a reasonable cost or a cost sufficient to cover taxes and depletion and return 6 per cent to stockholders. . . . Stock of the present coal companies is considered worthless by our banks to-day, and on the other hand the stock of the coal corporation would be on a paying basis and would be recognized at our banks." [7] Nothing further has been heard of the Paisley plan but it is interesting as a typical capitalist "solution," introducing fresh capital into an overcapitalized industry, squeezing out existing interests and reorganizing production in the hope of profits for a new set of investors.

For the mine workers, it matters little whether such a spectacular combine is suddenly achieved or capitalist monopoly is developed by the "normal" road of ever sharpening competition among larger and larger units. Either way, the capitalist class will pass on to the workers the cost of their search for profits. Miners will be displaced by the tens of thousands, perhaps by the hundred thousand. Management will become more "efficient" with speed-up, wage-cuts, "yellow dogs," and other devices for securing from the workers a maximum return with a minimum of independence. The crisis in coal and every move toward a capitalist "solution" show the irreconcilable conflict between the capitalists, with their demand for profits, and the workers' need for jobs, security, and a living wage.

CHAPTER IV

WHERE THE WORKERS ARE

Who are these 650,000 men who do the work of burrowing into the earth, digging out the coal, transporting it to the mouth of the mine, putting it through the breaker or the cleaning plant, and sending it forth on railroad cars or barges to feed the fires of industry and supply heat against the cold of winter?

The Workers

In the early days of American coal, Welsh and English miners were in the majority. They came to the United States hoping for escape from the miserable wages and the hazards in British mines. They brought with them a skill in mining craft and quickly found a place in the industry.

So long as the western frontier lands were unsettled and all industries were growing at an unprecedented pace, relatively few native white workers went into the mines. They could still dream of freedom on a western farm or take up some skilled trade safer than mining. Many were climbing out of the working class into the business world. Far more than most American industries coal mining throughout the nineteenth century was built chiefly on the labor of foreign-born workers.

After the Welsh and English, the Irish came in by the thousand; later, Slavs and Italians. As recently as 1910 nearly half the coal mine workers were foreign-born, and one in seven was the American-born son of a foreigner.

War years saw a change in the make-up of the mining population. Thousands of miners were drawn into the army, but the coal industry was expanding and tens of thousands of new workers went into the mines. The great incoming stream of foreign-born workers had been cut off, however, and by 1920 American miners born of native white parents outnumbered the foreign-born. Many more Negroes were working in the mines. The number of foreign-born workers had fallen to less than 40 per cent of all workers in the industry. In spite of these changes, coal was, in 1920—and still is—more dependent than most industries on foreign-born workers.

To-day fewer miners are employed than there were in 1920, and the foreign workers are a smaller percentage in this smaller total. The census of 1930 will probably show that the number of foreign-born miners has dropped well below 250,000. Negro miners are the only group which has actually increased in size. In 1920, there were about 60,000; to-day there are nearer to 70,000 Negroes in the coal mines, or more than one worker in ten, taking the industry as a whole.[1]

Age

Coal is one of the industries in which men grow old and die before their time. The worker is lucky if he escapes death on the job, since coal miners have a fatal accident rate much higher than that faced by men in any other occupation. And the lucky ones who are neither killed nor disabled are worn down by exposure to dampness and bad air. Thousands before they are really old grow stiff with rheumatism or crippled with miners' asthma so that they have to give up the hard work underground. Then a few find surface jobs about the mines. In the past this was easier in the anthracite than elsewhere, for old men could join the boys in the breaker. Now employers boast that "the human slate picker has disappeared."

During the war thousands of workers in their 40's and

50's who would ordinarily have been crowded out of industry were able to hold some kind of job in or about the mines. So in 1920, about 22 per cent of the mine workers were more than 45 years old as against only 17 per cent at the census of 1910. But even with this unusually large number of older men employed, more than half the mine workers in 1920 were under 35 years of age.

When the younger men came home from the army the industry was still expanding. The severe depression of 1921 failed to check the steady rise in numbers of workers. Only with the final collapse of the boom in 1923 began the elimination of mine workers by the tens of thousands. Since 1923 the older miner has faced a desperate situation. The total number employed in the industry has decreased by more than 200,000. The closing down of over three thousand mines has thrown men of all ages out of their jobs. Where machinery has reduced the working force, older men find themselves crowded out. *Coal Age* advises flatly that only men under 30 should be taught to operate a new machine, and there are plenty of young men to choose from. Other industries have been increasing production with a decrease in working force, and miners' sons—still dreaming of escape from the mines—find it harder than ever to get work elsewhere. If they stay at the mine they are preferred before their fathers. These changes cannot be measured until the census of 1930 is available, but the new figures will probably show a marked decrease in the percentage of mine workers over 45 years of age.

Young Workers

Nearly 200,000 or one-fourth of all the mine workers in 1920 were under 25 years of age, and nearly 45,000 of these young workers were boys under 18. Post-war changes have tended to increase the importance of young workers in every industry.

In the Soviet Union boys under 18 are not allowed to work underground, but no important American coal state has written on its statute books an 18-year age limit for underground workers. Several states have lists of dangerous occupations in which boys under 18 may not legally be employed, but the mining interests have seen to it that their industry, in spite of its terrific hazards, is not included.[2] In Pennsylvania, for example, boys may not legally work in certain dangerous occupations until they are 18 years old, but they can legally go into the mines at 16 and take a surface job at a mine when they are only 14 years old.

About 6,000 of the boys at work in coal mining in 1920 were less than 16 years old. Ten years earlier the census had reported over 15,000 young boys in and about the coal mines, but the introduction of breaker machinery and some slight improvements in child labor legislation had reduced their number. Child labor legislation, however, is often a dead letter. More than half the 450 boys *under 14* who were working in or about coal mines in 1920 were in Illinois, Indiana, Ohio, and Pennsylvania, states which had long been supposed to forbid such employment.

Since 1920, contradictory forces have been at work. Child labor laws have been further amended and now all the important coal states have a nominal 16-year age limit underground and at least a 14-year age limit for surface work at the mine. Machinery has more and more been installed to do the simpler jobs for which young boys used to be employed. The new census will doubtless show fewer boys under 16 in the breakers than the over 3,000 working there in 1920. But against these tendencies must be weighed the important fact that wage cuts and irregular work have made the miners' families much poorer than they were during the war. The need for children's earnings steadily pushes the boys out to earn as soon as they can land a job.

Miners' Families

Coal miners, like other workers, are mostly men with others to support, but the so-called "average home" where father, mother and three children live in privacy and health on the father's earnings is rare in the coal fields. About two miners in ten have more than three children and an uncounted number have also at least one parent to support.[3]

Only about three mine workers out of five are heads of households. One in five is living at home with parents or other relatives. One in five is boarding away from home. These boarders and lodgers include some 40,000 married men and widowers,—a wandering army hunting for jobs to support their families.

At least one mine worker in three is a single man. This figure was true even in 1920, when the number of older miners was exceptionally high. It doubtless understates the proportion of single men to-day. Single men outnumber by some 60,000 the total group of all workers married and single under 25 years of age. More than half of them are living at home with parents or other relatives, but whether living at home or boarding and working elsewhere few would be footloose and without responsibilities. Not only on the fathers of families but on young workers and unmarried men, capitalist industry throws a tremendous load. Without even a pretense of a social insurance system in the United States, older workers, dumped on the scrap heap of permanent joblessness, are saved from the poorhouse only if sons and daughters manage somehow to take up the burden of their support.

PRINCIPAL COAL FIELDS

Company "patches" with tumble-down shacks clinging to the steep sides of lonely ravines are the only homes for thousands of coal mine workers in the United States. But such villages are not the whole story. The hundred coal fields in 24 states present a varied picture. Even in the mountainous eastern fields where the great Appalachian coal beds extend from Pennsylvania and eastern Ohio south and southwest to Alabama, the composite makeup of the mining population and the conditions under which mining communities have grown up are more varied than the kinds of coal that the workers are bringing out of the earth. In the Middle West, the coal underlies a rolling country dotted with farms and small towns. Further west, mine villages are in rocky valleys or dropped here and there on the great plains and plateaus,—many of them as remote from other settlements as the mountain villages of southern West Virginia.

Pennsylvania has many more miners than any other state. Nearly all the anthracite in the country is concentrated in eastern Pennsylvania and the anthracite mines employ about 150,000 workers. About 130,000 are in the bituminous mines of central and western Pennsylvania. Both groups together give Pennsylvania 43 per cent of all the coal mine workers in the United States.

West Virginia comes second with about 105,000 workers in twenty-seven bituminous coal fields. Third and fourth are Kentucky and Illinois.

Before the World War, all the southern coal states together were producing only about one-fourth of the bituminous coal in the country, but the West Virginia and Kentucky share in total tonnage has increased rapidly. Lower wages and non-union operation have led operators to develop the rich coal veins in those two states in spite of chronic overdevelopment in the industry. West Virginia and Kentucky mines are producing much more coal than they produced in 1923, although the total for the country has fallen since that year. In 1929 some 42 per cent of the bituminous workers and 32 per cent of all the coal mine workers were in the South.

STEEL TRUST COAL MINERS IN ALABAMA

A PENNSYLVANIA COAL MINE VILLAGE

—Photo by Hine

Broadly, the coal fields of the country fall into three big divisions: the northern fields east of the Mississippi River where in spite of greatly decreased tonnage the mines still employ about 380,000 workers; the southern fields east of the Mississippi with some 212,000 workers; and the western coal fields—including bituminous and lignite—scattered in thirteen states from North Dakota to Texas and from Arkansas to the state of Washington. Here as in the North the annual tonnage has declined, but over 60,000 coal mine workers are still employed. Colorado with more than 12,000 workers is the largest coal state in the West. (For numbers of workers in each state and the shift in production, see tables on pages 240 and 241.)

Pennsylvania Anthracite

Mining is the dominant industry in the anthracite section of Pennsylvania, and in the four chief anthracite counties the mine workers and their families are nearly half the total population. Records of anthracite production go back to 1821, when 1,322 tons were raised during the year. With this century of growth the region has long been thickly settled. Castles of the rich still have unscarred bits of mountain beauty about them, but miners' families mostly live in the shadow of monstrous piles of rock and waste, or above a gaping cut where robbing of the coal beds has undermined the surface.

More than 15,000 mine workers live in the cities of Wilkes-Barre and Scranton in the center of the northern anthracite field. Other thousands are scattered in small, dreary towns strung close together along the steep shores of polluted rivers. Barely one-third of the anthracite workers are in little villages. About one-tenth—some 15,500 —are living in company-owned dwellings. No bituminous state except Illinois and Indiana has so small a percentage of miners' dwellings company-owned.

But while company villages are few in the anthracite, great companies dominate the region. The massive stone building which houses the Pottsville office of the Philadelphia and Reading Coal and Iron Company is popularly known as the City Hall. Throughout the anthracite, local banks, bus and trolley lines, and telephone and water companies have cross directorships with the mining corporations. Even hospitals, poor boards, and cemeteries are not beneath their attention. In some places an anthracite company not only controls the public water system but all other sources of water supply.

Pennsylvania Bituminous

In the Pittsburgh district, coal mining is closely tied up with steel and other industries. Cities, small towns, and villages line the shores of the Allegheny and Monongahela rivers where some of the earliest bituminous mining was developed. Through other valleys winding out in all directions railway lines gather in the coal from scores of mines, large and small. Few miners live in the cities that have grown up under the shadow of steel plants. Few have daily neighborly contact with workers in any basic industry other than coal.

Company villages are numerous in the district and many "independent" settlements have a row or a patch of company houses. Few of the settlements are beyond reach of one another. A miner in the Pittsburgh district is not hopelessly cut off from all life away from the mine where he is working.

The Pittsburgh district is only one of eleven bituminous fields in Pennsylvania. The domain of steel and coal extends south to the coking fields around Uniontown and Connellsville and east to the region surrounding Johnstown. Northeast of Pittsburgh are the mines of central Pennsylvania, some in wild valleys with little feudal villages, others in high open country where mining settlements are scattered among farming centers and county towns.

Taking all Pennsylvania bituminous fields together, eight miners out of ten live in villages with less than 2,500 population, and more than half are housed in company dwellings.

Even more than in other eastern states, coal in Pennsylvania has always been mined largely by foreign-born workers, but the balance is shifting. Many sons of the Slavs and Italians have gone into the mines and in 1928—for the first time in the history of Pennsylvania coal—native white workers outnumbered the foreign-born. In western Pennsylvania mines the number of Negro workers has been increasing ever since the war.

West Virginia

Coal mining has been a pioneer industry in West Virginia, taking thousands of workers into wild and lonely mountain valleys, remote from any other human dwelling. So villages built, owned, and controlled by the mining companies have multiplied. Always a railroad has threaded its way up the valley before the mine opened, but its chief purpose is to carry away the coal. Passenger trains are few. Roadways have followed slowly, so that for many miners' families the railroad track and the bed of the creek are the only paths to the outside world. Not all villages are so remote. Mines are clustered about the small cities in the northern part of the state. Some lie fairly near together in Kanawha County and within reach of Charleston. In the mountain valleys highways and scattered little towns are growing up. But throughout the state, the little village, company-owned, is the typical mining community. Over 93 per cent of the miners live in settlements with less than 2,500 population and about three-fourths of all are in company houses.

West Virginia workers have been drawn in part from the

mountaineer families who leave the poverty of their mountain huts in the hope of a better living at the mines. They
are a fighting stock and their past revolts against the
tyranny of the mine companies are a familiar chapter in
American labor history. The other workers were equally
divided in 1920 between Negro and foreign-born. But in
recent years more Negroes than foreign-born have gone
into the mines, especially in the southern counties where the
industry has been most rapidly expanding. In the northern counties the various foreign groups—Italians, Hungarians, Poles, and other Slavs—still outnumber the Negro
workers.

West Virginia has its full share of men who work and
board away from their families. The number, of course,
is not so great as it is in Pennsylvania where the total
number of miners is far greater; but the percentage is highest in West Virginia. More households in these two states
than in any other coal region have outsiders living with
them.

Kentucky and Other Southern States

Just over the border from West Virginia are the coal
regions of eastern Kentucky and western Virginia. State
boundaries do not bring any great difference in mine population or mining communities, but more markedly than in
West Virginia the native white miners are in the majority.
Villages are mostly remote and desolate, quite cut off from
contact with the outside world. Workers are too poor to
draw wandering salesmen, and the old line union officials
have never taken the trouble to reach these tiny widely scattered settlements. But the scores of little villages manage
to roll up a surprisingly large total number of workers:
over 44,000 in eastern Kentucky and over 12,000 in the
mountains of Virginia.

Western Kentucky coal fields lie west of the mountains

and are much closer to the coal fields of southern Illinois than to the eastern counties of Kentucky. Here about one miner in four is a Negro and very few of the white miners are foreign-born.

Distinct from all other coal fields is the important Birmingham region in Alabama. This is the southern Pittsburgh, dominated by a subsidiary of the U. S. Steel Corporation, and by two or three lesser steel companies.

The 25,000 coal mine workers outnumber the steel workers. Mines are in a limited area surrounding the city of Birmingham. About one miner in ten lives within the city limits, but most of the workers are in small company villages, and though the distances are short the villages are less easily reached from one another or from the city than are the mine villages of the Pittsburgh district. Few foreign workers have gone to Alabama since the early days of Alabama coal, and in 1920 Negro miners outnumbered the white workers. During the bitterly fought strike of that year many of the white and Negro strikers were blacklisted and hundreds, perhaps thousands, of strikers were replaced by Negroes brought in from the country. Now about three miners out of four are Negroes.

Illinois, Indiana and Ohio

The chief northern coal fields outside of Pennsylvania are now in central and southern Illinois. Here and in the western counties of Indiana coal beds underlie the rolling country characteristic of the Middle West. There are many small towns and cities in the mining districts and only about half the mine workers are village dwellers. Less than 10 per cent live in company houses. In Ohio, many of the mines—but not all—are in the hills, away from other settlements, and roughly one-fourth of the workers must depend on the mining company for their housing.

Mines in these states have always had fewer foreign-born

workers than the mines in Pennsylvania and fewer Negroes than the mines in West Virginia. Unlike Pennsylvania, West Virginia, and Kentucky, these mid-western states publish no data from year to year on the make-up of the mining population. After 1920, some twenty thousand more miners were taken on in Illinois, Indiana and Ohio, and then —after 1923—more than 90,000 were frozen out. Among the 97,000 who are still employed, we may roughly estimate that some 30,000 are foreign workers and perhaps 5,000 are Negroes.

Western Coal Fields

Coal villages of Colorado have been the scene of unforgettable industrial battles, and every one knows that a majority of the miners in that state are housed in company dwellings. The same thing is true in most of the western coal fields. On the plains just west of the Mississippi— Iowa, Kansas, and Missouri—some coal is being dug near the small towns; other mines are remote from a settlement. About one miner in five lives in a company house.

Foreign workers have been brought by the thousand into these desolate feudal domains. Negro miners are relatively many in Iowa and Missouri, but there and even in the Southwest they are fewer than the foreign-born miners.

West of the Mississippi, as in the northern fields east of the Mississippi, fewer miners are employed to-day than ten years ago. Probably 25,000 foreign workers are included among the 60,000 men still employed in western mines.

Negro Miners

From this brief sketch of the coal fields we see that the Negro miners are chiefly in three southern states: more than 25,000 in West Virginia (and most of these in the southern counties); some 17,000 in the Birmingham district of Alabama; nearly 10,000 in Kentucky (and most of these in the western Kentucky field). Perhaps 3,500 are in Virginia and Tennessee.

But while some 75 to 80 per cent of the Negro miners are south of the Ohio River and east of the Mississippi, there are probably at least 12,000 Negroes working in the northern and western coal fields. Pennsylvania has the largest number working in any one northern state, with some 3,500, chiefly in the Pittsburgh district and the coking region. In the southern counties of Illinois, near the border of Kentucky, many mines employ Negro workers, and in some of these one-third of the miners are Negroes. Perhaps 4,000 are in the other northern fields and 4,000 scattered through the western mines.

Chief Foreign Language Groups

Poles are on the whole the largest single foreign group, totaling in 1920 over 50,000 men. Only about one in six of the Polish miners had gone beyond the coal fields of Pennsylvania, and there were many more Poles in the anthracite than in the Pennsylvania bituminous mines. Some 2,000 Polish miners were also reported in West Virginia, Ohio, and Illinois, and small scattering groups in other states.

Italian miners were almost as numerous as the Poles, and on the whole they had traveled further inland. Some 10,000 were in the anthracite, some 17,000 in Pennsylvania bituminous, over 8,000 in Illinois, and about 5,000 in West Virginia. Many had gone west of the Mississippi.

Other important groups include Austrians and Slovaks (chiefly in Pennsylvania bituminous, but also in the anthracite); Russians and Lithuanians (chiefly in the anthracite); Hungarians (few in the anthracite, but several thousand in Pennsylvania bituminous, in West Virginia, and ten years ago in Ohio); Yugoslavians (chiefly in Pennsylvania, both sections of the industry) ; and Mexicans (chiefly in Colorado and the Southwest).

Foreign-born workers have not only dug most of the American coal produced during the past hundred years; they have also played an important rôle in the struggles of the mine workers. British miners, fresh from union membership in their native land, took the lead in organizing the miners here in the sixties and seventies. Hungarians, Italians, Poles and Slovaks—although often betrayed by mine union officials—have stood out in bitterly fought mine strikes from Pennsylvania to Colorado.

CHAPTER V

LIVING UNDER COMPANY CONTROL

Straight rows of double houses placed close together, painted all a dull and ugly red, each house exactly like its neighbors, small back yards cluttered with sheds and privies, houses and yards showered with smoke and dust from the railway and the big mine tipple—the whole settlement one hideous "patch" on a fair, open hillside.

Again, unpainted houses, lightly built and open to the piercing winds of a mountain winter, dotting a hillside or straggling along the steep banks of a creek,—no road, no plan, no pretense of comfort.

Very rarely a village well-planned, with houses well-built and not of a deadly uniformity.

Perhaps more than any other industries, bituminous coal mining has made its workers dependent on company housing. More than half are in company dwellings, and even this high figure is not so important as the fact that for most of these men no other dwellings are available. At hundreds of mines the worker must live in a company house or go elsewhere to find a job. What it means to live in a company village we shall see in a moment. First, let us look a little more closely at the houses themselves.

How Company Houses Are Built

Wooden houses with roofs of composition paper, usually without a cellar and often supported only on posts with the wind sweeping through under the floor—these are the prevailing type. There are exceptions, of course. More of the houses in the North than in the South have solid foundations, weather-proof walls and roofs of shingle or slate. But taking all the states together about one house in four is of the flimsiest board and batten construction, and even in the northern coal fields nearly 10 per cent of the company houses are board and batten. Such houses are bad enough in hot weather. In cold weather—and winter is cold even in southern mountains—they are cruelly unfit for human beings.

Where weather board gives an appearance of trim tightness, it has usually been slapped on to the studs with no wood sheathing between. Sometimes not even a layer of paper has been set in to keep out the cold. In the North, most of the weather-board houses are plastered inside but in the South a rough-wood finish is more common. The paper roof is almost universal in the southern villages.

Most of the houses have three or four small rooms. A few companies provide five- or even six-room houses for the workers. At the other extreme are hundreds of two-room shacks—and even one-room shanties. In every field, bosses and foremen have larger, better houses than the miners. In the South, and especially in Alabama, the housing for Negro miners is conspicuously bad.

Since nearly half the families consist of five or more persons, and thousands of families take in boarders or lodgers, serious overcrowding is common. From four to nine persons were sharing each sleeping room in one house out of seven when the Federal Children's Bureau studied a section of Raleigh County, West Virginia.

Water is piped through the streets of about two-thirds of the villages. But the companies' chief concern is to have water for putting out a fire. The daily convenience of the miners' families is not considered. Mining is at best a very dirty job. It means an enormous lot of heavy laundry work for the women. Theoretically, wash houses are provided at the mine mouth so that men can bathe and change their clothes before going home, but they are not popular with the workers. The wash-house—if it exists at all—is crowded and overheated when the men come pouring out of the mine. Lockers are seldom provided. The worker's street clothes must spend the day in a messy bundle slung from the ceiling and unprotected from pilfering. So he prefers to go home in his working clothes and use the tub of hot water which his wife or his landlady is expected to have ready for him in the kitchen. Plenty of hot running water, with shower bath or a stationary tub is more needed in a miner's house than in almost any other dwelling. But what is the real situation in this country that boasts of its bath tubs and plumbing?

In the anthracite the village with a water system usually has only one faucet in the kitchen, for the scale of water charges—whether in company villages or in the far more numerous "independent" communities—is so arranged as to tax heavily every additional outlet. Water is metered to "business, manufacturing, industrial, and commercial establishments" but the householder cannot secure a metered service. The miner's family can use an unlimited amount of water *provided* it is laboriously drawn by hand from the kitchen faucet, while a small amount passing through a boiler and running into a shower or a tub and a stationary hand-basin would double the bill.

Even the faucet in the kitchen is not universal in the anthracite and in the bituminous fields it is distinctly unusual. In six soft-coal villages out of seven the miner's family must carry in water from an outside hydrant or well, which is usually shared with at least two other families. The struggle for cleanliness is heroic, for as one miner's wife put it: "It's hard to get at keeping clean when you're tired out from carrying the water."

Outdoor privies are the only toilets provided for most miners' families, and few companies have taken the trouble to make even these modern and well-constructed. Even rarer are those which attempt the periodic cleansing of the pits which is necessary for health when scores or hundreds of persons are crowded into a congested village. "You can't never get a good breath down there you're so close to somebody's privy." Bad odors, polluted creeks, and a contaminated water supply are all too common.

Companies are in general negligent about repairs. Leaky roofs, broken windows, sagging doors may go long without attention. Even in many of the "better" villages, a coat of paint and some high-sounding welfare work may put up a good appearance while basic daily needs are neglected. "In the worst of the company-controlled communities the state of disrepair at times runs beyond the power of verbal description or even of photographic illustration, since neither words nor pictures can portray the atmosphere of abandoned dejection or reproduce the smells." [1]

Only two of the 713 villages studied by the United States Coal Commission were listed as meeting the modest standard set by the commission in both water supply and disposal of sewage and other waste. One other village was scored at 100 for housing, but here the water supply and disposal of waste were below the standard. Only 23 of the 713 villages were scored at 75 per cent or higher on all three of these basic points.

Housing for miners is not wholly a question of company villages. In the anthracite and in certain thickly settled sections of the northern bituminous fields several thousand miners had, during the better years of the industry, succeeded in buying a house, but these men are only a small minority among the 650,000 workers in the industry. And where they can build only on land leased from a coal-owner their position is by no means secure. Serious cave-ins are common in many anthracite settlements and land-owning companies and estates use a form of lease which clears the land-owner of any responsibility for damage to dwellings or to persons. A miner who has invested all his savings in a house built on leased land may suddenly have warning of collapse. Then he is lucky if the family and their belongings escape without damage. "After the house has gone under you can go in and get what lumber is left."

In coal fields, like parts of West Virginia, where all the land within reach of the mine is owned either by an operating company or by a land corporation that draws income from royalties on coal, miners who have acquired houses, built on leased land, have not thereby acquired freedom to organize, or to oppose the management of the employer. A few companies, operating away from any center of population or any other industry, are trying to lure their workers into buying houses from the company. They admit openly that this tends to anchor the workers at the mine and discourage revolt. They do not point out that if the mine were permanently closed the houses would be valueless.

Thousands who live in independent communities can—theoretically—choose their dwellings. Practically, their choice is everywhere strictly limited by the amount in the pay envelope, and this cannot usually be stretched to provide the space and the conveniences which are supposed to belong to an "American" standard of living. Landlords build to rent and make money and they give a grudging minimum of repairs. On the whole, the miner in a company house pays a lower rent and gets, perhaps, more for his money than the miner renting from another landlord, according to the United States Coal Commission study of housing in 1922-23. Since then company rentals have been pushed up in many villages. But even if the statement were true to-day—and miners question it—this is more than balanced by two other facts about company houses:

(1) At hundreds of villages the miner must live in a company house and thousands of families are forced to live in dwellings unfit for human beings at any price; and

(2) The terms on which a worker lives in a company village rob him of every bit of personal freedom.

Miners know these things so well that at mines operating near other settlements many company houses stand idle even when the mines are working at normal capacity. Almost always workers prefer when possible to shift for themselves rather than submit to the terms imposed in company villages.

One colored worker, employed for many years in the Sloss-Sheffield Steel and Iron Co. coal mines in Birmingham, Alabama, summed up the reasons why he was through with company houses forever. He had been evicted when his wife died and vowed then and there he'd never live in a company house again.

"Company knows too much about you! Besides, if they get stuck, the foreman sends up for you any time, even if you've just come off a 10-hour shift and maybe worked overtime and are tired. You can't refuse, or you'd be fired."

Living in a Company Village

Company stores, called "pluck-me's" or "grab-all's," are an outstanding daily grievance. In remote company villages they have a complete monopoly for the trade in food and working supplies; their only competitors are the mail-order houses to which miners' families have been turning for clothing and certain household necessaries, when they are able to muster the cash for immediate payment. But the post office is often in the company store and the manager can keep check on mail-order trade.

Pennsylvania state law forbids mining companies to operate stores at their mines, but the law has not prevented them from organizing subsidiary supply companies. President Morrow of Pittsburgh Coal Co. openly referred to "our stores" when he testified before the Senate sub-committee on living conditions at coal mines in April, 1928. He maintained that "at all our mines other stores are nearby. . . .

No. **TENNESSEE COAL, IRON & R. R. CO.**
PAY STATEMENT
EDGEWATER WORKS

SECOND HALF MONTH

COAL	TONS MINED	LESS DOCK-AGE	TONS PAID FOR	RATE	AMOUNT
PICK					
MACH			24 ?	49½	12 05
YARDAGE					
"					
"					
DAYS					
HOURS					
					12 05
TOTAL EARNINGS					12 05
GARNISHMENTS					
U. S. STEEL STOCK					
CASH ADVANCES					
GROUP INSURANCE					
STORE CHECKS					4 00
COMMISSARY					3 70
RENT					
WATER					
LIGHT					
DOCTOR					
DENTAL, HOSP. AND DISPENSARY					
TENNESSEE LAND CO.					
EXPLOSIVES					85
SUPPLIES					35
SHOP					05
SCHOOL					
COAL					
CHECK WEIGHMAN					10
BATH HOUSE					
BADGES					
R. R. TICKETS					1 00
TOTAL STOPPAGES					12 05
BALANCE DUE					

EMPLOYEE TO KEEP THIS PART
THIS IS YOUR RECEIPT FOR ALL STOPPAGES

PAY CHECK OF AN ALABAMA MINER

Deductions for mine expenses were $1.35. His net earnings for two weeks were $10.70, but he got no cash.

In addition . . . farmers, hucksters, peddlers, solicitors, and salesmen of all kinds of commodities . . . have access to our towns and trade with our employees." He was sure of this because over a thousand individual permits had been issued. Without a permit from the company no salesman could enter the villages.

Where other stores are within reach and workers are "free" to trade where they please, many companies keep an eye on the percentage of the payroll coming back to the company store. They will not admit that they compel workers to buy at the company store, but miners often feel that they are under coercion. If a family does too much buying elsewhere, the worker expects to find things made harder for him in the mine. Or as one miner in West Virginia put it: "If they caught me getting packages from Sears-Roebuck they'd fire me."

The old custom of paying wages not in cash but only in scrip which must be spent at the company store or exchanged there at a heavy discount for money is now everywhere illegal. But great quantities of scrip or coupons are still issued as an advance toward amounts due on the next pay day. It can be exchanged immediately for cash at a discount but it is accepted at face value for purchases at the company store. Other stores may take it also, but only at a discount, and usually they refuse to touch it. Scrip thus encourages trading at the company store, for with semimonthly pay-days and low earnings the worker finds it difficult to catch up and have cash ahead. The old "bob-tail check" of early days in the anthracite when every penny of wages stayed with the company for rent, mine supplies, and purchases at the company store is still common at many bituminous mines. Miners may receive on pay day, instead of cash, a statement neatly balanced with ciphers.

Company stores also allow installment buying of furniture and clothing, with a heavy charge for "overhead." If the mine stops running for a while or if the family is overtaken by illness, a current account may be allowed to pile up until it amounts to a considerable debt at the store. All this tends to tie the worker to the mine until he has cleared the debt. But in the total absence of social insurance to provide for sickness and unemployment, such "benevolence" is the best that workers can expect from their bosses.

Prices are usually higher at company stores than elsewhere. Where there is no local competition, prices are out of all relation to the cost of the goods. Where other stores are within reach, the company store receiving scrip can still charge a price above the current one and hold a good deal of trade without coercion. Since this form of credit entails no risk and no delay in payment—for the store cashes in the scrip at the mine office on the next pay-day—it gives the company store a clear business advantage over local competitors who extend credit to the workers. But this advantage is not passed on to the workers in lower prices. Stores are intended to bring in a profit to the mining company and most of them charge all that the traffic will bear.

The other basic grievance is the company's complete domination over the worker's daily existence. He has no voice in the management of the company village. No meetings for protest or organization are allowed on company land, and in many of the more remote regions this spreads so far around the mine that no public highway, no non-company land lies anywhere within easy walking distance.

Often the village is fenced off with a single gate kept constantly under guard. The West Penn Power Corporation, for example, owns a mining town near Logan Ferry surrounded by a high picket fence topped with barbed wire. The town is approached by only one road, watched by a coal and iron cop who stops all strangers. In this town all mail goes through the company post office.

Company police are, of course, at their worst in time of

strike, but through petty tyrannies they interfere daily with the freedom of the mine worker and his family. That they include unprincipled thugs imported from among the worst elements in the city population has been shown repeatedly in public hearings and reports.

Companies that go in for welfare work pay not only the policeman but the preacher. They usually supplement the county allowance for teacher's salary and select the teacher. They build a schoolhouse and perhaps a company clubhouse and a recreation field. They organize an employee association of some kind. But the workers for whom these benefits are arranged usually find much of the cost passed on to them through assessments or "dues" deducted from the pay check.

The Rockefeller companies and a few others have set up company unions. In Somerset County, Pennsylvania, after the defeat of the 1922 strike, the Consolidation Coal Company introduced so-called employee representation, but the committees were made up of those named by the strikers as "spotters," "scab herders" and gunmen. A striker who tried to attend the committee election meeting was barred out by a deputy sheriff.[2]

One steel company operating coal mines and company towns, in analyzing the men's output in tons of coal studied the returns from each company house. "This indicated that some of the houses were occupied by men whose productive ability was below the standard and gave an indication of those men who were occupying better quarters than was their worth to the company in comparison with others." At the end of six months "labor costs were reduced 30 per cent" without a change in wage schedules and "housing requirements were cut 33.1 per cent." Evidently men who did not speed-up production were thrown out of the company houses.[3]

THE COMPANY LEASE

Worst of all are the documents through which the miner, coming to one of these feudal villages, has to sign away his rights. To get a job in the mine he must sign a yellow-dog contract. To get a house for his family, he must sign a special form of lease forfeiting his legal rights as a tenant.

The yellow-dog contract is practically universal in the company villages of non-union coal fields, but is also required at many other non-union mines. It will be discussed in a later chapter. The special lease is peculiar to company houses. It ties the dwelling to the job. It explicitly provides for eviction of the family with little or no warning, and it places extraordinary restrictions upon the occupants of the house. Such leases have not only been common in non-union fields; they were tolerated at union mines before the breakdown of the United Mine Workers of America.

A few typical clauses are worth quoting. Most of the leases include some such agreement as this:

And said Employe shall not harbor or permit to use, occupy or otherwise be upon said premises, any person objectionable to the Company, and said Employe shall upon notice and demand of the Company, remove any person therefrom objectionable to the Company, and failing so to do the right of the said Employe and his family to so use and occupy said premises shall thereupon immediately cease and terminate.

In a non-union village this means that a worker who lets a union organizer come into his house is in danger of immediate eviction. Sometimes, as in the lease used by the Island Creek Coal Company in West Virginia, the worker has to agree that the company "shall at all times have the right to enter" the house to find and eject any "improper or suspicious persons." Leases frequently state that only the worker and members of his immediate family shall have access to the house, and the worker agrees "to not use, nor suffer or permit the use of the lands, ways, roads, or alleys to said leased premises for any other purpose or by any other persons." The lease used by W. J. Rainey, Inc., in Fayette county, Pennsylvania, elaborates this with gruesome detail:

The worker agrees "to do no act or thing, nor suffer or cause the same to be done, whereby the public or any person or persons whomsoever, may be invited or allowed to go or trespass upon said premises, or upon said private ways or roads, or upon other grounds of the Lessor, except physicians attending the Lessee and his family; teamsters or draymen moving Lessee and his family belongings into said premises or away from the same; and undertakers with hearse, carriages and drivers, and friends, in case of death of the Lessee or any member of his family."

Very common is a proviso in the lease that general rules and regulations of the company shall be strictly complied with. This opens the door to any kind of restriction. Very common also is the explicit statement that the company shall be the sole judge of the worker's failure to abide by the terms of the lease. The Coal Commission reported that in the Kanawha district miners leaving a village to look for work elsewhere expected their families to be evicted in ten days after the worker's absence was noted by the company.

Companies sometimes allow a family to remain rent free in a company house after the worker has been killed or permanently disabled in the mine. The charity of free rent may also be granted when a mine is shut down because the company has temporarily no market for its coal, but these occasional acts of benevolence toward docile workers only bring out more sharply the use of these unfair leases as a weapon in the class struggle. Thousands of families are evicted during every serious strike, and the companies always defend the evictions as reasonable since the worker has signed the lease and thereby agreed that the dwelling goes with the job. When men go on strike they leave their jobs, the company says, and they must expect to leave their dwellings also.

Operators have made interesting admissions about their methods. Thus, Samuel D. Brady of the Brady-Warner Corporation in the Fairmont field told the Senate sub-committee on coal (1928) the following story of May, 1924. Brady and five of his men, together with the sheriff, were moving furniture from company houses and dumping it in the Union Hall. . . . Then they went to the house of Joe Morton. We quote from the record of the hearing:

Brady: "We found the door locked and nailed. . . . I instructed one of the mine watchmen to break down the door. . . . The door was broken down, and I entered with two of the watchmen and found Morton standing in the front room, and I said to him, 'Joe, where do you want your furniture moved to?'"

Senator Wheeler: "You were advised by your lawyers, were you, that you could knock down their house?"

Brady: "Could knock down the door, so long as I did not disturb the tenants."

Attorney Townsend: "Isn't that violence?"

Brady: "No, sir; breaking down a door is not violence. The door is a door. Violence is to a human being. I had advice from my attorney."

President Baker and Vice-President Osler of Pittsburgh Terminal Coal Co. explained that instead of forcibly evicting tenants in certain villages during the 1927 strike they had turned off the water at certain hydrants. This did not really matter, Baker said, since there was no water in the houses and no flushing toilets; the families simply had to walk further to fetch the water they needed! Also the company had the roof taken off from one occupied house. "We thought that by making it rather uncomfortable for these people they would get out."

When a family is evicted the company assumes no responsibility for the household goods. One incident at Vintondale, Pa., in the 1922 strike illustrates what the miners may be up against if the company wants to punish them. Four miners who had conferred with a union organizer were "discharged and evicted the same afternoon; the men were held prisoners in the company office while their goods and families were trucked out of town in one direction; then after the company had taken $35 off them 'for the costs of the eviction' the miners were driven out in another direction." [4]

When companies and judges maintain that workers have freely agreed to the terms of these company leases and therefore cannot object to evictions, they are distorting the situation. Even if the worker knew what he was signing, what freedom has he to refuse? He needs the job and he knows that thousands of miners are out of work. In fields where the majority of the mines are tied to company villages with no non-company houses within reach of the mine, the individual unorganized worker has literally no choice but to take the job and the house on the company's terms— or join the ranks of the unemployed.

Only through mass organization can the miners resist the tyranny of the operators. Company houses, company police, company land, the company store,—the whole set-up of a company village gives the operator a powerful weapon which the yellow-dog contract makes it "legal" for him to use against workers who attempt to organize. But militant organizers can find ways to penetrate these fortresses, and workers suffering from wage cuts and more intense speeding up are ready to rise against unbearable conditions. No weapon of the capitalists can break the power of a united militant working class.

CHAPTER VI

THE CHANGING JOB AND JOBLESS MINERS

MINE workers' jobs have been changing and their work has been speeded up in recent years as more and more machinery has been brought into the mines. They are not yet standardized. Mine fields vary, and even two mines operated side by side in the same field may have a different arrangement of jobs.

One broad distinction runs throughout the industry. In every mine the workers fall into two groups of men: first, the miners who loosen the coal from the coal seam and get it loaded into the mine cars and, second, the so-called "company men" who do all the hauling, prepare the coal for shipment, and keep the mine generally in good condition.

Both groups have been affected by the new developments in mining technique. Both have begun to feel the bosses' drive for efficiency and speed-up. But the miners, far more than the company men, have seen their status changing. Miners used to work as independent craftsmen and prided themselves that "no damned foreman can look down my shirt collar." Now they are seeing their jobs subdivided; pick miners have been more and more displaced by cutting machines; mechanical loading is not only driving the hand loaders out but it brings a much closer timing and dovetailing of the various jobs. In some mines petty foremen are now installed to watch the men at the working face.

The changes can be most easily explained by a brief description of three arrangements, representing three stages of development. All of these—and many gradations in between—are present in the coal industry to-day.

The Pick Miner

In the mine without machinery, the miner's job includes all the varied work involved in shooting and loading coal. A place at the coal face, inside the mine, is assigned to a miner, or to two miners working together as buddies. In the anthracite they are not two certified miners but a miner and a "miner's laborer." Elsewhere also the second man may be a learner and not yet a fully experienced miner.

They may be set to driving an entry (haulageway); they may be given a point on an entry from which a narrow side passage or neck is to be broken through as a first step toward opening up a room. Or the room may have been already started. In the old days the boss assigned the place, with instructions as to direction and width, but allowed the miner himself to decide day by day just how the round of cutting, drilling, shooting and loading was carried out.

Wherever he is working in a non-mechanized mine the miner is responsible for keeping the roof safe over his head, setting timber props when necessary. He must put the bottom in condition and lay the track from the entry to the working face. In low coal seams he must himself push in and out of the entry the cars he needs for the coal or for any rock that has to be cleared away from the room. The miner drills holes for the charges of explosive by which the coal—or rock—is loosened and broken into manageable pieces. If he is "shooting off the solid" he makes the holes and blows off the coal without any preliminary cutting. For "pick-mined" coal, the miner first undercuts the coal with a hand pick, clearing out a space—or kerf—several inches high which extends in under the main body of the coal seam as far as he can reach. This cut relieves the tension of the coal when the explosive is touched off and makes it possible to get out the coal with smaller charges of explosive than are needed for shooting off the solid. After the shots have been fired, the miner must load the coal into cars and clean up the room for the next round of cutting, drilling, shooting and loading.

Most of this work involves a special skill. The miner must know how to test the safety of the roof and how to place the timbers to support it. He must be alert to recognize the sounds which often precede a fall. Undercutting is not only hard muscular work; it must be done with precision and delicacy to avoid premature falls of coal while the miner is lying at the face. Drilling of holes and the preparation of charges require good judgment, based on a knowledge of the coal or rock to be blasted and of the explosive itself. Loading the cars may sound simple enough, but when the coal seam is low and the miner cannot stand upright the loading is difficult. Often there is only slight clearance between the top of the car and the roof.

All these things the old time miner did—and does—with a minimum of supervision. As a "tonnage man" he is paid according to the amount of coal he sends to the tipple, and he is usually free to leave the mine before quitting time if he wants to. He provides his own tools and his own light. He buys his explosives. He uses the technique he has learned from other workers and, subject only to possible rules against shooting off the solid and possible insistence by the operator on a certain type of light or of explosive, he does the work as he thinks best.

In spite of this apparent freedom, there are many sources of perpetual conflict between this old time miner and the mine operator. The wage question is always the basic difficulty. For the miner this is complicated by the question of "dead work." Non-union operators have frequently paid nothing for the time the miner has to spend in such things as timbering, getting out rock and clay, and cleaning up bottom. The tonnage rate on the coal is supposed to cover the average amount of work involved. Obviously there are wide differences of condition and many sudden emergencies, sometimes involving whole days of work for which the miner receives no pay at all.

The boss and the miner also frequently disagree as to whether the carloads of coal are sufficiently clean of rock and clay. Often the miner is defrauded of part of his wage by deliberate and systematic short-weighing of his coal. Against this the miners have no redress unless they insist on employing a check-weighman to verify the weights. Even then the check which a miner hangs on each car to identify *his* coal may be now and then mysteriously "lost" before the car reaches the tipple.

Other conflicts arise at the working face. The miner has to depend on the boss for the timber to prop up his roof. Sometimes timber is not promptly available. Also the miner cannot load his coal unless cars are brought to his entry. Waiting for cars may mean a welcome pause in the day's work, but quite as often it means a serious delay which cuts into the miner's earnings.

Company Men in Old-Type Mines

While the pick miners—tonnage men—are working at the coal face, company men are employed on a time basis for all the other jobs inside the mine and for the surface work at the mine mouth.

Haulageways must be kept open. Roof and sides must be supported with timber or masonry. Tracks must be kept in repair. They must be kept clear of coal and rock which may be shaken off the loaded cars or dumped when a car is wrecked.

For the hauling of coal and rock a separate group of workers is responsible. In mines without motor haulage, the cars are drawn by mules, and each "trip" needs a driver with perhaps a "trip rider" to help him. On down-grades the driver or the trip rider must "sprag" each car with a piece of wood so placed as to drag against the ground and block the wheel from revolving. When the underground grade is too steep for mules, some mines still use a primitive rope and winch for the up-grade and depend on gravity for the down-grade.

If the entrance to the mine is a vertical shaft or a "slope" too steep for mules and men, some sort of power hoist is installed at the surface and a special crew is responsible for the cage (elevator) or the trips of cars carrying men or coal or timber or rock in and out of the mine.

If the mine is wet—and many mines cut across underground streams—crews of pumpmen have to be on duty night and day to keep the water under control.

Most mines make an attempt at artificial ventilation. This involves setting of doors and other barriers (brattices) to direct the air currents through the mine. When a door cuts across the haulageway a boy, called a trapper in bituminous mines, is stationed there to open and shut the door whenever a trip of cars comes along. Even the mines which have no machinery underground usually have set up a power fan on the surface to drive air through the workings; but a few still depend on an underground furnace so placed as to send hot air up one of the shafts,— the most primitive and dangerous device for drawing a current out of the mine and thus sucking fresh air down some other opening. Sometimes the main ventilation system is supplemented by underground fans. In old mines without electricity it is a boy's job to keep such a fan going.

The simplest surface workings have a place for weighing the coal and dumping it into railroad cars or barges. A blacksmith is employed for sharpening the miners' tools. In the anthracite, the coal has for many years been picked over and graded by size in the breaker, and some such preparation is increasingly customary at bituminous mines also.

Machinery Goes Underground

Cutting machines brought the first big change in the work of the old-time miner. A worker known as a machine runner, usually with a second worker as a helper, took over the undercutting of the coal which the miner had done with a hand pick. The "miner" still did as before all the other work at the face, and except that in course of time his hand drill was, in many mines, replaced by a compressed air or electric drill, his tools were the same that they had always been. His pick was still useful at times. His hand shovel was unchanged.

The cutting machine runner and his helper are assigned to a group of rooms, with a loader—or more usually two loaders—responsible for drilling, shooting and loading the coal in each room. Sometimes a pair of loaders are given two rooms side by side so that there may be no delay in waiting for the machine crew to make the next cut for them. Machine runners and hand loaders are still tonnage workers and not company men. Together they are responsible for the working places assigned to them.

The first cutting machine in the United States is said to have been used in Ohio in 1877, but no general figures on machine cut coal were gathered until nearly fifteen years later. By 1913, machines were cutting one-half the bituminous output and in 1929 three-fourths (75.4 per cent). The various coal fields have developed unevenly. Kentucky, Virginia, West Virginia, Ohio and Illinois show more than the average percentage cut by machine. In the anthracite, cutting machines have so far made little headway. Even in 1929 less than 2 per cent of the output was cut by machine.

For company men mechanical power first came underground in the shape of small steam locomotives for main haulageways. To-day electric motors (chiefly trolleys) are installed on main haulageways of most of the bigger mines, but in many of these mines mules and mule drivers have held their place for taking loads and empties back and forth between rooms and gathering points on the main lines. Recent development of reel cable lines, and the stress laid by the United States Bureau of Mines on the dangers from underground trolleys and the greater safety of rightly constructed storage battery motors, are beginning to bring electric haulage right up to rooms at the working face.

With electricity admitted underground for cutting machines and motor haulage, it has been turned to many other uses: lighting main haulageways, running booster fans, opening and shutting doors, firing shots, or providing underground telephones and signal systems. Mechanical braking tends to displace the primitive spragging.

Enter the Mechanical Loader

After the war boom collapsed and the crisis had driven the operators into a fever of competitive cost-cutting, engineers began seriously to study means of reducing the labor required for loading coal at the face. Their experiments with mechanical loading have brought the latest stage in coal mine mechanization underground.

Several different kinds of machines are being installed. A few mines with high seams are using a modified power shovel. Some mines with low seams use a dragging scraper. But more common than either of these is some type of shovel or revolving arms to gather up the coal and place it on the lower end of a short conveyor which lifts the coal from the floor level and dumps it in the car. Or the short lifting conveyor may do no shoveling but merely receive, on a low moving surface, coal shoveled onto it by hand.

The hand loaded conveyor does away with the hard muscular work—and the skill—of throwing coal into a car, and substitutes the steady drive of feeding the conveyor. The "hand loader" who was still an all round craftsman becomes an unskilled "shovel stiff," chained to the speed of a machine.

When any one of these loading devices is introduced the work at the face is subdivided and reorganized. Company timber men—instead of loaders or miners—set the timbers even at the working face. Trackmen work not only in the main haulageways and entries but all the way in to the point where the coal cars are loaded. Usually, but not always, the drilling of holes and firing of shots are done by a special crew. When jobs are so subdivided they must be fitted in together. This means a close supervision and speed-up alien to all the traditions of the industry. Tonnage rates and the privilege of quitting early are abolished. The men at the face become day men tied to a time schedule. In spite of this, "dead work" continues to be a grievance, for as emergencies arise which stop the machines, the machine runners may have to help clear things up at an hourly rate lower than their regular pay.

Seven per cent of the bituminous output in 1929 was deep-mined coal loaded by some one of these mechanical devices. Illinois leads in tonnage of machine loaded coal, with 18,252,000 tons, or about 30 per cent of its 1929 output. But Wyoming—a much smaller coal state—leads in the percentage of its output loaded by machine. In Wyoming, the 3,000,000 tons mechanically loaded were about 45 per cent of the state's output in 1929. In percentage Utah, Montana, and Indiana ranked next below Illinois. Pennsylvania and West Virginia mines reported increasing use of machine loaders, but less than 5 per cent of the output in these states was mechanically loaded in 1929. (See table, page 242.)

In the anthracite, more face conveyors and scrapers than loading machines proper have been introduced. Considerably less than five per cent of the tonnage is handled by any one of these devices.

The number of machine loaders and conveyors in use is steadily increasing. *Coal Age,* the leading paper of the coal industry, boosts this mechanization as the one way to meet the coal crisis,—naturally, since the makers of mining machinery are its chief advertisers. It says nothing of the fact that mechanization tends to increase the surplus capacity, which is one of the major problems of the industry. Already most of the mining companies which can afford the capital investment involved are experimenting with mechanical loaders. Mines in which the entire output is loaded by machine are still few, but the increase in this latest phase of coal mine mechanization is far more rapid than was the early progress of coal cutting machines and motor haulage.

STRIP MINING

Where the coal seam lies near the surface an increasing number of strip pits are being developed. Instead of burrowing underground and wrestling with the problems of using machinery in low, dark rooms, where falls of roof and explosions of gas or coal dust may wreck expensive equipment, some operators are having the overburden stripped off and mining the coal in the open. One such operation opened in 1929 at DuQuoin, Illinois, and the Rosebud mine at Colstrip, Montana, are using the largest power shovels in the world.

Most of the strip mines are in Indiana, Illinois, Missouri, Ohio, Montana, and Kansas. These states produced about 17,000,000 tons of the 20,300,000 tons of bituminous coal mined by stripping in 1929. About 1,700,000 tons of anthracite was strip mined in that year.

For the percentage of bituminous output cut by machine or loaded by machine underground and the percentage mined in strip pits in the several states, see table, page 242.

Speed-up

Besides underground loading machines and giant power shovels in strip pits, engineers are introducing all sorts of other technical changes that lead directly to speed-up in the mine. Cutting machines are more powerful and adaptable than formerly. They can be moved about with greater ease. Multiple drills mounted on a truck are coming in to replace the single drill held by the worker. The stretch of temporary track from entry to working face is in some mines replaced by a conveyor of adjustable length, carrying coal from a loading machine (or a lifting conveyor) at the face to a car on permanent tracks in the entry. Dumping of cars, whether at the foot of the shaft or at the tipple, is done with a minimum of hand labor and a maximum of speed. In a few slope mines, a slope conveyor carries a steady flow of coal from an underground dump to the tipple.

Coal operators are making heavy investments in new equipment of all kinds. Some 170 producing companies were said to be planning for 1930 a total capital expenditure of $44,000,000 for this purpose, and *Coal Age* (January, 1930) estimated that the total for the industry would be some $200,000,000.

The sharp competition of the present period is driving also toward a speeding-up and intensifying of labor apart from technical changes. Even where loading machines have not yet been introduced, the bosses are beginning to fix schedules and stints for the workers. Thus T. W. Gray, an engineer of the Pittsburgh Coal Company, writing in *Coal Age* (November, 1927), reported a working cycle for entry work, with a 6-foot undercut, at Montour No. 9 mine, as follows:

Cutting	35	minutes
Drilling coal and slate	20	"
Shooting coal	10	"

Loading coal .... 45 minutes
Shooting slate .... 10 "
Loading slate .... 20 "

They reckoned on making three cuts during each eight-hour shift.

A miner describes a similar speed-up in the Wyoming mines of the Union Pacific Coal Company:

Working in groups of four, they use the cutting machine and the duckbill loader. The speed-up is so terrible and terrific that the moment these men get the shots prepared, the match is touched to the fuse, the blast goes off, and within ten minutes' time the men are back in the smoke, loading and going on with their work.[1]

Tonnage men are sometimes kept on the job until they have produced a stated number of cars, and the daily stint is being pushed upward. If they had accepted a quota of four cars, for example, they are now forced to load five before quitting. More common, perhaps, is the clean-up system. Just what this means is clear from a notice posted by one of the wage-cutting Paisley companies in the summer of 1930:

Effective August 10th all mines will be on the Clean-Up System basis, that is, every loader has to clean up his place, regardless of the time it takes, before leaving the mines.

Every motorman has to do likewise.

Day men will stay in the section until the above is accomplished.

Any one who is not satisfied to go along with this . . . shall be gotten rid of. We find that practically all the other companies are working this system successfully. . . .

It is either a case of getting all of these things done or making another cut in wages.

Motormen and drivers have traditionally made the rounds as they could, leaving empties and gathering loads according to their own judgment—or their whim. They could play politics within the union or in a non-union mine they could curry favor with the boss by withholding cars from unpopular miners while they kept others well supplied. The miners' demand for a "square turn" has figured in many battles. Now the bosses' slogan is "Service to the men at the face," which would solve the problem of the "square turn" only to raise the new and far more serious problem of speed-up.

Timbering, track work, repairs,—all sorts of "company" jobs—are watched more carefully than ever before. *Coal Age* in June, 1929, gave the following advice:

Set your time on every job that is regular. When your assistants give out work have them tell the men how much time they can have on it. Have them enter the time in their books and make an inspection of the work immediately after it is completed.

That means discharging those men who don't meet the schedule. Exactly. The good men won't kick.

Time schedules, stints that must be finished before the worker quits, conveyors that must be fed without a moment's rest,—all these have robbed the miner of such "freedom" on the job as he formerly had. The mine is becoming "nothing but a goddam factory" as one worker phrased it, and a "factory" with much of the speed-up by which the capitalist class is trying to increase its profits during the present period.

Worker's Output Increasing

Bituminous

When a cutting machine can make three cuts an hour, a mechanical drill can drive a six-foot hole every minute, and a shovel can average over 500 tons in a two-shift day, the way is open for a tremendous increase in the worker's average daily output of coal and a corresponding decrease in the number of workers employed to produce the needed tonnage.

The new Wildwood mine of the Butler Consolidated Coal Company at Butler, Pennsylvania, 15 miles north of Pittsburgh, reported for the first few months of operation an output of 12.1 tons per man per day. Every point in the development of this new, completely mechanized mine called for speed, speed, and more speed. "Loading out a face at Wildwood is a matter of minutes rather than days. . . . Transportation geared to high-speed production. A brand new mine to load mechanically 6,000 tons per shift." So run the reports on Wildwood, the first mine planned from the start for complete mechanization.[2]

The situation is very uneven, and the general average is still below five tons per man per day. Mines which have introduced mechanical loaders or conveyors are still wrestling with the technical difficulties of adapting old mines to the newest methods. The engineer who tries to put over a complete reorganization of the working routine in order to get maximum output from the new machines usually meets with resistance both from miners and from old-time foremen.

And yet some old mines had, in 1928, already arrived at an increase in output per worker which clearly shows what operators and engineers are determined to accomplish. Six of the seventeen Illinois mines which loaded all their coal by machine in 1928 had, since 1926, doubled the worker's productivity. Two had pushed it up to at least eleven tons per man per day, counting all employees in and about the mine. This was a very exceptional record for underground mines. A good deal more numerous in Illinois and elsewhere were those which had speeded up to a seven-, eight- or nine-ton average per man per day, in deep-mined coal.

For strip mines throughout the country the workers' average output was over eleven tons a day in 1928, but several strip mines had pushed it still higher. Seventeen to eighteen tons per man per day were reported for groups of strip mines in Illinois, Indiana, Kansas and the North Dakota lignite field. The record was held by the Rosebud strip mine in Montana where three shovels and 75 men produced nearly

1,200,000 tons in the year, or an average of nearly 50 tons per man per working day.

Workers' productivity will always vary from one mine to another because of the almost infinite variety of natural conditions and differences in methods of mining. In spite of the intense drive for mechanization the coal mined in strip pits or mechanically loaded underground, up to 1929, was less than 12 per cent of the total bituminous output— too small a share to turn the broad average of productivity sharply upward. So the figures for the country as a whole have risen slowly, much as they had been rising ever since the first cutting machine was introduced more than fifty years ago.

From 1913, the last "good" year before the war boom, to 1929 the mine worker's average output rose from 3.61 tons to 4.85 tons a day, an increase of 34 per cent. Average yearly output had meantime wavered with the irregularities in mine operation. But during these sixteen years the rising daily output was such a basic factor in the situation that 69,000 fewer miners, working fewer days, mined more coal in 1929 than the total output in 1913. (For table, see page 240.) As mechanical loaders handle greater percentages of the coal, the average tonnage per man per day will move more sharply upward.

Anthracite

In the anthracite the story has been somewhat different. Anthracite reserves are strictly limited, both in area and total tonnage. Bituminous operators have commonly abandoned very old or difficult operations and passed on to exploit fresh rich fields; the industry is still skimming the cream off the huge bituminous resources of the country. But in the anthracite most of the cream was skimmed off many years ago. The peak of the anthracite worker's productivity thus far was reached in 1899, when the daily average was 2.5 tons per man employed. By 1914 the average had fallen to 2.06 tons per man per day.

During the war boom, operators had their culm piles ransacked for the finely broken coal which had no market in the early days. They set dredgers to work to recover coal from the river beds. While this coal, which had deteriorated from exposure to air and water, was keeping the home fires from burning brightly, the operators demanded in the name of patriotism that the miners underground fill an extra car a day. Daily output (including all the coal and all the workers) was pushed up to around 2.3 tons per man. Then with the passing of the boom—and the market for coal that would not burn—output fell to just two tons a day in 1924. From this point it has been pushing slowly upward again, but in 1928 and 1929 it had climbed only to 2.17 tons per man. Now the fresh drive for huge mechanical breakers, more serious experiments with cutting machines, loading machines and conveyors underground, and a greater emphasis throughout the industry on efficiency and speed-up in details of operation will shortly have marked effect on the anthracite worker's productivity.

UNEMPLOYMENT

Bituminous

The Union Pacific Coal Company of Wyoming employed 3,034 workers in 1923 but only 1,845 in 1929. The company's output in the latter year was only about 6 per cent less than the tonnage of 1923, but the working force had been reduced by nearly 40 per cent. During these six years the company had made a drive for mechanization, bringing the machine-loaded tonnage up from 3 per cent to 58 per cent of the company's output.

Increasing mechanization has been one important factor in throwing miners out of work. But even in Wyoming, Illinois, and other states where mechanical loading and strip mining have been especially developed, other changes in the industry have also contributed to the mass unemployment. Closing down of mines; slightly more regular operation of mines that continue to produce; and in most states a drop in total tonnage from 1923 to 1928 have all had a share in the problem. The loading machine and the strip pit hold a threat of much greater joblessness in the near future as their tonnage increases. More thousands of men will be directly displaced as more mines are mechanized and speeded up. Other thousands will be thrown out by the permanent closing of mines which cannot meet the sharp competition of the new machines.

Mass unemployment of miners began with the collapse of the coal market at the end of 1923. Every important coal state except Kentucky and Colorado produced less coal in the following year. Immediately more than 85,000 men were squeezed out of the industry. This first sharp reduction in numbers employed was clearly tied up with the closing down of 1,745 mines in every section of the country and in almost every coal state.

More coal was produced by fewer men in 1925 than in 1924. Then in 1926, exports to markets opened for American coal by the long strike of British miners, and an active industrial year at home, together pushed bituminous production above the tonnage of 1923. But this large tonnage of 1926 was mined by 26,000 fewer men than had been employed for the small tonnage of 1924. Everywhere fewer mines were in operation, and producing mines worked more regularly than mines had worked in 1923.*

The next great loss of mine jobs came after the defeat of the 1927 strike, when in the course of one year the northern

---

* In five states—Michigan, Montana, North Dakota, Washington, Wyoming—mines averaged fewer days of operation in 1926 than in 1923.

operators dropped another 55,000 workers, and 17,000 men were frozen out of the industry in the South and the West.

Northern mine workers have suffered most cruelly in the crisis of coal mine unemployment. One-third of the bituminous workers in Pennsylvania and Illinois, and more than half the workers in Ohio and Indiana, were permanently displaced. The total number employed in these four states and Michigan fell from 386,600 in 1923 to 230,500 in 1929. About 55,000 were frozen out of northern mines with the first collapse of the market; the other 100,000 were in part victims of the shift in tonnage to southern fields. In Ohio the drop in employment paralleled the loss of tonnage. Illinois and Indiana were rationalizing with machinery and speed-up, and the loss of jobs after 1924 was greater than the loss of tonnage. Pennsylvania mines, after the first collapse in 1923-24, had no further loss in tonnage, but the tonnage came from fewer mines operating on the whole more regularly. The number of Pennsylvania workers was thereby reduced.

Taking the southern states as a whole, they produced 44,500,000 tons more coal in 1929 than in 1923, with 25,500 fewer workers. In no southern state did these six years bring a marked increase in daily output per man, but his yearly output was pushed up by working more days in the year. Alabama had faced a sharp drop in tonnage and this was the chief factor in throwing 5,000 men out of the industry in that state.

Western coal miners numbered 80,600 in 1923, but only 60,400 in 1929, a loss of 25 per cent, though western tonnage fell by only 4 per cent. In seven western states, from 25 to 40 per cent of the coal mine workers lost their jobs. Mines in Wyoming, Montana, North Dakota and Texas were pushing up the worker's daily output. In most of the western fields, large mines were producing a larger share in the total tonnage, operation was on the whole more regular and the worker's yearly output rose more sharply than his average daily output. Iowa and Kansas were the only western states where a heavy loss in jobs ran parallel to a heavy loss in tonnage.

It is less important, however, to know how many of the 200,000 mine workers lost their jobs because the coal market collapsed, how many because southern mines increased tonnage and took away the market from northern mines, how many because machine loaders were introduced and workers were speeded up, than it is to know that all these "causes" are tied up with one another and with the chaos and cruelty of capitalism.

Anthracite

In the anthracite the year of peak employment was not 1923 but 1914, when 180,000 men and boys were at work in and about the anthracite mines. The war boom production of 1918 was accomplished with 33,000 fewer workers than had been employed four years earlier. Then the number wavered, without any direct relation to the amount of anthracite produced. From 1923 to 1927, total production declined from 93,000,000 net tons to 80,000,000 net tons, 22 breakers were closed, and the washeries and dredges were cut down from 142 to 67. But, on the whole, the men thrown out of work by these changes had been able to find other jobs in the industry, for the total number employed actually rose from 158,000 in 1923 to 165,000 in 1926 and 1927.

Meantime, of course, work had grown more and more irregular, and when tonnage dropped still further in 1928, nine more breakers were closed. The difficulty of finding new mine jobs had now become acute and within twelve months 4,600 fewer men were employed. The fall in anthracite tonnage was checked in 1929, but another 9,000 men were thrown out of work as additional mines and breakers were closed. The campaign of deliberate speed-up had begun—

concentration of work at the most modern breakers, fresh experiment with machinery underground, and lavish expenditure for displacement of surface workers by giant up-to-date breakers. Mass unemployment will grow steadily more serious in the anthracite.

Trying to Find Another Job

When the Consolidation Coal Company threw 2,500 men out of employment in May, 1928, the president of the company gave them the cold comfort of the following statement:

Further, in behalf of any former employees seeking affiliation elsewhere in the industry, it wishes earnestly to bespeak all proper consideration and courtesy for their applications arising out of this action.[3]

The mockery in these words is clear when we remember that other companies were also closing down mines; and in the course of that one year the total number employed in coal mining was reduced by 75,000 men. These 75,000 were added to more than 100,000 others who had been dropped since 1923.

These figures give only the net loss in numbers employed in the industry. Hundreds, perhaps thousands, of union miners in western Pennsylvania and northern West Virginia were replaced by new men brought in during the anti-union drive of 1924 and the following years. The modernizing of mines has included a drive to replace the skilled craftsman with cheaper labor. *Coal Age* (February, 1930) is quite frank about this. Writing of reorganization of work at the face when powerful pneumatic picks are introduced in a mine not suited for cutting machines, it says, "With a few key men available it is possible *to bring in inexperienced labor* for the actual loading." (*Italics mine.—A. R.*) Just how many new men have been brought into the industry even while the total number of mine workers has been sharply decreasing, we do not know. But clearly all the figures we have are an understatement of the actual numbers thrown out of coal mining and compelled to find a living elsewhere.

A good deal of cheerful guessing has been indulged in. We hear it said that "50,000 went to Detroit," or "they take up farming" or "they drift to the cities." In Pennsylvania, "they go into the steel mills." All of which means exactly nothing. For years before the big crash of 1929, basic industries were increasing the worker's daily output. They were raising production with a decrease in the total number employed in manufacturing and railroading. Even the rapidly expanding auto industry was a forlorn hope for the miners who found thousands of discouraged farmers, displaced mechanics, and young workers from all over the country standing beside them in the auto job lines. Also, management experts warn factory bosses against taking on miners; their tradition of independence makes them restless slaves on the belt.

When the crash tumbled all industries into a long period of serious depression, miners out of work became a part of the great mass of jobless workers.

But long before the crash, it was plain that cheerful guessing about jobs for displaced miners simply obscured a desperate situation. Whole towns in some of the coal fields had fallen into extreme poverty. In one Illinois center, for example, an enterprising pants manufacturer opened a factory. He had closed his union shop in another city and came to exploit at sweat-shop wages the wives and young daughters of jobless miners.

Operators assume no responsibility for workers they no longer want. The jobless miner has no security against starvation, for the American capitalist state makes no provision for the unemployed. Mine workers who have jobs and jobless miners can protect themselves only if with mass solidarity they demand that unemployment insurance, as a right for all workers, shall be provided at the expense of the capitalist class.

PART-TIME EMPLOYMENT

Bituminous

A miner's daughter in Illinois writes of the eagerness with which in mid-afternoon miners' wives stop their work and even the children in a mining village pause in their play to listen for the friendly whistle that announces work for the miners on the following day. For the same whistle whose sharp staccato blasts may startle them at any moment with news of disaster and death in the mine, blows a shorter signal every day when there is work ahead.

Naturally the question is uppermost in every mind: Will the mine operate to-morrow? For few mines in the country operate every working day in every week throughout the year. In 1929, coal mines averaged only four days of work a week, according to the official figures of the United States Bureau of Mines. Bituminous miners had work on the average 219 days, anthracite miners 225 days. For both branches of the industry, the 1929 average was 221 days.

Many mines in every state, and several coal states as a whole fell below this average. Illinois and Indiana mines averaged less than four days a week, or 177 and 172 days a year. Most of the western coal states averaged less than 200 days of mine operation in 1929.

AVERAGE DAYS OF BITUMINOUS MINE OPERATION

In "good" years	In "poor" years
1913......232	1919......195
1918......249	1921......149
1920......220	1924......171
1923......179	1925......195
1926......215	1928......203

Years vary with the ups and downs of total tonnage produced, and the brief boom of 1926 pulled up the number of days above the average in recent years. But no year since 1920 has given such regular work as 1929.

Mines which cannot find a regular market are, of course, the weaker units and in a long period of low prices and sharp competition they are slowly but steadily forced out of the industry. Big companies have deliberately cultivated a more regular operation of fewer mines, with fewer workers. So in 1929, although total tonnage mined was less by 30,000,-000 tons than the tonnage of 1923, the bituminous mines averaged 40 days more of operation in 1929 than in 1923.

All this has not only made thousands jobless. It has failed to benefit the workers who have held their places in the industry, for during these years they have suffered such drastic wage cuts that they may now work more days and still receive less pay than they had for a shorter year. And in spite of this increasing regularity, the bituminous industry still operated in 1929 less than three-fourths of full time. Also it is estimated that some 100,000 bituminous workers (or about 20 per cent of the total) were employed in mines that produced coal on less than 150 days during the year.

With the general crisis of 1930 and the sharp drop in coal production, mines again worked with greater irregularity.

Anthracite

In the anthracite, work was increasingly irregular up to 1928. From the peak of practically full-time operation, in 1918, the number of working days had slipped down to 217 in 1928. Omitting the strike years, 1922 and 1925, the figures were as follows:

AVERAGE DAYS OF ANTHRACITE MINE OPERATION

1913......257		1924......274	
1918......293		1926......244	
1919......266		1927......225	
1920......271		1928......217	
1921......271		1929......225	
1923......268			

The present drive for using fewer breakers and fewer workers will probably bring in the anthracite a turn toward greater regularity of operation.

WORKING HOURS

In their cost-cutting and speed-up, the operators drive not only for more days of work from each miner but for more hours of work each day. The principal point of attack thus far has been the fixing of definite hours for tonnage men and the shifting of tonnage workers to a time-payment basis. The privilege of early quitting which the old-time craft miner had always enjoyed in American mines is being withdrawn in one mine after another, as the efficiency engineer steps in. The full 8-hour day—or even longer—which has always been required of company men is more and more demanded of all workers underground.

Also, the number of men working in mines with a basic day longer than 8 hours underground had almost doubled from 1920 to 1928. From 18,500 on the 9-hour or 10-hour basis, the number had risen to nearly 35,500. These do not include the surface workers, who may have to put in a 9-hour day—or longer—at mines where the underground men have the 8-hour basis. Never before or since 1920 have so many as 97 per cent of the bituminous miners had an 8-hour day underground. By 1928, their number had slipped down to 93 per cent of the total.

After breaking the long Alabama strike of 1920-21, the operators in that state began to lengthen the working hours. Now at least three-fifths of the Alabama miners are employed at mines with a 9-hour day; almost one-tenth are at mines with a 10-hour day underground. Some mines have also been slipping away from the 8-hour day in West Virginia, Tennessee, Texas, Missouri, and Oklahoma. Kentucky has always been behind the old union fields. But Alabama operators have been the chief offenders. No other important coal state in 1928 had more than 10 per cent of its workers at mines with a 9-hour or 10-hour day underground.[4]

Company men in American mines, and tonnage men who have lost their privilege of early quitting, are now tied to a longer day than they would have in most European mines. The 8-hour day of British and German mine workers includes the traveling time underground. In the United States, the 8 hours cover only the time spent at the working face; men must travel through the mine and up and down the shaft on their own time. This adds, on the average, from 40 to 50 minutes a day beyond the time spent at the working face.

But conditions are much the best in the Soviet Union. There the mine worker spends no more than 6 hours underground and his actual working time at the face is limited to 5 hours a day. Every underground worker has a four-week vacation with full pay. And in case the mine is shut down by an accident or any other irregularity, the worker's lost time is covered by unemployment insurance.

Shorter Hours and the Jobless Miners

Miners in the United States can help themselves and their jobless fellow-workers by demanding and fighting for the 6-hour day (including traveling time underground) and the 5-day week with a full-time living wage for all workers in the industry. The operators have been allowed too long to talk about excess miners. They have met no effective resistance to the "quiet but relentless liquidation of excess plant-capacity and surplus man-power."

About 1,100,000,000 man-hours of work are now required at the mines to produce the coal that the country needs in the course of a year. These man-hours are distributed with the wildest irregularity. A few—certainly less than 50,000 including company men—work 300 days of 8, 9, or 10 hours and spend from 2,400 to 3,000 hours underground. Nearly 50,000 work less than 100 days of 8, 9, or 10 hours and spend less than 1,000 hours underground.

Mostly the yearly hours range between these two extremes, but they average nearly 1,700 hours, made up of days usually 8 hours long.

The 6-hour day and 5-day week for 48 weeks a year would cut the yearly average to 1,440 hours for each man. It would draw back into the industry most of the 125,000 men who have been displaced since 1924. The tonnage of recent years would require at least 780,000 men instead of the 654,000 employed in 1929. As productivity is further increased by the extension of new technique, a working day of less than 6 hours must be secured.

This equalizing and shortening of working hours must be enforced with an increase in the miners' pay. Even those men whose yearly days and hours of work now come up to the average for the industry can barely make ends meet on their meager earnings.

CHAPTER VII

WAGES AND WAGE CUTTING

Most of the coal mine workers do not earn enough to support a family. In no coal field in the United States do their average yearly earnings come anywhere near the cost of the budget set up for a worker's family by the United States Bureau of Labor Statistics.

Even among the men working at mines that operate regularly five or six days a week for fifty weeks, few can bring their yearly earnings up to $2,000 a year, for the average amount that coal mine workers can earn in a day is now considerably less than $7. In Alabama and Tennessee the average for some kinds of work has been pushed below $3 a day.

Machine runners in bituminous mines and contract miners in anthracite mines are far better paid than any other large groups of mine workers. The fact that about half of these men are earning more than $9 a day is often played up by the operators to cover the very low earnings of other tonnage men and of most company men in the coal mines. In the anthracite only about one worker in four is a contract miner, and in the bituminous mines only about one worker in twenty is a machine runner. Together these two groups include barely one-tenth of all the coal mine workers in the United States.

Even these relatively well paid groups include thousands of men who cannot earn so much as $2,000 a year, for in both branches of the industry the mines that operate from 250 to 300 days are balanced by mines operating less than half the full working time. Also possible daily earnings of tonnage men vary widely. One-third of the contract miners (anthracite) and almost one-half of the machine runners (bituminous) are unable to net a dollar in wages for each hour spent in the mine. Countless workers at the other end of the scale have hourly rates so low that even in 300 eight-hour days they could not earn so much as $1,500 a year. With irregular work they are close to starvation level.

ANTHRACITE

Earnings of anthracite mine workers average between $6 and $7 a day. Working 225 days (the average for anthracite mines in 1929) the total falls between $1,400 and $1,500 a year.[1]

Contract miners and consideration miners (who are contract miners temporarily employed at a day rate instead of a tonnage rate) are the only group of anthracite workers whose net earnings average more than $7 a day. Contract miners' earnings show a much wider spread above and below their average than any other group of anthracite workers. Wage studies of the United States Bureau of Labor Statistics failed to separate the contract miner who himself works as a pick miner and pays a "laborer" to help him and the contract miner who has a concession for getting out the coal from a section of the mine and sub-contracts to other miners who do the work while he bosses them like a petty capitalist and lives on the fruits of their labor. Contract miners of this petty boss type are employed only by certain companies in the northern part of the anthracite region. They are a small number in the entire group of contract miners, but their high "earnings" pull up the average and give a false idea of the wages earned by those contract miners who actually work at one place assigned by the operator.

The earnings reported for the entire group of contract miners show one-twelfth of them netting over $2 and more than one-fifth netting less than 90 cents for each hour spent in the mine. The usual earnings of contract miners are between these two extremes with more than half of them earning from 90 cents to $1.40 an hour, and a daily average of $9.07.

"Laborers," hired by contract miners to do their heavy work, average less than $6.50 a day. A small number of day men known as company miners are employed in the anthracite chiefly to cut and load rock or for entry work. They earn about the same as the contract miners' laborers, while their helpers (company miners' laborers) average about $5.70 a day.

Among the other inside workers average earnings for the several groups range from about $5.50 a day for the drivers to nearly $7 a day for such men as blacksmiths, motormen, and machinists. The largest numbers are in the groups earning from $5.50 to $6 a day.

Surface workers get less than inside workers. Only a few special crafts, such as blacksmiths and machinists, earn over $6. The prevailing wages are from $5 to $6 a day. Platemen (picking slate and sizing coal roughly before it enters the mechanical washer or breaker) earn less than $5. Boy slaters in the breakers and boy door tenders underground average between $3 and $3.15 a day.

Taking all anthracite workers together, they fall into unequal thirds:

The smallest third (about 29 per cent) are the contract miners and the consideration miners with a wide range of earnings and an average above $7 a day.

The middle third (about 34 per cent) are averaging from $6 to $7 a day. This includes the company miners and the laborers employed by contract miners, about two-fifths of the inside haulage and maintenance men, and about one-eighth of the surface workers.

The largest third (about 37 per cent) are in occupations where the average is less than $6 a day. This includes seven-eighths of the surface men, nearly three-fifths of the inside haulage and maintenance men, and the company miners' laborers.

Wages in the anthracite are based on a tri-district agreement between the United Mine Workers of America and the anthracite operators. The union has never fought for a scale which would give uniform earnings throughout the entire region. Union agreements have continued the old inequalities among different sections of the anthracite and even among different workings of a single company which were left undisturbed in the award of the Anthracite Coal Commission in 1903.

In one district company miners are now paid fifteen rates in 22 mines and in another district thirty-eight different rates in 65 mines, the hourly wage ranging from 59.4 cents to $1.02. Similarly in the same districts, an outside occupation, like carpenter, may have thirty-seven different rates in 22 collieries, with a range of from 52.5 cents to 72.7 cents an hour, while in the other districts the maximum rate for the same job is 90 cents and $1.00. Similar variations in wage rates for the same job are found throughout the anthracite region, the same mine paying five, six, or even seven different rates for outside laborers.

Even with the piece workers or tonnage men, the contract miners and their laborers, the rates paid in different mines cannot be directly compared. In one mine there is separate payment for each item of additional work, such as setting props and laying sheet iron, while in another mine in the same district, payment for these items is included in the car or ton rate for coal mined and loaded.[2]

These chaotic inequalities in rates plus the great variety in natural conditions make some working places far more profitable than others. Miners commonly believe that they cannot hope to secure one of the softer places without paying a good price to the mine foreman. Each good job is said to have its cash value, ranging from $50 upwards.

The U. M. W. A. has allowed the increases gained since 1903 to widen the gaps between the higher and lower paid workers. They have usually agreed to a uniform percentage added to the many basic rates of some earlier date. The officials have been more concerned in increasing the earnings of the more highly paid men than in pulling up to a decent standard the pay of the lower groups. So, for example, the laborers employed by contract miners were averaging less than the contract miners by $1.68 a day early in 1920. But five years later—after two increases in the tonnage rates—the difference in average net earnings had spread to $2.60 a day. While the contract miners' net average had been pushed from $6.85 to $9.07, the pay of their laborers had gone up only from $5.16 to $6.47. Meantime, the company miners' laborers, the poorest paid of all the workers who actually get out coal or rock from the mines, had seen their average raised only from $4.58 to $5.72 a day.

Union agreements have also left many details to day by day bargaining between the mine worker and the mine boss, with an elaborate machinery of appeal to grievance committees, a general Anthracite Conciliation Board (known as the Graveyard), and a so-called impartial umpire. Again and again operators have cut yardage rates, rearranged jobs, or juggled with the conditions covering deadwork, in a way that reduces the workers' earnings. Local strikes against such attacks on working standards have always been contrary to official union policy, which insists that men must remain at work and accept changes until and unless they are thrown out by the umpire. This slow-moving machinery representing operators and union officialdom has opened the way for cutting into earnings, a little here and a little there, without any change in the terms of the union agreement. So although basic rates fixed in September, 1923, and renewed in 1926 after the loss of the strike for an increase, are still in effect many anthracite workers are convinced that during the course of the seven years they have been getting less and less money for the same amount of work.

Annual earnings have certainly gone down with the drop

in the average number of days on which collieries are operated. Even if we assumed that the daily and hourly earnings reported by the United States Bureau of Labor Statistics for 1924 had not in the meantime been shaved down to lower figures, the greater irregularity of work would have cut annual earnings for 1929 to a point about 20 per cent below the annual earnings for 1924.

ANTHRACITE MINERS' AVERAGE ANNUAL EARNINGS
(based on daily average of 1924)

	1924	1929
Contract miners	$2,485	$2,040
Contract miners' laborers	1,773	1,455
Company miners' laborers	1,567	1,287

Among the contract miners whose average earnings were still around $2,000 a year, the wide variations bring more than half the group below this average. Also if the contract miners who employ gangs of workers could be sorted out and eliminated from the reckoning, the average itself would be much lower—probably less than $1,700 a year.

Most of the groups of day men were averaging from $1,200 to $1,300 a year in 1929.

The 1930 agreement between anthracite operators and the United Mine Workers of America still continues, in theory, the wage rates of 1923. But in providing for adjustments in the interest of "efficiency" it opens the way for operators to slip over further reductions in daily earnings.

BITUMINOUS

Wages of bituminous mine workers have been cut repeatedly in recent years until the average earnings are now from $5 to $5.50 a day. With mines operating only two-thirds of the working days, average yearly earnings are barely $1,100.

The wage-cutting drive of the operators began with the breaking of the Alabama strike in 1921 and the immediate reduction of nearly one-third from the tonnage rates which had been paid to Alabama miners under a union agreement. In the following years the U. M. W. A. retired from one southern outpost after another until by the end of 1924 it no longer played any part in fixing the wages of southern mine workers. Then powerful companies in Pennsylvania began to repudiate the Jacksonville agreement (and the supplementary agreement for central Pennsylvania) under which union wages in the northern fields had been held at the scale secured in 1920. After the strike of 1927, wage cuts were written into the district agreements of Illinois and Indiana, Kansas, Iowa, Wyoming, Montana, Missouri, and Michigan. In Ohio and central Pennsylvania the union district officials solemnly signed up for a drastic reduction in pay, but the agreements covered only a few thousand workers and the prevailing rates have been cut even below that nominal scale. The Pittsburgh region is now entirely non-union.

In coal mining as in other capitalist industries, employers tend always to pay the lowest wages for which they can secure the workers they need. If workers are scarce, wages go up; if there are more workers than jobs, wages go sharply down. With some 200,000 men crowded out of the industry in recent years, the operators have built up an enormous reserve of experienced mine workers. As more and more machinery is introduced and mines operate more regularly, the number of workers required is still being pushed down. The financial survival of each company depends on producing coal as cheaply as possible. At such a period in capitalist industry, general and drastic cutting of wages is inevitable unless the workers protect themselves through united, strong, aggressive action. But instead of militant, far-seeing leadership with a tradition of no-compromise, the U. M. W. A. had built up the bargaining habit and given themselves over to a corrupt and treacherous gang. How the strike of 1922 was betrayed and the membership and power of the union have dwindled is a story for a later chapter. Here we can only note briefly what the operators have been allowed to take from the pay-envelopes of the mine workers.

Miners and Loaders

In every bituminous field the men who cut and load the coal earned less day by day in 1929 than they had in 1924. The sharpest cuts in those years were in the northern fields, where operators were making drives to push wages down to the southern level. Southern operators had been cutting wages before 1924, and wages have been further reduced since these 1929 figures were gathered. But the averages from studies by the United States Bureau of Labor Statistics are the best gauge we have to measure the general trend.

DAILY EARNINGS (NET AVERAGE) OF MINERS AND LOADERS

	1924	1929
Northern States		
Pennsylvania (bit.)	$6.40	$5.27
Illinois	8.35	7.04
Ohio	7.17	4.87
Indiana	8.56	6.83
Southern States		
West Virginia	6.10	5.35
Kentucky	5.63	5.15
Alabama	4.57	4.03
Virginia	4.65	4.30
Tennessee	4.08	3.86
Western States		
Colorado	7.23	6.18
Kansas	5.92	5.03
Average for eleven States	6.56	5.50

They show that in the first quarter of 1929 Pennsylvania had come down to the level of West Virginia and Kentucky; Ohio, which had been higher than Pennsylvania, had fallen even lower. Miners and loaders in Illinois and Indiana who had averaged around $8.50 a day were earning barely $7.

In Tennessee and Alabama, at the other end of the scale, they were earning $4 or less.

Cutting machine men, who have higher earnings than any other bituminous mine workers, are roughly about one-twentieth of all in the industry. The much smaller number of men who operate loading machines are averaging less than the machine cutters but they are better paid than the hand loaders and the pick miners.

DAILY EARNINGS (NET AVERAGE) IN ELEVEN STATES—1929

Pick miners	$5.33
Hand loaders	5.15
Machine loaders	7.00
Machine miners (cutters)	8.68
Machine miners' helpers	6.34

This same relation among the groups of miners and loaders appears in each of the separate states, except that hand loaders average higher earnings than pick miners in Illinois and Indiana. In those states, also, the two men on a cutting machine are paid equally. In most of the other states one man is classified as a helper and earns less than the machine runner.

The fact that operators are installing mechanical loaders and that the skill needed for operating a machine earns more than the hand loader can earn, does not contradict the other fact that operators are determined—and, in a capitalist economy, compelled—to pay the lowest possible wages. When two men running a machine (or a loading machine operator with machine helper and one or two hand shovelers) can between them load from two to ten times as much coal as the same number of men without a machine, the operator can pay each worker on the machine crew more than he pays to hand loaders and still cut his wage bill. But the workers on the machine get their higher wages at the expense of other workers who are out of a job. Less money comes to the mine workers as a class. And as skill in operating a loading machine loses its present scarcity value operators will cut the wages of loading machine men, just as they have already pushed down the wages of cutting machine men.

Actual net earnings vary, of course, above and below the averages for the several states. Union agreements have included some adjustment of tonnage rates for differences in coal seams and require some payment for deadwork, but miners have always been able to earn more in some mines than in others. Even a single mine will show variations in the earnings of tonnage men in each occupation.

In unorganized fields wage rates vary from one company to another. While every non-union operator is determined to push labor costs to the lowest possible point, some companies pay more than others. They reckon that a wage rate slightly above the average in the field makes for "loyalty" and steadiness, and is in the end cheaper to the company than "restlessness" among the workers. Others think only of the immediate cost and push their wages below the average.

The drive for cost-cutting and speed-up has made the operators more and more insistent that men on cutting or loading machines should be paid by time instead of by tonnage, since the miner hired on a day rate must accept closer supervision and must work a full day without breaks or early quitting. So each of the union agreements in 1928 not only accepted a drastic cut in tonnage rates but fixed alternative day rates for workers on machines. In Illinois this was set at $10.07 for eight hours of work, with lower rates for helpers on loading machines and for men loading on to conveyors. In Indiana it was set uniformly at $9, including helpers. Under the Jacksonville tonnage rates, machine runners in Illinois and Indiana had averaged from $11.50 to $12.50 a day, and about one-seventh of them had netted $2 or more for every hour at the working face. The union day rate not only pulled down the average but eliminated the lucky machine runner's former chance of earning from $14 to $20 a day.

Non-union day rates for machine cutting and machine loading are even lower. Seven dollars and $6 a day were reported from Pennsylvania companies to the Senate sub-committee on coal in 1928. Certain southern West Virginia companies gave rates ranging from $5.20 for an 8-hour day to $4 for a 10-hour day.

Company Men

Daily and hourly rates for the various groups of inside men working on haulage and maintenance and for surface workers have been uniform throughout a district under the union agreements in the bituminous fields. From the fall of 1920 until 1927, the basic union rate for most of the inside men was $7.50 a day. A few inside occupations had a $7.25 rate. Trappers (boys and old men) had less. Rates for surface workers were mostly from $7.25 to $7.45 a day.

When the U. M. W. A. officials accepted defeat of the Jacksonville scale in 1928, the basic $7.50 was cut to $6.10 in Illinois and Indiana district agreements. Ohio officials signed up a handful of operators at a $5 basic day rate, but most of the mines opened up non-union and have pushed the rate below $5. In the mountain states of the West, union wages have always been slightly higher than in other fields but the 1928 agreements cut Wyoming from $7.92 to $6.72 and Montana from $8.39 to $7.19. Southern mines, of course, pay the lowest rates.

In all the southern states company men average less than in any northern state. Tennessee is again at the foot of the scale with motormen averaging only $3.90 a day and "inside laborers" only $2.93.

Yearly Earnings

Average yearly earnings of bituminous mine workers are everywhere less than $1,200 a year. In Ohio, Alabama, and Tennessee the yearly average has been cut to less than $900.

Miners and Loaders (*Bituminous*)

	Average days of operation [3]	Average yearly earnings [3]
Northern States:		
Pennsylvania		
1924	180	$1,152
1928-29	218	1,149
Illinois		
1924	148	1,265
1928-29	156	1,098
Ohio		
1924	143	1,025
1928-29	171	833
Indiana		
1924	136	1,164
1928-29	150	1,024
Southern States:		
West Virginia		
1924	182	1,110
1928-29	223	1,193
Kentucky		
1924	174	980
1928-29	212	1,092
Alabama		
1924	220	1,005
1928-29	222	895
Virginia		
1924	226	1,051
1928-29	226	972
Tennessee		
1924	159	649
1928-29	226	872
Western States:		
Colorado		
1924	178	1,287
1928-29	193	1,193
Kansas		
1924	151	894
1928-29	128	644

Miners in Kansas, where work is more irregular than in any other state, have the lowest yearly average with less than $650 a year. Even more important than these low *average* yearly earnings is the fact that one-fifth or more of the bituminous miners and loaders in 1928 and 1929 had work for less than half the year. Less than 5 per cent of them could work a full 300 days.

During the brief boom of 1926 when American industry was active and coal exports were raised by the British coal strike, *yearly* earnings of miners were higher than in 1924 or in 1928-29. Mines operated more regularly; non-union employers found it worth while to check the downward drive on wages; the Jacksonville scale was still in force in several union districts. But this was a temporary break in the general trend.

In 1928-29 miners and loaders worked more days and produced more coal than in 1924, but except in three states this meant no increase in their yearly earnings. Pennsylvania miners worked harder and longer and barely kept the yearly average of 1924. In the other seven states for which we have figures the yearly earnings had fallen. Also, fewer men were employed, so the total wages paid to mine workers as a class had been cut even more sharply than the average earnings of the individual men who still held a job in the industry.

Bituminous mine workers average less for each hour spent in the mine than most of the A. F. of L. "aristocrats" are earning for each hour on the job. With irregular work they make less in the year than the average for all men and women factory workers. Except in Alabama and Virginia this is true within each separate state of the eleven for which mine wage figures are available.

Wage Cutting Continues

More wage cuts have swept through the bituminous fields since April, 1929. The Pittsburgh Coal Company, which had taken the lead among western Pennsylvania operators in breaking down the Jacksonville scale in 1924 and 1925, led off again with a wage cut in April, 1929. Other operators

in Pennsylvania, eastern Ohio, and northern West Virginia
followed suit and posted cuts in their turn. By the end of
1929, company men who had had $7.50 under the Jackson-
ville scale were getting less than $5 a day throughout these
fields.

Tonnage rates, deadwork conditions, and day rates have
been attacked in the southern fields also—operators claiming
that they must push their wages down still further to underbid the reductions in northern mines. Miners have resisted
with local strikes. But the drive against the workers' living
standards has not ended. Nothing can check it but united,
organized resistance by workers in all the fields, North and
South, white and colored, fighting together in the new militant industrial union of the mine workers.

TRYING TO SUPPORT A FAMILY

Men with families—and about three-fifths of the mine
workers are family men—cannot on "average earnings" provide even the food and clothing listed in the meager budget set
up for a father, mother and three children by the United
States Bureau of Labor Statistics. About one miner in five
has a family larger than this standard.

So children must go to work as soon as the law allows—
or as soon as an employer will take them on. But possible
jobs are few. Unless there is a town nearby, the boy must
usually go to the mine or leave home to find work elsewhere.
The girl may fit in as a house servant or a child's nurse in
one of the two or three comfortable homes of the salaried
men, but there is little else she can do in a soft coal village.
In the thickly settled anthracite regions more of the children
are at work. Silk mills, cigar factories and clothing plants
have moved into the anthracite districts especially in order
to take advantage of the cheap labor of miners' daughters.

At least one wife in six adds a small amount to the family
income. Her one outstanding occupation is taking in of

boarders or lodgers. For a woman with a large family and a small house this is an almost impossible job. Most of the 65,000 miners' wives who were doing this kind of work in 1920 had few children or none at all. In the soft coal villages, laundering or cleaning in the home of a mine official is usually the only outside work at hand for the miner's wife. So it often happens that the mother of a large family, who needs most desperately to supplement her husband's earnings, is unable to help. The little house is already overcrowded, and she cannot find a job outside.

Where the miner's wife or daughter had regular work she was adding less than $7 a week to the family income in the bituminous villages and about $8 a week in the anthracite, when these earnings were studied in 1922-23.[4] Such a very small addition to the mine worker's wage leaves tens of thousands of mine families with an income too small to buy even the most meager necessaries.

The averages of the mine workers themselves are, as we have seen, between $25 and $30 a week in the anthracite fields and between $20 and $25 a week in the bituminous fields. But behind these averages are the still lower earnings of three groups that together make up more than half the mine workers in the country: (1) workers in Ohio, Alabama, Virginia, Tennessee and Kansas, where wages have been pushed below the average for the country; (2) workers everywhere in the lower paid mine occupations; and (3) the men in all mine occupations and in every field who have work less than 4 days a week. For these workers and their families the "average" earnings range downwards to a point of near starvation.

The new militant union has not only led local struggles against wage cuts. It puts at the head of its immediate demands a steady minimum wage of $35 a week.

CHAPTER VIII

LOSING LIFE, LIMB, OR HEALTH

ABOUT 40 men killed and more than 2,000 injured is the *weekly* average in and about the coal mines of the United States. During the 10 years ending with December 31, 1929, coal mine workers on the job were the victims of nearly 22,500 fatal accidents and at least 1,500,000 non-fatal injuries serious enough to compel a loss of working time.

Coal mines are more hazardous than metal mines, steel mills, railroads, lumbering or structural iron work. Speed-up and mechanization are increasing the death toll. In spite of safety campaigns, the death rate in bituminous mines has been higher since 1921 than it was for several years previously. It is now higher than the death rate in the anthracite mines, but the new drive for speed-up in the anthracite is increasing the hazard there also.

Coal mine workers in the United States have a fatal accident rate about twice that of German miners and about three times that of the British. In the American coal mines, out of every 10,000 full-time workers about 45 are killed on the job in the course of a year; in Great Britain less than 15. Even the coal mines enrolled in the National Safety Competition in the United States in 1926 and 1927 had brought their average death rate for the two years only about one-fourth below the death rate in other mines. The average hazard for the 25,000 workers in this group of selected mines was still far greater than the hazard for coal miners in European countries.

The Toll of Great Disasters

Since the Avondale disaster in 1869, when 179 anthracite
mine workers were trapped by a fire which blocked their way
to the only shaft, 22 great disasters have killed from 100 to
nearly 400 workers at a time. Such disasters reached their
climax in the first 10 years of the present century when 10
great explosions and mine fires rolled up a total of nearly
2,000 victims. They have been fewer in recent years but
Stag Canon (New Mexico) in 1923, Castle Gate (Utah) and
Benwood (West Virginia) in 1924, and Mather (Pennsylvania) in 1928 have been horrible reminders that mine workers may still, at any moment, be trapped for wholesale
slaughter.

	Total Deaths in Major Disasters	Number of Coal Mine Disasters Each Killing		
		100 or more	25-99	5-24
1915 to 1919....	933	2	3	39
1920 to 1924....	1139	3	8	38
1925 to 1929....	1257	1	12	47

Smaller "major disasters" killing anywhere from five to
99 men at a single throw have continued with a deadly
monotony. Exact numbers of victims vary from year to
year, but the number of these smaller "major disasters" and
their total death roll have been rising even while the number
of mine workers has been decreasing.

Other Accidents Kill More Men

Disasters killing five or more men at a time account for
a very small part of the total deaths in coal mine accidents.
It is disasters that are most dreaded by the workers and their
families: it is only disasters that have headlines in the newspapers. But the great death toll of more than 2,100 workers
a year is made up chiefly of one man here or two there, occasionally three or four together caught by one of the many
underground hazards which are less spectacular than fires

and great explosions but which kill seven, eight or nine times
as many men year by year.

Falls of coal or rock are the greatest of all hazards to coal
mine workers. About half of all coal mine deaths are due
to this one cause.

Haulage accidents come next in importance. About one
coal mine death in six happens to a man crushed between the
underground train and the side of the entry, or caught un-
awares on the track and run over, or mangled in the process
of coupling the cars, or thrown while jumping on or off a
moving train.

Explosions of gas or coal dust come third and electricity
comes fourth. These two causes overlap, since electricity is
not only killing by direct contact some 80 to 100 workers
underground every year but it has become an important factor
in setting off underground explosions.

The hazards from these four chief causes of underground
deaths have clearly increased, so that while other types of
underground accidents have been slightly reduced, the total
underground death rate has risen. The present speed-up
drive started later in the anthracite than in bituminous mines;
the increase in mine hazards also appeared some years later.

COAL MINE DEATHS IN UNDERGROUND AND SHAFT ACCIDENTS
(rates per 10,000 full-time underground workers)

	Bituminous	Anthracite	Total
1911-1915	52.1	52.4	52.2
1916-1920	45.5	49.1	46.1
1921-1925	54.1	45.0	51.6
1926	54.1	41.0	51.1
1927	50.6	47.7	49.8
1928	55.0	46.6	53.0

When changes in the length of the working day are taken
into account and the hazard is measured in relation to the
number of man hours worked by the underground men, we
see even more clearly that hazards have been increasing in

recent years. (Death rates per million man-hours are given in the Appendix, p. 244.)

Mine workers killed in 1928 and 1929 numbered 2,176 and 2,181 as against an average of 2,300 during the preceding ten years. The victims were fewer simply because fewer men were employed.

COAL MINE DEATHS IN 1928

	Number	Rate per 10,000 full-time workers
Surface workers	84	11.3
Underground workers:		
Bituminous	1,675	52.2
Anthracite	417	46.6
Both	2,092	53.0
All bituminous	1,729	49.0
All anthracite	447	38.5
TOTAL, U.S.A.	2,176	46.4

Death rates for 1929 are not yet available. Serious disasters were fewer than they had been in 1928, but ordinary accidents, each killing less than five men, had increased. Also more men were killed in surface accidents in 1929 than in 1928.

Most of the mine accidents happen underground, but the surface workings have their own hazards from mine cars and railway cars, machinery and electricity, powder explosions, boiler explosions or falls. The death rate among surface workers at coal mines is higher than the fatal accident rate among railroad workers, men in steel mills, or workers in any manufacturing industry.

NON-FATAL INJURIES

In and about the coal mines at least every sixth man is injured on the job in the course of the year. Among those who have full-time work, and therefore more than the average exposure to coal mine hazards, every fourth or fifth man loses time because of an injury. This takes account only of accidents serious enough to keep a man home from work. But the boss who is under orders to improve his safety record sometimes threatens a worker with discharge if he stays home the day after a minor accident. The United States Bureau of Mines' estimate that 111,000 mine workers have non-fatal injuries in the course of a year is certainly an understatement. No exact figures are available, but at least 150,000 non-fatal injuries every year would come nearer the truth.[1]

Anthracite workers run a greater chance of being injured than bituminous workers in the mines enrolled in the safety competition. On the basis of their records, it appears that every bituminous worker has at least one non-fatal accident in the course of 10 years. Among those who have full-time work throughout the 10 years, the chances are that every man will be injured twice. In the anthracite, every worker would expect two accidents in 10 years, and those who have steady full-time work, three accidents in 10 years.

Most of these accidents leave no permanent injury, but over 2,000 men are permanently disabled every year. For every man killed in a mine accident there is another man somewhere in the industry who has lost a finger, a hand, an eye, or a leg, or who has suffered some other injury from which he can never recover. A few are totally crippled or disabled for life. The temporary injuries also include many that are very severe. In the records of the "safety" mines, they averaged 19 working days of lost time.

Why Accidents Happen

Operators driving for output and profits criminally endanger workers' lives. "Safety" has become a trade slogan, but actually day by day the underground hazards continue. Real safety in a mine with power lines, motor haulage, and machinery is expensive. It is technically difficult. It checks the speed-up. And most operators think it is cheaper to pay the meager compensation required if a worker is killed or injured than to make the mine safe and prevent accidents before they happen. In a capitalist economy costs and profits for the employing class are more important than the lives and well-being of the working class.

The United Mine Workers have talked about safety. When the union was strong, some of the organized states built up better mining laws than most of the unorganized states have ever had. But these codes always lagged behind the best safety technique of the time. Union officials played politics to secure soft jobs for their friends and relatives as mine inspectors. They never pushed a state to appoint only inspectors who were trained in the technical details necessary for safety in a modern coal mine.

So the states have pretended to regulate coal mines while the underground hazards continue to injure and slaughter the workers.

Falls of Rock or Coal

Every week some 20 mine workers are killed by falls of rock or coal. Newspapers in the mine regions and reports of state mine inspectors are full of items like the following:

One man was killed and seven injured when falling slate crashed upon a man trip entering the Arnold City mine in Fayette County, owned by the Pittsburgh Coal Company. Three of the injured are not expected to live.

Granville Channell, American, machine miner, experience 45 years, married, 8 children, employed at the Boulder Valley mine, Weld county, was killed by a fall of top coal. The mine foreman had instructed deceased to prepare his place for cutting a pillar by taking down the top coal into which a shot had been fired the night before, throwing down a portion of the coal. Deceased was cutting the top coal on the right side next to the breaker prop, to let down the remaining portion, when it gave way, and deceased in some manner slipped and was caught by the falling coal. He was so severely injured that he died a few hours later. Deceased was known as a practical miner, especially efficient at this kind of work.

Buried alive in a sitting position for twelve hours, Edward Warning, a miner, spent the time while waiting for what seemed certain death for himself in a futile struggle to keep alive one of his mates. Rescuers after a frantic struggle finally reached the buried men. Warning and another worker were still alive, but four others were dead. The cave-in occurred as the men were setting tunnel supports in the south side of the Buck Mountain colliery workings of the Lehigh Valley Company. Warning is on the road to recovery. Mokaitis, the other man rescued, was caught only by the tail end of the fall, suffering a dislocated shoulder and head injuries.

Such accidents happen day after day in the coal mines. They kill more than 1,100 men every year. No mine field escapes. Coal seams vary in natural roof conditions, but treacherous falls of rock or coal are a universal underground hazard. And the hazard has been definitely increased by the speed-up and changes of recent years.

The condition of the roof in the entries has always been the company's direct responsibility. At the working face, the setting of props used to be done by miners and loaders on their own time and according to their own judgment. Union tonnage rates were supposed to be high enough so that men could afford to protect themselves. When the roof was exceptionally bad and required more work than usual, the union miner could demand an allowance for dead work. The unorganized miner has no such protection. His tonnage rates have been cut repeatedly. With low wages and irregular work he is driven by desperate need to take chances and do a minimum of propping. Companies making a drive to cut down the death rate from falls of roof stiffen up the rules and standards for timbering, but they seldom make any adjustment of pay to cover the additional work involved.

In mines which have been reorganized for speed-up and mechanization, the former tonnage men are usually on hourly pay, but here the drive for steady production, the close scheduling of the working cycle at the face, and the pressure for loaded cars to be collected at regular times have compelled the miners to take chances on the roof. When shots are fired during the day while miners and loaders are in the mine, the roof should be tested after each shot and before the full crew resumes work at the face. New and more delicate methods of roof testing have been devised, but minutes are counted. Testing is too often neglected, or men are pushed to take a chance with a roof known to be tender and to need more support. "Speed-up and finish loading the coal; props can be set later."

Miners know the cracking sounds which usually precede a fall. But more and more the noise of machinery is drowning out these warning signals. Machines also require more open space between timbers than is safe under certain roof conditions. The Colorado state inspector of coal mines in his 1929 report admits this when he says: "I am informed that in some of the mines, the mine foremen insist upon the loaders timbering their places to suit the mining machines, instead of timbering them to protect themselves."

Roof hazards cannot be entirely eliminated. O. G. Sharrer, assistant mine superintendent of the Union Pacific Coal Company, pointed out in *Coal Mining* (August, 1929) that "Even with the best of mining skill and material there is the ever-present danger of sudden falls of overburden or sides of excavations, with the accompanying hazard of having expensive machinery buried and ruined." (He says nothing about the burying and ruining of miners.)

Roof hazards can be very greatly reduced. Instead, the death rates from falls of rock or coal have been rising. They have risen in the mines as a whole, and especially in the states where the speed-up with mechanical loaders has been most developed.

Explosions of Gas and Coal Dust

The year 1929 and the first eight months of 1930 saw 13 "major" explosions which piled up a death toll of 234 men.

Four of these disasters are briefly described in the following news items:

Sixteen men were trapped a mile and a half back under the hills in a mine of the Pioneer Coal Company (Kettle Island, Kentucky) late to-day by an explosion that tore out the brattice work. Little hope is held for their survival as débris fills the tunnel entrance. Mine officials were unable to determine the cause of the explosion definitely, but it is thought that a gas pocket ignited. One victim was 17 years old and the 15 others had wives and children. [Two days later]: The blast had crippled the ventilating system, and over 30 rescue workers, who believe the remaining bodies may not be found for several days, are themselves in danger from the fumes.

Twelve miners perished to-day in the dark recesses of the Yukon Mine of the Crown Coal Company (Arnottsville, W. Va.) in an explosion of gas. Nineteen men were in the mine at the time and seven escaped unhurt. The blast occurred at 2 A.M., with only the small night crew of loaders in the mine. Two hundred workers are employed in the underground plant during the day time. The belief was expressed that the workers in No. 8 heading struck a gas pocket and that it might have been ignited by a spark from a motor.

Twenty men died in an explosion in a Standard Coal Mining Company shaft at Standardville last night. The deaths are attributed to carbon monoxide gas, and five miners who were rescued had successfully barricaded themselves against the fumes when rescuers reached them. Four others were partly overcome when they were dragged out. [The following night three of the rescue crew were killed by a fall of slate.]

Seven coal miners were killed and fifteen others escaped injury in a localized explosion at Old Ben Mine 8 (West Frankfort, Illinois) at 2:30 A.M., to-day. The victims were blasted beyond recognition, identification being possible only through their numeral checks. The blast occurred during the night shift when only 22 men of the maintenance crews were at work in the mine. In spite of the cold blistering winds, hundreds of miners with women and children watched for hours the hoisting of relief crews.

Sometimes the number of victims is larger. At McAlester, Oklahoma, for example, in December, 1929, miners were driving an entry in a gassy mine, with makeshift ventilation from an electric fan. Either an open light or a spark from the switch of the fan set off the gas in the entry. A wave of flame swept instantly through the mine. Sixty-one men were killed.

Partly the number of victims is a matter of chance. When the explosion spreads a sudden blast of flame through all the underground workings no man in the mine can escape. An explosion may be local. Then only the men near the spot where it occurs are killed or seriously burned, but every man working on return air between the explosion and the surface is exposed to the deadly after-damp.

The fact that explosions happen is no longer a matter of chance. The hazard has been analyzed. It can be done away with. Safety experts of the United States Bureau of Mines have stated that: "Mine explosions are the least excusable of the accidents which occur in or around mines, but they will continue to occur as long as mining men continue to select a few of the known precautions against explosions and reject the others." [2]

Explosive gas (methane) is constantly present in many coal mines and occasionally present in most of the mines which are classed as non-gassy. Safety requires that all possible precautions against this danger be taken at all times and in every coal mine.

Adequate artificial ventilation is one universal basic necessity. Scientific standards have been worked out on all the details: what volume and speed of air circulation are required; how the fan should be installed; how the air currents should be directed; how exact tests should be made to find out whether the amount of methane is at all times and at every point in the mine far below the percentage that makes an explosive mixture, and so on. But few operators provide the equipment or take the trouble to apply all the known standards of ventilation technique.

Special emphasis is placed by the United States Bureau of Mines on the importance of withdrawing from the mine all workers except a small specially trained crew the moment the percentage of methane at any point has risen toward an explosive mixture, either because the work has uncovered a pocket of gas or because an air course has been unavoidably blocked. But how many bosses order or permit the workers to leave the mine whenever the amount of gas approaches a dangerous percentage? Almost none.

Instead, many gassy mines supplement an inadequate ventilating system with auxiliary underground fans operated only when the full shift is in the mine. In such mines workers every morning are sent down into an accumulation of methane.

Bituminous coal dust also is explosive. Most underground explosions originate in gas; then they are swept through the workings by the explosion of coal dust in the passageways. Clouds of bituminous coal dust in direct contact with an open flame will also explode when no methane is present at all. This fact has been established by repeated laboratory tests in several countries, and some disastrous explosions have clearly originated in dusty entries near the mouth of a mine on fresh intake air.

Rock dusting of all entries and unused working places is one necessary measure for safety. It serves to localize any explosion that may originate at the working face.

Many bituminous mines still make no pretense of rock dusting: only seven state mining laws mention it at all. Some mines go through the farce of sprinkling a little white dust a few hundred feet from the mine mouth. But: "It is improbable that there are half a dozen adequately rock-dusted mines in the United States," according to the chief safety engineer of the United States Bureau of Mines.[3] Too often, also, mines use the cheapest rock dust at hand which may or may not be such as to create a new danger for the lungs of the mine workers.

Safety also demands that even in rock-dusted haulageways, tracks should be well laid and mine cars kept in good order to prevent the spilling of coal—with dangerous clouds of dust—from wrecked cars. Miners paid by the ton or the carload have always resented the high topping of cars, which meant a loss of coal shaken off the car along the haulageways. Now such a needless scattering of broken coal and dust is recognized as adding to the explosion hazard.

Rock dust cannot be applied at the working face. And the use of top cutting machines and mechanical loaders creates clouds of coal dust which increase the hazard of explosion even at a well-ventilated working face. Mechanical spraying of cutter bars and the face of the coal is therefore important for safety.

Dangers from explosive gas and explosive dust can be greatly reduced by thorough ventilation and rock dusting, but emergency hazards will still arise. Therefore safety measures are not complete until all possible ways of igniting explosive gas and explosive dust are also analyzed and reduced to an absolute minimum. The main sources of ignition fall into three groups: (1) open lights, including carbide cap lights, "safety" lights that can be opened in the mine, and smoking; (2) electric arcs from unprotected switches, slipping trolley poles, and sudden breaking of any power line; and (3) explosives used to shoot down the coal.

Permissible electric cap lights to replace the open flame carbide cap lights are now required by the management in most of the coal mines classed as gassy. The miner must usually pay for the daily charging of the battery. Some companies deduct this even for days when the mine is not operating. Workers object to this safety tax. They know that the electric cap light is often used as a substitute for good ventilation. They are compelled to work beside electrical equipment quite as dangerous for explosions as the open flame of the old carbide lights. In the earlier models the battery sometimes leaked and made an acid sore on the miner's back. Weight is also a factor; one of the lightest models claims a total of 83 ounces. Altogether the "bug light" seems to many of the workers simply an expensive and burdensome substitute foisted upon them by operators who refuse to take safety measures for which they cannot make the miners pay.

That all open lights should be excluded from every coal mine, even from those which are not commonly gassy, is the opinion of safety experts. But closed lights are only one among many measures, and explosions are still occurring in mines that require the permissible cap lights. Safety engineers of the United States Bureau of Mines comment thus on the present situation:

The time has come when all mine operators, especially those who recognize the gas hazard by installing permissible lights, should cease pretending to a condition of safety because they have merely installed closed lights; instead of relaxing vigilance after equipping the mine with permissible lights, true safety should further be secured by the installation and careful use of permissible electrical machinery and by the most rigid safety practices as to ventilation, dust prevention, and dust dissemination.[4]

Electricity

The explosion hazard from electricity in coal mines has risen with the increase in non-permissible open-type electric equipment, such as mining machines, locomotives, fan motors, and rock-dusting machines. These are less expensive than the permissible machines with explosion-proof power connections, and most operators continue to subject the workers to these clearly known hazards, taking a chance that nothing will happen, and unwilling to pay the cost of safety.

"Trolley locomotive haulage is too dangerous to be allowed in any mines that really wish to operate safely; this is true even when the trolley installations are protected by the most advanced safeguards known." [5] In actual practice trolley lines are mostly unprotected. They cause many electrocutions every year. And sputtering trolley poles in gassy or dusty haulageways offer a constant peril of explosion.

Other power lines which could be effectively insulated and buried are commonly left exposed. Carelessly installed electric lighting underground makes a new fire (and explosion) hazard.

The whole question of safety in a mine electrically equipped involves many technical details. Safety can be achieved, but only by painstaking, intelligent concern in the installation and maintenance of lines and equipment and in the daily use of the machines.

Explosives

Explosives used to shoot down coal or rock set off nearly one-third of the gas or dust explosions. They are also a direct cause of death and of many non-fatal accidents underground. The death rate from explosives—apart from gas or dust explosions—is especially high in the anthracite.

Much work has been done on the testing of explosives, so as to find the exact balance required to provide the necessary force with a minimum of flame. "Permissibles" (explosives approved by the United States Bureau of Mines) are now available for all underground uses, but less than one-third of the coal is shot with permissibles. Only one state has prohibited the use of any other explosive in shooting down coal.

But any explosive is hazardous. Really to guard against accidents many other points are involved besides the kind of explosive: how explosives are transported and stored underground; how holes are drilled and the amount of explosive used for a given shot; what is used for tamping; how the shot is fired, and so on. The United States Bureau of Mines recognizes that even with the utmost care explosives cannot be made entirely safe. Shots should be fired only by specially trained men and only when all other workers are out of the mine. To protect also the shot-firers themselves, a mine should be specially wired so that shots can be set off from the surface after the firers have prepared the shots and left the mine. Power currents should not be tapped for shot-firing.

Other Underground Hazards

Seven or eight men every week are victims of underground traffic accidents. Such accidents kill more mine workers than any other one cause except falls of rock or coal. With the increase in motor haulage and the speeding up of heavy trains, without use of the possible safeguards as to clearance, braking, coupling and switching, this hazard has risen markedly.

All sorts of other underground hazards kill on the average two mine workers every week, and every second week a man is killed in a shaft accident. Fires, as distinct from explosions, are still a common occurrence, although the number of deaths in mine fires—other than explosions—is now relatively small. Every two weeks, on the average, a worker is killed by a mining machine. This hazard has definitely increased. A worker may be suffocated by mine gases. He may be drowned by an inrush of water. Or he may be fatally injured by a fall, or a tool, for besides the hazards peculiar to underground work, the miner shares the hazards common to all other workers.

Mining will always call for men of vigor and courage. Emergencies and special dangers can never be entirely foreseen and eliminated. But the present death toll of 40 men a week and over 2,000 men every year is in the main a criminal sacrifice to the drive for speed and low production costs in a fiercely competitive capitalist industry.*

* Every phase of safety technique is discussed in the publications of the United States Bureau of Mines. Of special interest to mine

State mining laws are below the highest safety standards. As with other legislation for the protection of workers under capitalism, efforts to strengthen the laws or strictly to enforce their provisions meet with strong opposition from employers. The Federal Bureau of Mines has no authority and seeks no authority to enforce high standards of safety. The use of equipment and explosives approved by the Federal Bureau of Mines as "permissible" is not required by law.

Mines will never be as safe as modern technical knowledge can make them until the workers themselves compel the universal enforcement of the highest standards.

HEALTH HAZARDS

That the miner grows old before his time is proverbial. Gases, dust, lack of sanitation underground, and hard work in stooping, strained positions, are the most important health hazards peculiar to coal mining. Miners and their families who must live in congested little villages, with no drainage and only a tainted water supply, are also more exposed to sickness than the working class families in cities.

Various gases injurious to health may be present in a coal mine. *Black damp* is the common term for air with too little oxygen and so much carbon dioxide that a flame burns only dimly and men breathe with difficulty. *Carbon dioxide* comes from the coal seam and from the lungs of the workers themselves and may become oppressive in a poorly ventilated mine. Carbon dioxide, usually with other poisonous gases, is always present in the *after damp* which follows a fire or explosion. Blasting creates noxious fumes, which are especially deadly (with nitrous fumes and carbon monoxide)

workers are three recent pamphlets which can be secured from the Superintendent of Documents, Government Printing Office, Washington, D. C., for the prices indicated: *Safety in Coal Mining, a Handbook* (Bureau of Mines, bulletin 277), 25 cents. *Coal-Mine Ventilation Factors* (Bureau of Mines, bulletin 285), 25 cents. *Coal-Dust Explosions in Mines* (Bureau of Mines, technical paper 448), 5 cents.

when any of the charge burns without exploding. These fumes may include "rotten gas" or "stink damp" (hydrogen sulphide), but more commonly rotten gas is suddenly released from some underground pocket. The most treacherous gas is the colorless, odorless *white damp* (carbon monoxide) which is usually present in the after damp following a fire or explosion and in the fumes from an imperfect detonation of explosives.

Repeated exposures to carbon monoxide, too slight to cause death or loss of consciousness, undermine the health of a worker. Dr. Alice Hamilton says of carbon monoxide: "Slow gradual gassing causes much more severe permanent damage than does more rapid poisoning. . . . Glaister [another expert on industrial diseases] believes that it is the victims of gradual gassing in coal mines and garages who are most likely to develop pneumonia, weakness of the heart, paralysis, and mental disease." [6]

The death rate from respiratory diseases other than tuberculosis is relatively high among coal miners, and epidemics of influenza-pneumonia are especially severe in mining camps.

Miner's asthma is traced to dust irritations. The daily breathing of coal dust brings on a chronic bronchial catarrh. Silicosis has been a special hazard in the United States for metal miners and tunnel workers, but rock dusting with the wrong kinds of dust will increase this hazard for coal miners.

Lack of sanitary sewage disposal underground helps to spread intestinal diseases, notably typhoid, dysentery, hookworm disease, and other parasitic infections. "Miner's anemia" is now identified as hookworm. It has been especially prevalent in the southern mine fields.

Heavy lifting, and the jarring from drills or other machines, especially in seams where the worker cannot stand upright and the body is continuously cramped and strained, wear down even a vigorous physique. Beat hand, beat knee, or beat elbow are common ailments among miners. They are the miners' names for an infection developing under the hard callous of a joint. As years go by, the miner is almost certain to grow stiff with rheumatism.

LACK OF SOCIAL INSURANCE

What happens to a mine worker and his family when illness, injury or death cut off the pay envelope? For the miner is not the only one to suffer from the hazards of the industry; at least three-fifths of the men have dependents for whose bread and shelter they are responsible.

Average earnings are too low to provide a decent living when all goes well. They leave no reserve for carrying the worker's family through a period when wages are cut off. And no coal mining state in the country provides any social insurance as a matter of right to the workers, beyond a meager system of compensation for a worker and his family when a miner is killed or injured on the job. For other deaths and illnesses the miner and his family are thrown entirely on their own resources.

This haunting insecurity of the worker's family has been exploited to the full by the great industrial insurance companies. Thousands of miners are included in the mass of workers who squeeze out somehow from an inadequate wage the weekly payment for a small sickness and death-insurance policy. But many a policy has been forfeited when work is scarce and immediate hunger presses harder than the dread of illness or death.

A few districts of the United Mine Workers have tried to set aside a fund for benefits to members in need. Such funds, supported by the mine workers themselves, are no substitute for the complete system of social insurance which should be set up at the expense of the industry and not at the expense of the wage-earner. Only under the workers' government of the Soviet Union is such a system provided.

UNDERCUTTING AND DRILLING

—Photo by Hine

—Photo International News Reel

For injuries and deaths while at work all the coal states but two have made a meager provision through workmen's compensation laws. Arkansas has no compensation law. Oklahoma provides small benefits for injured men but nothing for the widows and children of men who are killed.

The men who draft compensation laws in a capitalist state say they are afraid of making the benefits so attractive that workers will stay off the job when they are able to go back to work. Capitalists pride themselves on having regular income from investments, and salaried men are paid as a matter of course through vacations and sick leave. But reformers, employers, and legislators carefully guard against allowing any wage-earner to share their privileges. It is a class issue; they are determined to make the workers carry a large part of the burden. So the highest cash benefit allowed to an injured worker under any state compensation law is two-thirds of his regular wage, with a maximum sum of $25 a week. In most of the coal states the compensation law is below this "standard." For the family of a worker killed on the job or dying as the result of an injury, the benefits for all dependents together are never higher than the amount allowed to an injured worker while he is totally disabled. The American Association for Labor Legislation, which has worked with the A. F. of L. unions to secure workmen's compensation laws, recommends that for a motherless child under eighteen years of age, the benefit allowed after the death of the father should be only 25 per cent of the father's wage. Two children should together have only 40 per cent.

Every worker knows that besides giving utterly inadequate amounts, the compensation benefits are so administered that delays in payment are notorious. Also the doctors whose services are provided under the laws often work together with the employer or with the insurance company whom the employer has paid to carry his risk. Many an injured worker is convinced that his case has been misrepresented, and that he has been compelled to go back to work before he had really recovered. Workers' claims are also sharply contested—often to the advantage of the operator.

Coal miners' illnesses, apart from mine accidents, are not usually included in any state compensation laws. For various lists or classes of occupational diseases, workers are supposed to receive benefits on the same principle as for industrial accidents in eleven states and the District of Columbia. But only in Kentucky, North Dakota and Ohio does any one or more of the illnesses characteristic of coal mining come within the scope of the law.

Workmen's compensation laws in the United States are a glaring example of class legislation, giving a false appearance of fair treatment and actually leaving the workers and their families with no genuine, adequate security against the hazards of industry. For old age, unemployment, and ordinary illness the coal miner has no pretense of social provision.

CHAPTER IX

EARLY STRUGGLES IN COAL

EARLY strikes of coal miners in the United States show the class line-up of workers and mine owners, with the power of the state at the service of the employers. Strikebreakers were protected, pickets were fined, strikers and their families were evicted from company houses.

Long before the workers were organized the fight was on against low wages and wage cuts; against unfair weighing, long intervals between pay days, and unfair dockage; against scrip and the company store; against long hours; and against obvious and unnecessary hazards in the mines.

Local unions would grow and die. The first of these seems to have been the so-called "Bates Union" in the anthracite in 1849. First efforts at national organization came from the Belleville tract in Illinois in 1861 and were led by a group of British miners who had had experience in unionism in the old country. Financial panic and depression had meant years of falling prices and wage cuts. The various coal fields had been brought into closer competition by the steadily increasing railroad mileage. Miners, like other workers, were beginning to realize the need for wider and more stable organization. In 1861, at St. Louis, the American Miners' Association was formed to unite local lodges into districts, with a body of national delegates to direct policy. Daniel Weaver, Thomas Lloyd and the others who set up the A. M. A. hoped great things of legislation and education. They were quite unprepared for the struggles to raise wages, when prices soared during the Civil War, and to prevent the wage reductions which swept the country in 1865 and the following years. So the fights went on locally, with defeat for the miners. The American Miners' Association had built up connections in Illinois, Indiana, Ohio, and Maryland, but by 1868 it "had dwindled away."

CLASS WAR IN THE ANTHRACITE

Pennsylvania anthracite fields were the scene of the most bitter and determined struggles during the next few years, and no chapter in American labor history has been more generally distorted than the story of the, so-called "Molly Maguires."

Many Irish miners in the anthracite had resisted the Civil War draft. Like the bituminous miners, they had fought for higher wages when prices soared, and struck against wage cuts when the war inflation collapsed. But they had no union. Mine bosses commonly carried firearms, and "when labor in many instances sought relief, it was answered with an oath supplemented by the pointing of a revolver." [1] In the course of these hot years, several of the most hated mine bosses were waylaid and shot. How many workers also fell in this guerilla war is not recorded. No one on either side was arrested and convicted. The anthracite miners had no union and no press, so only the bosses' side of the story could be told to the country. It quickly grew to a legend of widespread "criminal conspiracy" with no reference to the violence of the bosses.

Meantime the struggle was becoming more and more a mass conflict. In 1868 nearly 20,000 men were out four months in an unsuccessful strike for the 8-hour day. By the next year they had organized county unions, of which the strongest was the Workingmen's Benevolent Association of Schuylkill County, with John Siney as the leading figure.[*] The W. B. A. accepted the principle that wages should go up or down with the price of coal, but immediately it struck

* The name was later changed to Miners and Laborers Benevolent Association, but the initials W. B. A. continued in use.

for a minimum rate below which the sliding scale should not fall. Miners were now up against the notorious Franklin B. Gowen, president of the Philadelphia and Reading railroad (the largest coal owner in the southern anthracite field). This strike also was defeated after Siney had carried on futile negotiations with the company. Another strike, in 1871, originated in the Scranton region and spread throughout the anthracite.

Even a union with bargaining officials and without a closed shop was too much for Gowen, who was determined to have a free hand in exploiting the workers. Also he knew that many of the Irish miners had no patience with bargaining and might carry thousands with them in striking to the limit of endurance. The tradition of the Molly Maguires would make it easy to do away with the militant Irish leaders if only he could get something on them as a pretext for criminal prosecution.

Whenever strikers had marched from one colliery to another, or a tipple had been burned down or coal cars had been wrecked in the course of a strike, a whispered terror of the "Mollies" had been started on its rounds. The legend now ran that a secret band of criminals was at work within the union and that they also controlled in the anthracite counties the Ancient Order of Hibernians, an Irish fraternal order.

So Gowen thought out the idea of planting spies in the miners' union and in the A. O. H. to uncover anything on which he might start a crusade to "get" the militant Irish leaders. Pinkertons were brought into the Schuylkill field in 1873—the first recorded use of spies against labor. But they accomplished nothing until after the Long Strike of 1875. Industrial espionage was a new game and it took time to work out the art of provocation.[2]

Gowen also organized an anthracite pool so that all the operators in the southern counties could work together to hold prices up, push wages down, and destroy the miners' union. The result was the bitterest labor struggle the country had yet seen. Even after repeated wage cuts, the union officials had protested that they could not attempt to resist, but the militant Irish carried the day. In January, 1875, the Long Strike began.

The Industrial Congress, meeting at Indianapolis in April, 1875, authorized an appeal for relief funds. "These men with all their sufferings and wrongs are now engaged in a contest with the most powerful Anti-Trade-Union combination that has ever been formed in this country. . . . The miners have been denounced as conspirators, vilified by the press, and charged with lawlessness and crime. . . . Your duty demands that you sustain them." But the relief was inadequate.

In the closing weeks of the contest there were exhibited scenes of woe and want and uncomplaining suffering seldom surpassed. Hundreds of families arose in the morning to breakfast on a crust of bread and a glass of water, who did not know where a bite of dinner was to come from. Day after day, men, women and children went to the adjoining woods to dig roots and pick herbs to keep body and soul together, and still the strike went on with no visible sign of surrender. But workingmen must work that they may eat, and must eat that they may work, while capital can wait. The end came at last in the unconditional surrender of the miners. The force of nature could go no further.[3]

The Pinkertons meanwhile had been active, commanding the company's special police and promoting trouble in the Ancient Order of Hibernians of which the Irish miners were members, and which survived after the union had been wiped out in the defeated strike. It is a long and very instructive story, the preparation for this first great American frame-up. Three facts stand out: (1) The chief spy, McParlan, by his own confession, had brought into the A. O. H. several disorderly characters and managed to fasten certain crimes of theirs upon one or another local group of the order. (2)

After the strike was lost and the miners were desperate, three bosses were shot. On the witness stand, McParlan told how he had known beforehand that these shootings were to take place but *he had made no move to prevent them.* (3) After McParlan's friends had made a safe getaway, some twenty Irishmen—many of them miners who had been active in the strike—were sent to the gallows. They were tried and convicted in an atmosphere of hysterical prejudice, with contradictory testimony, glorification of McParlan as the hero of the occasion, and flowery appeals to patriotism for the support of capital. Gowen, president of the largest coal company, acted personally as the chief prosecutor, assisting the district attorney at several of the trials.

The hangings of the Molly Maguires in 1877 and in 1878 ended this first period of class war in the southern anthracite counties.

The Knights of Labor was beginning to draw in anthracite miners, especially in the Scranton region, which had not been involved in the Long Strike and the anti-Molly drive. During the big railroad strike of 1877, the miners and laborers of the Lackawanna Coal and Iron Company at Scranton came out also. A posse of special police fired on a strike demonstration and killed three of the miners' leaders. Two years later another union, the Miners and Laborers Amalgamated Association, was attempted, chiefly in the middle and southern anthracite fields. Both organizations pinned their faith on conferences with the operators, and in 1885 and 1886 tried to secure higher wages without a strike.

Operators meanwhile had organized another selling pool, dominated by J. P. Morgan and Co., which had secured control of the Philadelphia and Reading company. But in September, 1887, the miners having gained nothing by attempts at bargaining, 10,000 men in the Lehigh valley struck for higher wages while the Philadelphia and Reading miners continued at work, intending to help the strikers with relief.

They soon realized that the companies were playing into each others' hands, and in January 22,000 workers in the Reading territory joined the strike. Engineers and firemen of the Reading railway who belonged to the Knights of Labor went out in a spirit of solidarity, but their places were filled by scabs from the railroad brotherhoods. Slavs and Italians were imported to take the places of the striking miners. The strike was not taken up by the workers in the northern counties and defeat was inevitable. By March the strikers were starved out. The unions were destroyed. The anthracite workers were left completely at the mercy of the operators. Now and then a local battle flared up in the darkness of those years. At Lattimer, near Hazleton, 19 unarmed foreign miners were shot and killed and 40 others were wounded by a sheriff's posse.[4]

BITUMINOUS STRIKES AND UNIONS BEFORE 1890

Tuscarawas Valley in Ohio, the Connellsville coke region in Pennsylvania, and the Shenango and Mahoning valleys on the border of the two states were the scene of some of the most spirited, hard-fought strikes of the years just before and after the panic of 1873. All the strikes of this period were local struggles. No nation-wide strike was attempted by the miners until after 1890.

John Siney, of the anthracite miners, John Hinchcliffe, who had edited a miners' paper in Illinois, and others saw the need for nation-wide organization. The Miners and Laborers Benevolent Association with Siney as president (anthracite, 1870) actually did establish correspondence with local unions in the principal bituminous fields. Both Siney and Hinchcliffe took part in the general Industrial Congress at Cleveland in July, 1873, and immediately afterward Siney called a convention of miners at which the Miners' National Association of the United States was organized with Siney as president.

The panic in September opened another industrial crisis and miners flocked into this new union so that by 1875 it had 347 lodges in thirteen states with a membership of 35,000, or roughly one-fourth of the workers in the industry. Officially the M. N. A.—like the Industrial Congress—had recognized the growing power of organized capital and stated that workers must combine on their side to protect their rights and interests. But they believed in moving slowly, trying to bargain and arbitrate, and never striking except as a last resort. Especially they tried to hold the rank and file miners back from local strikes.

But the abuses the workers had to endure were too glaring. Bad times had meant a drive of wage cuts. Hungry miners could not wait for the slower plans of their well-paid president.

In the Tuscarawas Valley, strikes with evictions, blacklisting, and imported strikebreakers had been fought in 1870 and again in 1873. After the panic, Mark Hanna led a group of operators in wage negotiations with the union; a 20-cent wage cut was compromised at 19 cents! The miners at the Crawford Coal Company which had refused to negotiate went on strike for a checkweighman, and were promptly offered nine cents a ton more than the other operators were paying if the miners would accept the company's weighing. The other miners who had been "done" in the negotiations immediately demanded and secured the higher rate. But this was only temporary. More cuts followed, and by March, 1876, the struggle was on again. Union officials tried again to secure a compromise, but the miners "declared their willingness to eat grass, stone, dried leaves, etc., rather than submit to mine coal for any such price."

Mark Hanna, the Republican boss who made McKinley president, was one of the first coal operators who realized that employers would benefit from negotiation with compromising union officials. In most bituminous fields, as in the anthracite, the miners had long struggles to establish any organization. Local leaders would be locked out, evicted, and blacklisted even before any strike was attempted. When a strike was on, the authorities could be counted on to support the operators.

Two Pennsylvania courts gave a sharp illustration of this fact in the Connellsville and Clearfield strikes of 1875. In the Connellsville strike, an operator named Armstrong who owned several mines "imported Italian strikebreakers, arming them with breech-loading rifles and warning them to shoot every English-speaking white man who came near them, informing them that unless they did so they would receive injury. The result was that a riot ensued, in which the Italians used their rifles, killing two men and wounding others." The grand jury found a true bill of murder in the second degree against the Italians and also against Armstrong, but the court sent only the Italians to the penitentiary and let off Armstrong, the operator, with a fine of five dollars and costs.[5]

The Clearfield strike had been approved by the Miners National Association. When the strikers succeeded in persuading a trainload of scabs to leave the region and paid their fares back to the city, thirty-six union members were arrested and charged with conspiracy and riot, because they had organized and picketed. Some of those convicted were several miles away from the mine the day the strikebreakers were sent away. Siney, the national president well known for his moderation, was acquitted, but all the others were convicted and sentenced.

It was already a common practice to call out the militia to protect strikebreakers. McNeill summed up the situation in 1875 as follows:

Strikes continued through the year, imported labor everywhere taking the places of the strikers. In some places it was colored men; in others, Germans, Italians, Swedes, Polanders, Hungarians, and everything else they could employ, who took the places of the miners. It was only the coolness, fortitude and sagacity of the leaders that prevented bloodshed in every coal-mining district. The military were called out to serve the purpose of the operators in Indiana, Illinois and Iowa, and every effort was made to incite the men to some rash act, to give the authorities an excuse for the arrest of the men or an attack of the militia.[6]

Workers deeply involved in their local fights resented the counsels of moderation from the officials of the national union, especially as neither strike relief nor aggressive strategic plans for united action were forthcoming. The Clearfield cases drained the small national treasury at the very time when local unions were dropping out of the organization. By the summer of 1876, the Miners National Association had ceased to exist.

The Knights of Labor

Local strikes and local organizing continued. District organizations began to develop, and in 1882 a state-wide union was formed in Ohio. Meanwhile the Knights of Labor was drawing in miners as individuals and a good many of the miners' local unions. This order, which until 1878 was entirely secret, had been started by garment cutters in Philadelphia nine years before and by 1875 it was spreading westward, with a varied membership, including both skilled and unskilled workers in all sorts of industries. The railroad strikes in 1877 sent a fresh wave of workers' solidarity sweeping through the country and opened the way for the growth of the Knights.

Secret organization made a strong appeal to the miners who had endured persistent persecution for their open union activities. By 1878 District Assemblies of the Knights of Labor with miners as an important group in the organization had been set up in Pittsburgh, Maryland, West Virginia, Ohio, Indiana, and Illinois. In 1882 the Knights were organizing coal miners in Colorado and New Mexico and the following year a "practical coal miner" was appointed as a national organizer for the industry.

Like unions that had preceded it, the Knights of Labor deplored the growing power of capital. Terence V. Powderly, the Grand Master Workman of the order, would talk of abolishing the wage system, but he never had a clear program of class struggle. The Knights looked to education and workers' coöperation as a way of escape from the tyranny of employers. In so far as open action was to be undertaken the program sought to substitute arbitration for strikes, and to secure laws for the protection of labor. Yet in spite of official policies, the local and district assemblies were compelled by their membership to carry on strikes.

Employers magnified the peril they saw in the Knights of Labor and began compelling workers to sign a yellow-dog contract—known in those days as an "iron-clad"—in which workers agreed not to join the Knights or any other secret union. The Knights of Labor did have possibilities of danger to the capitalist class, for it was one of the few unions in American labor history which organized skilled and unskilled workers together. "An injury to one is the concern of all" was the motto of the order. But it never developed its full possibilities as a fighting class organization in the industrial struggle of the wage earners.

Throughout the 15 years of its activity among the miners, the Knights of Labor included many workers who were also members of some other union. Sometimes—as in Maryland and West Virginia—coal mine strikes were entirely Knights of Labor affairs. Sometimes only a local miners' union was involved. Sometimes, as in the hard-fought Hocking Valley strike of 1884, an open union and the Knights were both in the struggle.

Hocking Valley Strike

New grievances had developed with the introduction of cutting machines and the operators' insistence that coal must be screened before weighing. During the eighties also more foreign workers were brought to this country than during any other ten years of the nineteenth century, for industry was expanding and until 1887 employers were still free to import contract labor. Thousands of unskilled foreign-born workers were brought into the mining regions to compete with the miners already at work. Industrial depression in 1884-85 brought wage cuts in every industry, and the coal miners suffered more severely than any other group of workers, with a 40 per cent average reduction in pay.

Of all the mine strikes in the eighties scattered from Maryland and West Virginia to Colorado, the Hocking Valley strike of 1884-85 against a reduction from 70 cents to 50 cents a ton and the introduction of an "iron-clad" (yellow dog) was the most notable. It marked a new stage in the class struggle of the soft coal miners, for the forces of capital and of labor were both more closely organized than they had been before. Two corporations controlled most of the mines in the valley. The miners were backed by a state-wide union. From miners' unions in Ohio and elsewhere, from the Knights of Labor, and from other workers, the Hocking Valley miners received unprecedented strike relief, totaling $70,333.48 in cash and over $25,000 worth of food and clothing. But with 4,000 miners on strike even these large sums did not go very far and the long struggle called forth heroic endurance by the workers and their families.

The operators sent out agents to import strikebreakers from Europe. Meantime "the Hocking Valley was made the dumping ground for the worst kind of refuse the principal cities could supply as strikebreakers." [7] Spies worked as provocative agents among the strikers, trying to stir up jealousies and break their solidarity. The militia was on the ground and stood by while armed thugs attacked unarmed miners. "Men who preached and taught temperance had barrels of beer and whisky rolled among their hirelings to make them fighting mad. In their hurry they sometimes shot down each other, and the coroners rendered a verdict of accidental shooting. When arrested the judges and jury set them free." [8]

Striking miners were finally crushed into submission. The corporations were strong and could afford to wait. Active mass support of miners outside the valley and of other workers would have brought them to terms but for this the unions and the rank and file were not yet ready.

New Organizations in the Eighties

The years 1885 to 1887 marked another stage in the American labor movement and in the organization of the coal miners. A great wave of strikes, involving masses of unskilled workers, swept over the country. The Knights of Labor had brought Jay Gould to terms, temporarily, in a strike of railroad workers, and within a year their total membership in all industries rose from 104,000 to 703,000.

A few trade unions had federated in 1881, with Samuel Gompers as one of the outstanding figures, and they asked the Knights to join in a united demand for the 8-hour day to be presented to all employers on May 1, 1886. Powderly, the Grand Master Workman of the Knights of Labor, sent out secret instructions to the Knights to disregard the call, but most of the district and local assemblies went ahead with plans for a May Day strike. The militant labor movement had a strong following in Chicago and led the 8-hour demand in that city. Eight-hour day demonstrations and strikes on that first May Day in world labor history swept into a great mass movement that distressed both Gompers and Powderly while it stirred fresh alarm in the capitalist class.

While the masses were stirring in what historians like to call The Great Upheaval, union officials were setting up three new organizations. In September, 1885, delegates from miners' unions in Illinois, Indiana, Ohio, Pennsylvania, West Virginia, Iowa and Kansas, organized at Indianapolis independently of the Knights of Labor, a National Federation of Miners and Mine Laborers. A very loose and ineffective Amalgamated Association of Miners representing parts of four states had been set up two years before. This new federation started with the definite purpose of coöperating with employers in the adjustment of wage rates so as to avoid strikes and secure for both operators and workers greater returns from the sale of coal. Hanna and another Ohio operator were ready to help them round up other operators and in February, 1886—at the very time when the great May Day movement was stirring the masses of workers—the union officials signed their first interstate joint agreement with operators from western Pennsylvania, northern Illinois, Ohio, and Indiana.

About the same time, the general executive board of the Knights of Labor authorized the organization of National Trades Assembly No. 135 to bring together the miners' assemblies in the K. of L. and push organization in the coal industry. From the beginning, many of the miners' local unions had a double affiliation. John McBride, Christopher Evans and others prominent in the new National Federation were also members of the Knights of Labor.

In December, 1886, officials of the National Federation of Miners and Mine Laborers helped to organize the American Federation of Labor with Samuel Gompers as president. For the labor movement as a whole, this new American Federation of Labor sharpened the conflict between the craft unions and the Knights of Labor with its broader basis of solidarity. But the solidarity of the Knights was a vague ideal of brotherhood with no clear-cut understanding of the class line-up of workers against capitalists. The weakness of Powderly, himself a dabbler in small money-making projects and a vain, wavering man, and the weakness of the Knights as an order were revealed by the failure to build on the militant class consciousness of the workers in 1886. Powderly's "solidarity" turned more and more to the petty bourgeois Americans who were fretting over the tyranny of big business, and failed to reach the foreign-born unskilled workers who were flocking into American industry. Thousands of skilled workers retained a feeling of loyalty to the Knights while they found a stronger practical weapon against their employers in the growing craft unions and the A. F. of L. Except among the miners and brewers the craft unions won out, while the Knights of Labor gradually weakened and died.

In 1888 the National Federation of Miners and Mine Laborers changed its name to the Miners' Progressive Union and included a small group who split off from the Knights of Labor. Two years later, in 1890, the two organizations, National Assembly 135 of the Knights and the Miners' Progressive Union, combined as the United Mine Workers of America. This was from the beginning affiliated with the American Federation of Labor and, until 1894, with the Knights of Labor also.

STRIP MINING WITH A GIANT POWER SHOVEL

—Photo International News Reel

CHAPTER X

THE UNITED MINE WORKERS OF AMERICA

THE new union had almost no foothold in the anthracite fields. Among the nearly 200,000 soft coal mine workers, less than 25,000 were in the union and these were scattered over 16 states. Theoretically all workers in the industry were eligible for membership—thanks to the strong influence of the Knights of Labor—but in many local unions only the miners and their helpers were organized, and no systematic drive to bring in company men was attempted until after the great strike of 1897.

From the beginning the United Mine Workers of America was one of the most important organizations in the American Federation of Labor. John McBride, retiring as president of the miners in 1894, became president of the A. F. of L. for one year,—the only break in the long reign of Samuel Gompers. After Gompers' death, his successor William Green was promoted from the post of secretary-treasurer in the U. M. W. A.

In 1890 the U. M. W. A. still had a long slow road to travel before it drew in so many as three-fourths of the mine workers in the country and became for some years the second largest union in the world. When the organized mine workers in the United States numbered from 300,000 to 400,000 members, only the German Metal Workers Union had a larger membership.

Conference and arbitration rather than strikes were from the beginning the official goal of the United Mine Workers of America. But the first joint interstate agreement of 1886 had broken down entirely and the union realized in 1890 that some strikes would be necessary to secure recognition. Strike relief was to be granted from the national treasury, but only for strikes approved by the officials. No strike was to be approved until all efforts at conference and bargaining had failed.

Local struggles continued, sometimes with and sometimes without the approval of the national union. Coal mines were growing faster than the demand for coal, and the early nineties were years of falling prices which the operators passed on to the workers in drastic wage cuts. "One of the most awe-inspiring strikes in the annals of our trade" was fought out by some 10,000 Connellsville coal and coke workers in 1890-91. As in the Westmoreland strike twenty years later, men, women and children spent the cold Pennsylvania winter in tents. It was a revolt of foreign-born workers, chiefly Hungarians, against starvation wages and the tyranny of company towns. Another strike the same year, in the Tuscarawas Valley, was hailed as one of the first in which Negro miners stood out "side by side with their white brothers."

Among the most militant struggles of that period were the strikes in Tennessee against the use of convict labor in the coal mines. Tennessee miners had been organized in 1888 and the next year began a series of local strikes. Armed miners in April, 1891, took the convicts out of the mines at Coal Creek and escorted them back to the prison in Knoxville. They then called on the governor who promised to summon a special session of the legislature to pass laws against convict mine labor. But the convict-leasing companies were on the job. Convicts were returned to the mines and militia were stationed at Coal Creek. Miners made friends with the militia and succeeded in releasing 1,500 convicts. More soldiers were sent in and permanently stationed near the convict mines. In August, 1892, the miners renewed the struggle, first at Tracy City, then at the iron mines at Inman, and the coal mines at Oliver Springs and

Coal Creek. At first the miners were successful in battling the militia. "In several instances entire train loads of militia were taken captive and disarmed, but the final victory was with the militia. The mines were retaken from the miners and the prisoners were put back to work." [1]

With less notable conflicts in other states, a total of 22 strikes against convict labor in coal mines are reported from the years 1881 to 1900. They were all defeated. Convicts continued to work in Alabama mines until after the war. Convict leasing has been abolished in Tennessee, but in state-owned mines at Petros prisoners are still mining coal for sale in the commercial market.

After the panic of 1893, the miners were in a desperate situation with low wages and irregular work. The union had lost members, for it had been unable to meet its promises of strike relief, and most of the local struggles had been defeated. Both officials and workers saw that the only hope was now in a nation-wide shut-down to bring the operators to terms. So when the union in April, 1894, with a membership of less than 20,000 miners, issued a call for a nation-wide suspension, 125,000 men walked out of the mines, demanding an increase in wage rates. As the weeks went by more and more miners joined the strike, but they could not hold out long enough to gain their increase. In June, the union accepted a compromise wage rate, with the promise of semi-monthly payments and a union checkweighman. But the operators who signed up in the several districts were too few and the union was too weak to enforce the terms agreed to.

1897 STRIKE

Another nation-wide strike was called three years later, to start on July 4, 1897. Union membership had gone down to its lowest point, less than 10,000 men, but the unorganized miners responded in a "spontaneous uprising of an enslaved people." The tie-up was complete in Ohio, Indiana and northern Illinois. Thousands in other fields were also out from the beginning, including some West Virginia miners chiefly in the Kanawha region. More and more men joined the strikers in western Pennsylvania and the Panhandle. John Mitchell, young and not yet corrupted, won promotion in the union by bringing out the miners in southern Illinois. Without relief funds, the strike meant twelve weeks of hardship and hunger, but the workers' front held solid.

The market for coal was rising and in September a committee of operators agreed to a temporary increase pending the outcome of a joint interstate conference for the Central Competitive Field (western Pennsylvania, Ohio, Indiana, and Illinois). For outlying districts nothing was gained, but the union called off the strike.

Virden and the Fight for Union

Having been promised an increase in pay, the 8-hour day, and a union checkweighman at the tipple to see that their coal was fairly weighed and recorded, the miners were determined in 1898 that all operators in the Central Competitive Field should live up to the agreement. Several local strikes had to be fought to a finish to bring individual operators into line.

At Pana and Virden, in Illinois, strikebreakers and armed guards were imported by two companies which refused to let the union miners come anywhere near their properties. Some of the imported men were Negro convict miners from Alabama; some were free Negroes lured by promises and ignorant of the strike. The Alabama Miners Division of the Afro-American Labor and Protective Association was campaigning in Alabama against the strikebreaking but it was too weak to accomplish much. When the strikers at Pana and Virden attempted to reach the trainloads of Negroes to release them from the armed guards and send them back to Alabama, the guards opened fire on the strikers. The first battle, at Pana, the end of September, was indecisive. But on October 13, 1898, at Virden, the miners won completely. Seven union miners were killed, and eight wounded. Five mine guards were killed, and about a dozen wounded, but the train loads of scabs went back the way they came and until 1922 no more strikebreakers were brought to Illinois mines. Virden Day is still remembered by miners in Illinois.

In most of the outlying fields recognition of the union was won only by a struggle, and the same familiar weapons against the workers—strikebreakers, armed guards, evictions, arrests, injunctions—kept reappearing in every fight. The militia was frequently used against the strikers. In Hopkins County (western Kentucky) during the strike that began in November, 1900, operators secured an injunction forbidding the U. M. W. A. to furnish the strikers with any food and supplies.[2]

In the Southwest, the largest four companies yielded in 1900 only after their workers had stood out solidly for more than a year.

Bargaining vs. Militancy

Never once did the national officials call out workers in the Central Competitive Field to back a struggle elsewhere. They bound themselves to the operators in these four states and signed time agreements which made no provision for such strike emergencies. In return for this, the operators under the agreement of 1898 began to collect union dues through the check-off.

During the anthracite strike of 1902, as we shall see, leaders in certain bituminous district strikes, together with a militant minority throughout the union, demanded a general coal strike. But President Mitchell was close to Mark Hanna and other operators who dominated the Central Competitive Field, and he maneuvered successfully for loyalty to the operators instead of loyalty to the needs of the striking miners.

Again in 1906, the rank and file, resenting the wage cut that Mitchell had helped the operators put over two years before, were ready for a fight. All agreements were expiring together. Outlying organized districts were demanding admission to the one Joint Interstate Conference. But the operators of the Central Competitive Field had always stood firm against enlarging the territory covered by a single agreement. So Mitchell, in 1906, won out against the militants. No strike was called. The demands formulated at the national convention of the union were compromised in district agreements.

Never except in 1922 were the anthracite and bituminous workers allowed to strike together.

Bargaining and coöperation with the employers—class collaboration and business unionism—were always the official aim of the United Mine Workers of America. But within the union there was a minority who opposed this subjection to the operators and compromise time agreements. A handful of delegates from the U. M. W. A. took a leading part in fights against the official policies at A. F. of L. conventions. In the U. M. W. A. itself they were securing resolutions for nationalization of coal mines,—the first, in 1894. They compelled John Mitchell to resign his job with the National Civic Federation or give up his card in the mine workers' union.

But this minority never guided union policy in the most basic matters. It lacked far-seeing leadership. The Socialist Party, to which many of the militant miners belonged, was itself divided, and men like Eugene Debs who believed in revolutionary class unionism did not formulate its policy.[3] The executives of the party would not admit that business unionism is a betrayal of the workers to the capitalist class. Instead they made the party steer clear officially of union policy and activity. So the Socialists within the U. M. W. A.

were not united and they followed no consistent revolutionary line. Also some of them were personally weak and allowed themselves to be corrupted by racketeering officials.

Practically all the U. M. W. A. officials have been capitalists at heart. Before the days of the Civic Federation, President Ratchford of the U. M. W. A. had left the union to become a "labor commissioner" for the operators in Illinois. In 1904, D. C. Kennedy passed from the presidency of District 17 (West Virginia) to become "commissioner" for the Kanawha Coal Operators Association. John Mitchell stepped from the presidency of the U. M. W. A. to a job with the National Civic Federation. When he died he left a fortune of $250,000, largely in coal, railroad, and steel company securities. Tom L. Lewis who followed Mitchell as president of the U. M. W. A. became himself an operator in West Virginia and secretary of the anti-union New River Coal Operators' Association. John P. White, who was successor to Tom L. Lewis, is now attached to the Union Pacific Coal Company in Wyoming as a labor arbitrator to help the company in its program of speed-up and cost cutting. District officials and organizers too numerous to mention have followed these examples, leaving the union in order to become operators or openly the servants of the operators.

Within the union, personal struggles for power and office have played a large part since the very beginning. Charges that membership rolls had been padded and official funds used to secure friendly delegates at union conventions were passed back and forth before the turn of the century. The notorious corruption of officials and the breakdown of the union since the war are simply the rotten ripe fruit of ideas and methods which became the dominant policy of the union machine the moment the strike of 1897 in the soft-coal fields had turned the corner toward success.

MITCHELL AND THE ANTHRACITE STRIKES

When John Mitchell, president of the United Mine
Workers, went into the anthracite in the fall of 1899 it was
his second attempt at organizing outside of his home state of
Illinois. As vice-president, the year before, he had gone into
West Virginia where the union had less than 300 members
and had shortly withdrawn before the armed guards and injunctions with which the West Virginia operators had greeted
the organizing campaign. In the anthracite the operators
were equally opposed to union organization, but the mines
were more closely gathered about large centers of population
and immediately Mitchell turned to the local business interests
and the church for help in his organizing attempts. He persuaded certain outstanding priests and tradesmen that they
would benefit if the miners had more money to spend.

The miners were desperately poor. They had had no wage
increase for 20 years and they were without protection against
unfair weighing and unfair docking. They were working 10
hours a day or longer. Older men remembered their lost
strikes of 1875 and 1887. They had seen the steel workers
brutally defeated in 1892 by interests close to the anthracite
operators. Then too, while railroads under powerful financial control had been building up their dominating monopoly
of anthracite mining, they had made the most of the language
divisions among the workers. English-speaking workers
were petty bosses, contract miners, and skilled workers. The
newly arrived foreigners were unskilled workers and miners'
laborers. Mitchell was clever enough to realize that the union
must include the foreign-born, who greatly outnumbered the
English-speaking workers.

After a year of organizing had brought in more than
10,000 of the 150,000 anthracite mine workers, Mitchell
called a convention representing the three anthracite districts
and formulated demands to put before the operators. The

national executive board in Indianapolis authorized a strike if the demands were not granted. But the strike was not called until Mitchell had tried to secure a conference and offered to accept "impartial" arbitration of the demands.

On September 17, 1900, the strike began. Unorganized workers responded along with the new union members. From the first day some 112,000 men were out. Nearly six weeks the strike continued with unbroken ranks.

Early in October the operators posted offers of a 10 per cent increase to workers who would return immediately. But the strike continued.

It was a presidential year and McKinley was running for his second term. Hanna, the manager of the campaign, felt that the anthracite strike might be disastrous for his candidate. "During all of this time, Hanna was busy. When he found the operators firm against any discussion, he went over their heads to J. P. Morgan and arranged an interview for Mitchell. The desire for political victory commingled with admiration for Mitchell's personality. No public announcement of the result of this interview was made, but the railroad presidents received their orders." [4]

Mitchell evidently received his orders also. He called another convention which was steered into accepting the 10 per cent increase, provided it was made definite for six months; a marked reduction in the price of powder sold by the companies to their miners; and recognition of workers' committees for adjustment of grievances. But no shortening of the working day; no standardizing of the mine car or the ton; and no checkweighman. The operators duly posted fresh notices with the 10 per cent increase and the two slight concessions besides, and the union officials dutifully called off the strike.

As months went by, the anthracite miners realized how little they had gained. Spies were brought in and workers active in the union found themselves discharged and blacklisted. Some of the companies built stockades around their mines in preparation for another struggle. By March, 1902, the workers had lost patience with the negotiations which Mitchell and the district officials carried on more or less under Hanna's guidance. At their convention in Shenandoah the anthracite miners drew up fresh demands including a 20 per cent increase, a uniform ton, the 8-hour day, reinstatement of discharged union men, and recognition of the union.

In spite of clear-cut demands from the convention, Mitchell offered to compromise on a 10 per cent increase and the 9-hour day, and the district officials offered to accept arbitration. On May 12, 1902, 140,000 workers walked out of the mines. Hanna was meanwhile telling Morgan that Mitchell would settle for a 5 per cent increase, but until October 23, 1902, the strike was almost 100 per cent effective.

Workers' families were evicted from company houses, and their credit was exhausted long before the end of the struggle. Coal and iron police and state troopers were a constant danger to the workers. Hostility increased as the weeks went by. In June a young boy was killed. In July the troopers fired on a meeting of strikers at Shenandoah. The Philadelphia and Reading took the lead in posting notices in September that strikers returning to work would be protected and those staying out longer would lose their jobs, while the Governor sent in militia to protect the scabs. But the strikers could not be bullied. They stood firm.

Meanwhile, the summer of 1902 had brought out the conflict within the union between those who wanted to play the employers' game and bargain for hard and fast unbreakable time agreements, and those who demanded a nation-wide strike to organize the entire industry. Organizers had been at work in West Virginia and about half the mine workers in the state had gone on strike early in the summer. One-third of the Alabama miners were out. The Michigan district was tied up, and several thousand miners were out in western

Pennsylvania. When five striking districts united in demanding that Mitchell call a special national convention to consider a nation-wide strike, "Mitchell did not want to use the call immediately. He kept it in his pocket almost a month."

He conferred with friends among the operators, in Ohio and Illinois. Then having "gained seven weeks"—as his biographer puts it—the special convention came together the end of July. Mitchell put over a skillful compromise: the agreements must be respected, but a strike would be called against any operator who shipped bituminous coal into the anthracite market; bituminous miners would be taxed a dollar a week and union officials would contribute a quarter of their salary for relief in the anthracite. Miss Glück who describes this arrangement as "peace with honor" says nothing of the failure to back the strikes for union in Alabama and West Virginia.

The "Graveyard"

In the end, the anthracite strike was compromised. As cold weather approached the scarcity of hard coal had brought the usual tirades in the capitalist press against the strikers for causing the "public" to suffer. President Roosevelt staged a spectacular but useless conference at the White House, and then began figuring how he could follow the example set by President Cleveland, when Federal troops were sent in to Illinois to break the Pullman strike in 1894. But the bargaining of Hanna and Mitchell brought results. Mitchell had again persuaded a convention of anthracite delegates to authorize arbitration. Then J. P. Morgan told Roosevelt that the anthracite operators would accept the award of a commission to be appointed by the President. On October 23, the strikers returned to work.

Public hearings before the commission brought a picture of brutal exploitation and poverty. The miners' case was ably summed up by Clarence Darrow. The hardness of George

F. Baer, president of the Philadephia and Reading Railroad, who claimed a "divine right" for the companies to own and manage the coal mines, aroused popular feeling and increased sympathy for the miners. If "justice" could ever win against the self-interest of the capitalist class, here was a chance for a righteous award!

But the anthracite miners, whose determined solidarity had brought them close to victory, were tied up with a system of compulsory arbitration and the agreement not to strike on a grievance while action was pending before the board. No pit committees were allowed until some years later, and workers' grievances had so little chance that the board was soon dubbed the Graveyard,—a name which it retains to this day. Presidents of the anthracite districts were allowed to serve as the miners' representatives on the board. Otherwise the union gained no recognition in 1902, but this was enough to place the union machine strategically near to the operators. Operators kept the absolute right of discharge. They could continue to pay for coal by the carload, unless the workers might persuade the management of a colliery to obey the state law requiring payment by weight. Thus the commission's announcement that miners had the right to employ a checkweighman and a check docker might help on the unfair docking for impurities in the coal but it meant nothing in the basic day by day method of payment.

No wonder Mitchell was acclaimed by the capitalist press and the "progressive" employers as the greatest labor leader of his time!

COLORADO, 1903 AND 1914

Even more openly treacherous was Mitchell's betrayal of the Colorado miners in 1903. The United Mine Workers had organized the coal miners in the northern part of the state but they had gained no foothold in the mines of the southern fields operated by the Colorado Fuel and Iron Company and the Victor American Fuel Company.

The Western Federation of Miners was a militant, revolutionary union of metal miners with a small membership in the coal fields. Big Bill Haywood, the outstanding leader in the W. F. M., understood workers' solidarity as reaching beyond the boundaries of any one industry and had offered during the coal strikes of 1902 to call out all the metal miners if the U. M. W. A. would call a general strike of all the coal miners. Also the workers in the W. F. M. had contributed to the anthracite relief fund more cash, per capita than any other outside union.[5] So when the Western Federation of Miners pulled out the metal miners in 1903, they called on the western coal miners to back them up.

Colorado coal miners lived and worked under a tyranny unequaled in the coal fields of the more thickly settled states in the East, and the new District 15, in northern Colorado, had been talking of a strike on their own account. Many of the coal mines in the Rockies were even then owned by the great metal mining corporations and the call to the coal miners found the workers eager for a struggle. National officers of the U. M. W. A. were pushed into endorsing the strike, which early in November, 1903, brought out thousands of miners throughout Colorado and over the border in New Mexico and Utah.

The U. M. W. A. promised relief but immediately Mitchell began advising a separate compromise settlement in the northern Colorado field. A coal famine threatened in the West, which meant that if the miners stood firm they could bring the operators to terms. But Mitchell was busily conferring at Denver with operators, business men, and the Governor. Three times the union miners of northern Colorado refused to obey Mitchell's orders and break the ranks. Then the national office withdrew relief in the northern field and this time on a secret ballot referendum it was claimed that the workers voted to yield. The coal famine was relieved and the great strike of the unorganized miners was betrayed to defeat.

Evicted strikers and their families spent a bitter winter in tents on mountain hillsides. Militia came in to the chief strike area in southern Colorado and martial law was declared. Tent villages were blockaded and spies were sent to watch the trains leaving Denver for the south, but, with the help of the railroad workers, Mother Jones and others who had not given up the fight got through anyway. Tents and houses were searched and strikers bullied, thrown into jail, or forcibly deported. In the course of the fight at least two strikers were shot. Some of the strikers refused to be registered and finger printed by the military and an Associated Press dispatch from Trinidad, Colo., May 19, 1904, pictures the brutality that was then let loose upon them:

Trinidad, Colo, May 19.—Eighty striking miners were marched on foot from Berwind to Trinidad this afternoon by a troop of cavalry. The men had all refused to register at Berwind. . . . The men were brought to military headquarters here and photographed in groups and registered according to the Bertillon system, after which they were turned loose. They had been marched a distance of twenty miles over the mountains in a scorching hot sun. Several fell by the roadside from fatigue. They were given water by the military authorities when they arrived here, but no food. . . .

All men arrested are Italians and have created no disturbance whatever. They were either living at home or in strikers' camp. One man, through an interpreter, told the following story of their trip: . . . The troop drove us as I see men drive cattle, and they repeatedly struck us and several times when men would lag behind they would run their horses against them and compel them to run or stagger out of the way to keep from being killed. . . . One Italian about sixty years old became so weak he could not walk and two of the soldiers struck him on the head until he fell by the roadside, where he was left in the broiling hot sun, and I do not know but what he is dead. He had been sick and was not fit to walk and only got a few miles when he fell. Several men became weak, but they bore up rather than take the blows of the soldiers.[6]

In June, 1904, all official union relief was withdrawn by the United Mine Workers, and local unions in the East were warned by the national officers against contributing to the Colorado strike.

Nine years later the workers of Rockefeller's Colorado Fuel and Iron and of other companies in Colorado rose in a fresh revolt. Again there were evictions, and a tent colony, spies, injunctions, shootings—all the weapons of the capitalist class. Baldwin-Felts thugs fresh from battles in West Virginia were imported and worked with the state militia. This time the militia let loose a rain of shot and fire on a tent colony at Ludlow, and killed 19 persons, including 11 children.

The state of Colorado made no move to punish the men responsible for this massacre. On the contrary, the commanding officer at Ludlow, Major Pat Hamrock, was in February, 1930, given command of the state penitentiary.

Another officer of Ludlow fame, Lewis N. Scherf, was commanding militia at Columbine during the I. W. W. coal mine strike of 1927 when eight miners were killed and twenty miners were wounded by the militia. Scherf was also called to the penitentiary in 1930—not as a prisoner. He was placed second in command with his old chief Hamrock.

STRUGGLES IN ALABAMA

"Free" miners in Alabama had responded eagerly to the U. M. W. A. organizing campaign. Not only in 1902 but again in 1903 several thousand were out in short local strikes. They secured an arbitration award with a slight increase in pay and some improvement in working conditions, but the Tennessee Coal, Iron and Railroad Company, which dominated the situation in Alabama and Tennessee refused to pay the scale of the arbitration award, and in 1904 some 10,000 men employed by the T. C. I. and R. and other "furnace" operators went on strike. Both Federal and state courts issued injunctions against the strikers. "The climax . . . came when the governor ordered the state militia to cut down the tents used to shelter the evicted mine workers and their families. In addition to this order, the soldiers were directed to take possession of the tents, and orders were issued that public meetings could not be held. The governor also threatened to call a special session of the legislature to repeal the vagrancy law of Alabama, so that every striking miner could be arrested and sent to prison." [7] Two years later all union agreements in Alabama had been broken up and membership declined steadily.

During the war boom, the union was revived, and in May, 1920, when Alabama operators refused to accept the award of the Bituminous Coal Commission, a strike was called which spread throughout the coal fields of the state. But the coal interests, headed now by U. S. Steel, which had taken over the Tennessee Coal, Iron and Railroad Company, were determined to destroy the union completely. They secured from the governor the use of the state militia which proceeded to break up the picket lines and prevent all meetings and speeches, even including regular business meetings of union locals inside their own halls. The old story of blood, evictions, tent colonies, and imported strikebreakers was repeated.

Even peaceful picketing was strictly prohibited and one day just before Christmas the militia shot at sight a sturdy old miner, John Northcutt, who had persisted in leading a picket line. The soldier who killed him was shot in his turn, and Will Baird, an active striker who was son-in-law to the murdered picket, was accused. Baird fled into the woods, but later gave himself up to the sheriff. A gang of soldiers broke into the jail at midnight and carried off Will Baird for a lynching. His body was found in the woods, pierced by 22 bullet holes. The lynchers were known and the grand jury indicted them, but capitalist court machinery cleared them all.

In February, 1921, the U. M. W. A. agreed to arbitration of the strike by the governor. Naturally he ruled against the union on every point. All recognition was refused, and every miner who had been an active leader in the strike was blacklisted by the operators. John L. Lewis's chief assistant, Van A. Bittner, was sent in to take charge of the weakened district, and under his guidance its destruction was completed.

War and Treachery in West Virginia

Several thousand unorganized miners had answered the union strike call in West Virginia in 1902 and stood out with great determination and solidarity. One bloody battle was fought at Stanniford. But only in a small area in the Kanawha field did the union gain recognition. There a two-year district agreement was signed with the operators, including an increase in pay with semi-monthly payday, shortening of the day to 9 hours, the right to employ a checkweighman, the right to buy elsewhere than at a company store, and reinstatement of strikers without discrimination. Operators agreed to check off the union dues.

For 20 years the Kanawha district remained a union stronghold in West Virginia. But less than half the miners who had joined the strike were within this union area. Thousands scattered in other mines were left to settle as best they could. Union officials hoped that as time went by other operators would see the smooth working of the Kanawha agreement and come to a more friendly attitude toward the union.

Much of the West Virginia mining was already controlled by outside interests. They were beginning the long fight for northern coal markets, and they set out deliberately to underbid the northern fields in their production costs of which the chief item was the mine workers' wages. The fields in the northern part of the state were near the southern Pennsylvania counties where the mine operators were consistently hostile to the union. The southernmost counties were just being opened up, largely by companies close to the interests which had fought to a finish the unions in steel and metal mining.

So instead of considering how they might bargain with union officials, the operators who had not yielded in 1902 began systematically to sharpen their weapons against the union. During the strike a court had readily granted an injunction to prevent union organizers from "holding meetings at or near the mines of the companies." Then operators secured a court ruling which deprived the union of the legal right to organize. [8] To make even stronger the barriers against organization, the yellow-dog contract was gradually introduced; the worker who wanted a job was compelled to sign away his right to join any labor union. Some companies with the help of state officials specialized in importing under contract foreign workers who were then held in a state of peonage until they had worked out their "indebtedness" to the company.

A system of private armed guards was developed as a continuous routine, even when there was no strike in the offing. Deputy sheriffs, commissioned by the county, were paid by the operators and stationed at the mine camps. The notorious Baldwin-Felts agency at Bluefield built up a business of supplying spies and gunmen to coal operators. Private mine guards had roused protests which led the governor of the state in 1907 to refer to them in his message to the legislature:

They [mine guards] are used at some of the collieries to protect the property of owners, to prevent trespassing, and especially to prevent labor agitators and organizers of a miners' union from gaining access to the miners. . . . Many outrages have been committed by these guards, many of whom appear to be vicious and dare-devil men who seem to add to their viciousness by bulldozing and terrorizing people.

But fine words were wasted against the wishes of the coal interests and the mine guard system remained.

When the Paint Creek operators withdrew from the Kanawha agreement in April, 1912, and set up the conditions that prevailed in the neighboring non-union Cabin Creek Valley, Paint Creek miners went on strike. They were joined by unorganized miners in the Cabin Creek and New River fields, but the Kanawha union district was not called out. Officials had signed up for another time agreement in spite of the withdrawal of the Paint Creek operators.

The strike was a long hard-fought battle. Some new variations appeared in the old story of class war. Some evicted strikers could not get their mail from post offices on company property. At least once mail was deliberately burned by a store manager. The roads up the creeks were guarded by machine guns and no stranger or known union organizer was allowed to pass. Mother Jones in her *Autobiography* tells a stirring tale of wading and driving up the creeks to encourage the strikers and give unorganized men the union obligation.

Union officials were eager to prove their reasonableness and urged the governor to send in state militia, but as usual the militia was turned against the union. Three times martial law was declared and all the constitutional rights of free speech and free assembly were formally suspended—just as they had been informally destroyed by the mine guards.

Presence of the militia did not prevent a trainload of Baldwin-Felt guards, with machine guns and rifles, from roaring past a tent colony at Holly Grove, killing a miner and a woman and wounding 16 more. A military commission took over the administration of "justice" and arrested and detained scores of strikers without regard to such details as the nature of the offense or the penalty provided by the state laws. They worked in close consultation with the governor, and later admitted that they were simply keeping certain miners out of the way until they "had peace and order in that territory." Meantime they were aiding the mine guards to protect imported scabs.

After more than a year of struggle and suffering, a compromise settlement was secured. The union gained a foothold in all three fields, but in none of them were conditions brought up to the standard of the Kanawha agreement.

Until the war boom the paid-up union membership in West Virginia was barely one-tenth of all the coal mine workers in the state. In 1916 and 1917 the union was strong enough to gain recognition in the Fairmont field (northern West Virginia), and in spite of the operators' terrorist tactics, workers were organizing in the wild mountain regions about Logan and south of the Kanawha district.

Miners on the March

Three thousand union miners from the Kanawha field came together in September, 1919, rifle in hand, to march over the mountains to Logan and do battle with the operators. The governor rushed to the miners' camp and begged them to disband. He promised a full investigation of the miners' grievances in Logan County, and the miners heard that Federal troops were on their way to Logan. So they yielded to their officials' advice and turned back, misguided into believing that the governor and the troops would enforce fair play.

A number of Mingo County operators during the following spring (1920) tried to break the organizing wave by locking out their miners and bringing in strikebreakers. At Matewan, Mayor Testerman and chief of police Sid Hatfield protested as illegal the eviction of union miners by the Felts brothers and a band of their gunmen. Then Albert Felts tried to arrest Sid Hatfield and in a five-minute battle ten men were killed, including the mayor and both the Felts brothers. This was only the most important of many skirmishes of which the record will never be complete. Troops were brought in and stationed about the mines while nearly 3,000 striking miners and their families spent the winter in tent colonies.

Mingo County miners were almost solidly organized and several local unions had been formed in Mercer and McDowell counties. Chances of success were promising, even in the McDowell County area dominated by a subsidiary of United States Steel, when John L. Lewis withdrew support from the work in Mercer and McDowell counties. This betrayed the Mingo County miners into a hopeless position in their fight for union.

Still the conflict continued through the summer of 1921, with the county under martial law. On July 31, Sid Hatfield and his friend Ed Chambers were shot on the courthouse steps at Welch, in McDowell County, by an ambushed gang of Baldwin-Felts men, led by a stool pigeon who had been active in the union. This was a spark that set aflame the fighting spirit of union miners in the Kanawha field. Three weeks later seven thousand men gathered again at Marmet, 10 miles from Charleston, for an armed march to Logan and Mingo counties. They wore a uniform of blue overalls and a red handkerchief around the neck. They had organized a commissary and a small band of nurses to care for the wounded, for they were set to win the county for the union and they knew that this meant war.

Again the governor of West Virginia and district president Keeney tried to hold them back. Lewis was begging President Harding to arrange a conference of union officials and Mingo County operators. The miners had gone half way to Logan when they did actually start to disperse. Then they heard that the miners' outpost near Sharples had met the state troopers and three miners had been killed. Once more they headed southward, with reënforcements. They swarmed over the mountains in several divisions. But the delay had given the operators time to increase their forces.

Gunmen, legionnaires, business men and militia, with rifles, machine guns, and airplanes lined up to resist the marching union miners. The battle lasted nearly a week—with over 50 men killed—and the miners were breaking through the lines when Federal troops arrived and turned the tide against the workers. Martial law continued, and little by little the strike was smothered and the union destroyed in Mingo County.

Lewis's desertion of the miners in the three most southerly counties of West Virginia was only the beginning of withdrawal and defeat throughout the state. In 1920 the U. M. W. A. was at its peak of membership, with a paid-up enrollment in West Virginia of nearly half the 100,000 mine workers in the state. By 1929, there were barely 600 paid-up members in West Virginia.

Kanawha and New River operators early in 1922 tried to force a district agreement without waiting as usual for the outcome of negotiations in the Central Competitive Field. When the union refused this, the operators announced a wage cut and open shop operation. The miners walked out, independently of the nation-wide strike call of 1922, and stayed out in the Kanawha field long after the big northern strike was over. In spite of hunger and suffering, many were still refusing two years later to work in non-union mines. A few Kanawha operators had signed up separately in 1922, but by 1924 the union had lost its foothold in the field. Then the wave of destruction swept northward to the Fairmont field where most of the operators had signed up after the 1922 strike. A smaller group went through the forms of an agreement in 1924 only to break it the following year. Again a strike with evictions, barracks, tent colonies—and defeat. Operators and official U. M. W. A. policies between them had destroyed the union throughout the state.

CHAPTER XI

THE REIGN OF LEWIS

John L. Lewis slid into the presidency of the United Mine Workers just at the end of the war, when the class lineup of workers on one side and capitalists on the other was to be more clear-cut than ever before. Workers who had been fighting for "democracy" were coming back to the post-war depression of severe unemployment. The masses were stirring in Europe, and even the most persistent and poisonous anti-Bolshevik propaganda could not conceal the fact that the workers had taken over the control of government and industry in Russia. In the United States, a wave of militancy brought several hard-fought strikes. Most notably, in 1919, steel workers were battling for union against the strongest corporations in the country. Employers were beginning their more systematic drive to undermine the labor movement by company union and welfare schemes. For the competition among capitalists was even sharper than it had been before the war, and they were determined that the cost of their battles should be passed on to the workers in the cost-cutting and speed-up which have been an outstanding feature of the post-war years.

For the United Mine Workers the situation made clearer than ever the old conflict between militant union policy and a business bargaining that kept the favor of operators by playing into their hands. Official traditions were for the second course, and to carry it out John L. Lewis was the man of the hour. He and his lieutenants have accomplished more bald betrayals of the miners to the operators and more unprincipled autocratic suppressing of a militant rank and file than are revealed in the annals of any earlier régime.

199

1919 Strike

Long before the organizing campaign had been given up in southern West Virginia, Lewis had begun his strike-breaking career in the North. Pushed by the rank and file whose wage increases during the war had not kept pace with the cost of living, he called a nation-wide bituminous strike to begin on November 1, 1919. Over 70 per cent of the bituminous workers responded. But the government, deeply concerned for the operators' wishes, opposed the strike and a Federal judge issued a sweeping injunction against all union strike activities. The union in 1918 had agreed to a wage scale which was to hold for the duration of the war. The armistice had been signed twelve months before the strike began and war-time regulations of coal prices had been withdrawn. But no treaty of peace had yet been signed between the United States and the Central Powers, so the operators and the capitalist court maintained that the miners' war-time wage agreement was still in force.

Lewis immediately accepted the operators' viewpoint and announcing patriotically, "We cannot fight the government," he ordered the workers to return to the mines. But most of the strikers stayed out until early in December when a slight increase was granted and operators and union officials agreed to accept whatever terms an "impartial" commission might award. As usual the award was a compromise, granting the miners less than half their demands. Illinois workers refused to accept the compromise and in spite of Lewis and the district president Farrington they led an outlaw strike which won from the operators a further increase for the company men.

1922 Strike

Another great strike in 1922 was even more openly betrayed. Before the wage agreements expired on April 1, bituminous operators proposed district settlements and the breaking up of the Joint Interstate Conference of the Central Competitive Field. They talked openly of wage cuts below the scale of 1920. The union held out for renewal of the scale, in a joint interstate agreement, with shortening of hours, special rates for overtime, and abolition of the penalty clause under which heavy fines were levied on unauthorized strikes. In the anthracite, the miners demanded an increase above the scale awarded by a special anthracite commission in 1920, while the operators insisted that wages must go down.

A nation-wide strike was called, but the day before it began union officials in western Kentucky (District 23) quietly signed up for a renewal of the old terms until April, 1923. A few days later union mines in southeastern Kentucky and Tennessee (District 19) were signed up for a two-year agreement. This withdrew from the strike two districts where the operators were in sharp competition with northern coal fields and set an official seal upon scabbing by union miners on their striking fellow workers. After Farrington broke with Lewis, he helped to circulate the report that Kentucky operators had paid Lewis $100,000 for letting them operate while northern mines were closed.

In spite of this, the strike brought out nearly three-fourths of all bituminous miners in the country. It tied up the anthracite fields. It spread to the Pennsylvania non-union mines in Somerset county and the Connellsville coke region, drawing out in all nearly 100,000 unorganized miners. The midsummer strike of railroad shopmen further strengthened the miners' position.

Herrin and Cliftonville

At Herrin, in the solidly organized southern Illinois fields, a new stripping mine was being uncovered. Union officials had agreed that this work of removing the overburden might continue during the strike. (Later Lewis charged that Farrington and Fishwick, president and vice-president of District 12, had secretly agreed to permit actual production of scab coal provided the operator would split his profits with them.) Early in June the union men were discharged and a trainload of strikebreakers were brought in from Chicago, to get out coal under protection of armed guards hired from a detective agency.

After three miners had been killed, union men from nearby mines rushed to Herrin. They remembered the union victory at Virden, and wrath over the bringing of scabs into 100 per cent union territory rose to fever heat. In a pitched battle the mine superintendent and some twenty of the guards and scabs were killed. It was a spontaneous outburst of rank and file workers to defend their right to organize and strike. Even the coroner's jury put the blame for the deaths squarely on the mine superintendent.

Another battle was fought in July, 1922, at Cliftonville, in the Panhandle of West Virginia. Several hundred union miners from around Avella, Pennsylvania, marched over to the Richland mine, where strikers had been evicted and scabs had been brought in. When a small delegation went ahead to talk to the scabs at the tipple, the mine guards opened fire without warning and killed an old miner. In the battle that followed, seven union men, thirteen strikebreakers and the county sheriff were killed. All the union marchers that could be rounded up were arrested, and over forty of them were sent to prison.

Non-Union Fields Betrayed

In the non-union fields evictions and tent colonies, armed guards and strikebreakers, were an everyday occurrence. At least six strikers were killed in the frequent clashes between pickets and police. But the strikers, newly organized and hopeful at last of relief from the special tyranny and unfairness of non-union operators, held firm.

By August, union victory was in sight and the operators in the organized fields were ready to bargain, withdrawing the wage cut if the miners' demands were withdrawn. Miners who realized the power of mass solidarity were demanding that all agreements must expire the same day. Instead, the officials signed bituminous agreements to run until April 1, and let the anthracite run until September.

But the worst betrayal in the entire strike was Lewis's desertion of the newly organized strikers in the Connellsville and Somerset fields and other anti-union strongholds of southern Pennsylvania. Miners in union districts were sent back to work before these non-union operators had yielded an inch. Rockefeller's Consolidation Coal Company and Davis Coal and Coke, Bethlehem Mines Corporation, Hillman interests, and others were allowed to reopen union mines in the Pittsburgh or Fairmont fields, while the workers at their non-union mines remained on strike. The struggle dragged on for months. The officials of District 2 (central Pennsylvania) levied relief assessments on the district membership and kept organizers in the strike area. But the Lewis settlement at Cleveland had knocked the main props out from under the Connellsville and Somerset strikers. By the summer of 1923 the last of the non-union mines had reopened, most of them with a yellow dog contract.

United States Steel through the H. C. Frick Company is the strongest interest in the Connellsville field, just as another subsidiary, United States Coal and Coke, dominates McDowell County in West Virginia and its Tennessee Coal, Iron and Railroad Company dominates Alabama. Lewis had withdrawn organizers from McDowell County. He had left the Alabama strikers at the mercy of the anti-union governor's arbitration. When he also flagrantly deserted the Connellsville strikers the rumor began to spread that

Lewis had sold out to the United States Steel Corporation. Later, after Farrington and Lewis had fallen out and were telling what they knew about each other's crooked dealings, Farrington, the paid agent of the Peabody Coal Company, reported that Lewis had received money from non-union coal companies.

The actual result of the Lewis policies has been defeat and loss for the union. Instead of pushing for nation-wide organization he has played for favor with the operators in the old union strongholds. For 10 years he has echoed their statements that at least 200,000 miners must be frozen out of the industry and that anti-trust laws must be amended to encourage concentration and "stabilize" production. Outlying districts have been sacrificed, one after another. Betrayal and defeat in Pennsylvania in 1922 marked just another important milestone on the downward road. With the rapid shrinking in union membership and union territory, the old union strongholds themselves were threatened.

JACKSONVILLE AND THE 1927 STRIKE

At Jacksonville in 1924 the Lewis machine signed up for a three-year agreement, continuing the 1920 wage scale in the Central Competitive Field. Most of the outlying union fields followed suit with district agreements renewing the 1920 scale, but operators in the Kanawha field and western Kentucky refused to negotiate. Alabama had been lost in 1921. Tennessee and eastern Kentucky had been lost in 1923. Colorado, Utah, Texas, Maryland and Virginia were operating 100 per cent *non-union*.

Within twelve months after Jacksonville, operators who had signed three-year agreements began to cut wages, locking out and evicting union men who refused to work at less than the Jacksonville scale. Consolidation Coal Company and Bethlehem Mines Corporation, whom Lewis had helped in the Somerset strike of 1922, now took the lead in breaking the Jacksonville agreement in the Fairmont field. Pittsburgh Coal Company, Youghiogheny and Ohio Coal Company, and the Paisley mines led the drive in western Pennsylvania. Companies tied to railroad interests scrapped the agreement in central Pennsylvania. In all, 110 mines in Pennsylvania and 50 in West Virginia changed from union to non-union operation during the year 1925.

The Southwest—once a stronghold of the union—had begun to break up. The Southwest agreement of 1924 had included less than one-fourth of the mines and the miners in Oklahoma and less than two-thirds of the miners in Arkansas. By the end of 1925, the union had lost other important mines in these states.

Operators who had kept the Jacksonville agreement were united in demanding a wage cut from April 1, 1927, as the basis for further negotiation. Lewis, who had led the most disastrous retreats and betrayals, called a bituminous strike under the slogan "No Backward Step." But as the months went by, instead of keeping a solid front throughout what remained of union territory, and throwing the full force of the organization into calling out miners throughout the country, Lewis prepared fresh disaster by authorizing temporary agreements before the busy season in Illinois, Indiana, and a few other districts with any operators who were willing to reopen for the winter at the old scale.

Thousands of miners in Illinois and Indiana went back to work. Left-Wing leaders and progressives protested against this break in the solid front of the strike, while Lewis and his publicity staff were busily setting forth the "victory" that had been secured. Meantime the temporary agreements had granted the operators one vital point: nominally the Jacksonville scale was continued, but day rates lower than the average earnings under the Jacksonville scale were allowed for machine cutters and machine loaders, and joint committees were set up to discuss and recommend adjustments of machine loading rates in relation to the needs of the coal market and union and non-union cost of production.

Most of the operators in Pennsylvania and Ohio had decided to break entirely with the union. They were evicting strikers, bringing in scabs, increasing their private armies of coal and iron police, and using the courts against the union miners. That the strike was a life and death struggle for the union in Ohio and the bituminous mines of Pennsylvania, was clear long before Lewis and the district officials (including Fishwick of Illinois) had ordered the strikers in other fields back to the mines under temporary agreements. The Pennsylvania and Ohio miners were deserted. Once more the union machine had cleared the way for defeat.

Relief was continued by the International U. M. W. A., but only for those who had no connection with the rebellion against Lewis which had grown to a considerable movement. Few families received even $5 a week and the average was far below this amount. Stories began to leak out about the rakeoffs taken by officials who were buying supplies. And strikers remembered that at the last convention (in January, 1927) the union machine had put through a salary raise for the international officials. So Lewis was sure of his thousand dollars a month and Philip Murray and Thomas Kennedy had their $750 a month—besides "expenses"— even when the rank and file were close to starvation.

Some barracks had been built after Pittsburgh Coal Company and others began throwing out the union families. Now in 1927 more and more strikers were evicted and more of these makeshift dwellings were built, some by the union and some by the Left-Wing relief committee, until from 8,000 to 10,000 families were facing the choice of a cold and hungry winter in crowded barracks or giving up the fight for union.

Injunctions

Rule by injunction is a special device of American capitalism. Employers expect the state to protect them in autocratic exploitation of the working class. But before the end of the nineteenth century labor unions had through many years of struggle won a legal right to exist throughout the United States. So employers, still determined to prevent organization or to destroy a union, have turned to the courts and quietly secured from their capitalist judges injunctions against one or another form of union activity. Injunction orders issued at various times and in various states have made "illegal" all the organized activities essential for effective struggle by the workers. The United Mine Workers has appealed various injunction cases to higher courts, but only Left-Wing militants have led mass revolts, risking arrest and imprisonment for defying injunction orders.

Injunctions against mine workers have played an important part in building up this body of court-made capitalist law, but it is a long story. Here we can only refer to a few of the typical sweeping orders issued at the request of coal operators.

Long before the strike of 1927 courts had proved themselves the obedient servants of operators against mine workers. In the famous Hitchman case, dating from the reign of John Mitchell, an injunction against all union activities at a mine where workers had signed the yellow dog contract had been upheld by the United States Supreme Court. The southern West Virginia struggle had brought forth an injunction against the union's maintaining tent colonies and the Somerset strike in 1922-23 had brought a similar order from a Pennsylvania court.

One of the most far reaching writs before 1927 was a Federal injunction secured by the Pond Creek Coal Company (southern West Virginia) in 1920 which prohibited the workers "from advertising, representing, stating by word, by posted notices, or by placards displayed at any point in the State of West Virginia or elsewhere, that a strike exists in the Pond Creek Field, or at plaintiff's mines, and from warning, or notifying persons to remain away from said Pond Creek Field or from plaintiff's mines." [1]

During the 1927 strike an epidemic of drastic injunctions swept through western Pennsylvania and eastern Ohio. They added some new restrictions. At Rossiter, Pa., for example, Judge Langham, who admitted he had a $6,000 investment in one of the coal companies involved, obligingly forbade meetings and singing on a lot more than a quarter of a mile from the mine or at any other place or places within hearing of the scabs when they were going in or out of the mine. Judge Schoonmaker of a Federal court obliged the Pittsburgh Terminal Coal Corporation by enjoining further union activity or support for the court appeals in 450 eviction suits brought by the company against striking miners. Federal Judge Hough announced that pickets must be English-speaking American citizens. The Circuit Court at Wheeling forbade strikers at Elm Grove from entering upon roads, railroads or street cars passing through the company property or adjacent thereto, for any purposes connected with the strike; the ladies' auxiliary of the local union was also forbidden to meet.

Practically throughout the strike area mass picketing was made illegal, and picket lines and strikers' meetings were attacked and broken up. At St. Clairsville, Ohio, when the wives of militant strikers went in a body to the jail where their husbands were imprisoned more than 50 women were arrested.

How many strikers were arrested for defying injunctions and sheriffs' proclamations it is impossible to know. Mass picketing was carried on by thousands of rank and file workers who revolted against the official United Mine Workers' policy of obedience to capitalist law.

Operators' Gunmen

Even without resorting to state militia, the coal operators have had various little armies at their disposal in the war against striking miners. Pennsylvania and West Virginia furnish the employers with state police. Private guards hired by the coal operators are sworn in as deputy sheriffs. Perhaps most notorious are the coal and iron police of Pennsylvania—now officially known as industrial police—hired by the operators and licensed by the state to act as police openly in the service of the employers. In Ohio, Federal marshals have helped in the enforcement of Federal injunctions.

Pennsylvania has stood out above all other states in recent years in the brutality and lawlessness practiced by the police against striking coal miners. Blocking public highways, provoking disorder by riding roughly into peaceful meetings, drunken raids on tent colonies, frame-ups, lawless arrests of local leaders followed by beating and torturing to extract "confessions"—they have stopped at nothing in their campaign of terror against the strikers. In every struggle, uncounted miners have been knocked down, beaten up, or otherwise injured. Women and children do not escape. Now and then a striker is killed.

Deputy sheriffs and state police were most conspicuous in the non-union Pennsylvania fields during the 1922-23 struggle. In Fayette County alone (Connellsville region), when that fight was hottest 2,500 deputy sheriffs were at the disposal of the operators. That meant one deputy to every twelve miners in the county. In Somerset County, the army of deputies was much smaller, but the county sheriff admitted that he personally had earned from $30,000 to $40,000 in fees from the coal companies for the deputies commissioned during the first twelve months after the strike began.[2] The army of state police numbered over 6,600 on March 1, 1923, when Governor Pinchot's investigating committee examined the official records.

In 1927, the coal and iron police were the most conspicuous force used by the operators in the Pittsburgh district. Operators' deputy sheriffs and coal and iron police have always been largely recruited through strikebreaking detective agencies, who send in to "enforce the law" men chosen for their skill in wielding a rifle and a blackjack.

Even capitalist law is far less important to the operators and their private armies than any tactics, legal or illegal, that may break down the spirit of the strikers.

State troopers were also active, however, in 1927. It was they who rode into the meeting of 1,500 men, women and children at Cheswick, near Pittsburgh, on August 22, when striking miners were holding a Sacco-Vanzetti protest meeting in an orchard. One of the miners described what happened:

The police waited to one side. They had horses, but stood beside them—not mounted yet—while the last of the crowd was forming in the orchard. Then a sergeant and a lieutenant came up to the speakers' stand. I was in the crowd first, but when they went up to the stand, I went up there too. They ordered the meeting to stop. The chairman turned to the crowd and said that whether the meeting would be held was up to them as citizens of the United States. The crowd called out that they wanted to have a meeting. A man yelled: "I was in the army in the War. I fought for liberty. We have a right to liberty and free speech!"

Then one of the officers on the platform fired his pistol three times and yelled, "Get on horseback!" A lot of them jumped on their horses and charged while the others threw bombs at the crowd. They exploded and the gas got all around us. It got in our eyes and we couldn't hardly see. The crowd began to run south, while the policemen clubbed them and threw more bombs and rode them down with their horses. Many people, including women and children, were knocked unconscious. They picked them up and threw them into some trucks. I don't know where they hauled them to.

For half an hour they rode up and down the public highway near by, clubbing and beating up people. They also smashed the windshields of some automobiles which were passing.[3]

One of the troopers swaggering along the highway hit one man too many. "Clubbed across the knees and then cracked over the head as he doubled up with pain, the man, who is unknown in that section, became infuriated, drew a pistol, killed the trooper and escaped." Pittsburgh papers, loyal to the ruling class, played up the trooper's death and the bravery of the police in quelling a riot. Twenty-one union miners were arrested on charges of "unlawful assembly, rioting and inciting to riot and resisting officers." Later an Italian miner named Accorsi who had left Cheswick and moved out of the state was brought back by the authorities to be framed for "murdering" the trooper. When his case came to trial in 1929, long after the excitement had died down, the frameup had been thoroughly exposed in the Left-Wing papers. And in the meantime, the unprovoked and vicious killing of the miner Barkoski by the coal and iron police had taught even a Pittsburgh jury something of police methods in their state. The Accorsi frameup was too raw; this miner was acquitted.

John Barkoski was beaten to death in February, 1929, by coal and iron police of the Pittsburgh Coal Company, after they had assaulted and arrested him at his mother-in-law's house. The company doctor testified at the trial of the policemen that he had watched one of them kicking and beating Barkoski on the floor of the barracks. "I warned Lyster, 'This will have to stop now because his condition is serious.'" But having said this the doctor left the barracks. After more than four hours of torture, Barkoski was sent to the hospital to die. The policemen were defended by a high-priced Mellon lawyer and acquitted of murder. On a second trial for "involuntary manslaughter," one of the thugs was sentenced to a year and another to 10 months in the workhouse.

The full story of how the police have carried on a reign of terror for the operators cannot be told here. It is too long a record of tyranny and brutality against striking miners and local union leaders.

More and more during the 1927-28 strike the forces of the operators were turned with special harshness against the Left-Wing miners. After the U. M. W. A. had given up the fight for union operation at most of the Ohio and Pennsylvania bituminous mines and had signed up practically on the operators' terms in Illinois and Indiana, the union machine turned more openly against the militant rank and file among the strikers, joining forces with the police and courts in attacking the "reds." We shall see how this reached a climax in Pittsburgh at the September, 1928, organizing convention of the National Miners Union and in southern Illinois during the N. M. U. strike 15 months later.

Official Settlements in 1928

The temporary agreements with which Lewis had broken the solid front of the strike in the fall of 1927 were renewed in the spring by Illinois and Indiana operators. Then three days after the Frick subsidiary of United States Steel (in Pennsylvania) posted a wage cut, Lewis called the international scale committee together and ordered district settlements on the basis of wages below the Jacksonville scale. Illinois and Indiana were the only major soft coal states in which district agreements covered most of the mines in the states, but even there some operators tried to starve their workers into accepting a still more drastic cut.

Under the Illinois agreement, which runs for four years,

an arbitrator was appointed to insure "peace" in the mines. Disputes on which the joint conciliation bodies could not come to an agreement would be referred to him for final decision. Operators were granted the right to install mechanical loaders without any provision against wholesale discharges and the speeding up of men kept on the machines. Day rates were fixed for loading machine men and machine cutters, and again a special joint commission was appointed to study and fix tonnage rates for machine loaders "on a basis that will be fairly competitive"—that is, with low wage non-union fields. Dead work conditions were made far less favorable to the miners. Illinois and Indiana agreements were carefully timed to expire in different years.

Harry Fishwick, president of District 12, headed the miners' committee which negotiated this Illinois agreement. President Lewis took part also in the final sessions. Fishwick hailed the agreement as a step toward *improving* the miners' conditions.

When the terms of the 1928 agreements were submitted to the membership in secret referendums, they were declared carried in the various districts by narrow majorities. Rank and file miners, well aware that feeling against the new terms was running high, charged crookedness in the counting of the referendum votes, and many mines were tied up by local strikes until the workers were driven by hunger to accept the settlements.

Fall in Bituminous Membership

As a result of these various betrayals and defeats the membership of the United Mine Workers in the bituminous fields has dropped from the high point of 1920, when it included 386,000 workers at bituminous mines in the United States—or nearly two-thirds of the workers then employed in the industry—to about 80,000, or barely one-sixth of the

1929 total. Canadian membership also fell from 20,600 to 12,900.

Illinois was, in 1929, the only important bituminous district in the union, with more than half the bituminous membership of the United States. Barely 30,000 members were scattered in other bituminous fields, and only in Illinois, Wyoming, Michigan, and Montana were the organized miners so many as 80 per cent of the total in the state.

BARGAINS FOR ANTHRACITE OPERATORS

With this narrowing of the bituminous domain from which the national treasury of the United Mine Workers could replenish its funds and furnish the high salaries and expense accounts of Lewis and his lieutenants, the union machine was set to tighten its hold on the anthracite districts and to work out a still closer coöperation with anthracite operators.

Anthracite workers demanded an increase in pay when their tri-district agreement expired August 31, 1925. They authorized union officials to bargain for a two-year contract on that basis, but the operators insisted that wages must be reduced. The resulting strike lasted until the operators had sold off at high prices the coal stocks which they had been accumulating during the summer. But the strike was not a spectacular struggle. Operators intended to renew the agreement and they did not attempt to bring in scabs to run the mines.

In February, 1926, after secret conferences between Lewis and Richard F. Grant, then head of the Hanna anthracite interests, the miners' demands were scrapped, the operators withdrew their threat of a wage cut, and an agreement was signed to run until August 31, 1930. Lewis boasted of the great achievement—the longest joint agreement in the history of American coal mining.

Broad powers given in 1923 to the Board of Conciliation to "equalize wages" were renewed. The board was also authorized to work out a program of "coöperation and efficiency." As for basic wages, either side could move once a year for a change in the joint agreement, and if negotiations broke down final decision would be left to two men, or three if the two came to a deadlock. This agreement marked a definite further stage in placing the union at the service of the operators.

But the "peace" and "stabilizing of the industry" promised by the agreement have not been forthcoming. Operators driving for efficiency and cost-cutting have been closing down high cost collieries for months at a time, or even permanently, throwing thousands of workers and their families into hopeless poverty. No formal proposal to cut basic wages was put forward under the agreement, but the workers are convinced that their earnings have been reduced and their jobs speeded up by countless little changes put over by the operators and the union machine. Again and again the rank and file have revolted in local strikes, which district officials have always tried to suppress, insisting that all grievances must be dealt with by the joint bodies for conciliation and arbitration.

Various officials within the U. M. W. A. have played on this unrest for their own advantage, trying to build up a separate anthracite union which they could control without paying tribute to John L. Lewis. But the Lewis machine has been too strong for them and one after another Capellini, Brennan, McGarry returned to the Lewis fold. Genuine militants—Campbell, Reilly, Lillis, and Frank Bonita—were murdered in cold blood by hired thugs brought in from outside the anthracite. Sam Bonita, Moleski, Mendola—going as a committee of protest on the sub-contracting system to the office of Agati, a cog in the Capellini-Lewis machine—were threatened. Agati and Bonita both drew and fired. Agati went down and Bonita, Moleski, Mendola, all three, were framed for the penitentiary. Later, when the

National Miners Union had been organized, hostility of U. M. W. A. officials was focused on N. M. U. representatives. The struggle between the U. M. W. A. and the Left-Wing union is still in its early stages in the anthracite, but already frameups have been attempted and several N. M. U. organizers are now awaiting trial under the sedition law of Pennsylvania. U. M. W. A. officials, local authorities in anthracite towns, and state police have worked in apparent harmony against the Left-Wing organizers.

Early in 1930, Lewis began secret bargaining with anthracite operators for renewal of the long time contract, but the rank and file insisted on a convention, in the vain hope of heading off another betrayal. Demands were drafted, to satisfy the restlessness of the workers : a wage increase, abolition of the sub-contracting system, equalization of working time among the various collieries of a single company, etc. Negotiations dragged on for three weeks and included another secret conference with Richard F. Grant—who now links the Hanna interests with one of the strongest Morgan anthracite companies. Then Lewis and his subordinates on the anthracite scale committee signed a five-and-a-half-year agreement from which these rank and file demands have disappeared. In their place has been inserted still another joint body for the fixing of terms and conditions to promote efficiency. The operators' demand for a frankly lower wage scale was withdrawn for they have gained something far more important to their interests. Union officials accept the drive for concentration and speed-up. They will help operators keep "peace" in the industry while more thousands are thrown out of their jobs and the "lucky" ones must work harder than ever to earn what they earn to-day.

As a reward and symbol of this service to the employers, the union machine wins for the first time a modified check-off of union dues by the anthracite operators. This assures steady revenue for the U. M. W. A. treasury in spite of the workers' increasing restlessness under Lewis policies. Also the check-off has been proved a useful weapon in Illinois against the growth of the Left-Wing union.

REVOLT AGAINST LEWIS

The first lineup of an organized opposition to Lewis within the union came with the Kansas fight in 1921. Howat and Dorchy, Kansas district officials, had defied the state com- pulsory arbitration law and called a strike to secure back pay due to a miner, a widow's son. Lewis denounced the strike and when Howat was convicted and sent to jail Lewis placed the district under a provisional government and expelled Howat and Dorchy from the union without entering charges or permitting an investigation.

Progressives and others who posed as progressives because they were at outs with Lewis demanded reinstatement of Howat and Dorchy. The progressives put up a fight to force the issue onto the floor of the national convention but the Lewis steam roller crushed all discussion of Howat at the conventions of 1922 and 1924.

Nationalization of coal mines was another rallying point for the early opposition to Lewis. A committee was ap- pointed in District 2 to draft a definite plan for nationaliza- tion. When the committee report was ready, the *United Mine Workers Journal* refused to print it and the national conven- tion machinery never allowed it to be presented on the floor.

After Lewis' betrayal of the 1922 strike progressives and Communists within the union began to organize a definite revolt against his régime. They drew up an indictment of Lewis' methods and Lewis' policy, and set forth a program of action. Forces of revolt were united in demanding a genuinely aggressive campaign to organize the non-union fields.

They protested against the squandering of union money for Lewis lieutenants who were appointed as organizers and yet rarely set foot on non-union territory, spending all their time playing Lewis' politics in the union districts.

They protested against the appointment of provisional district governments. Kansas was only one of several fields from which Lewis had ousted the elected officials, sending in a personal representative and turning district funds over to the national treasury. In one field after another the district union has been destroyed by these emissaries of Lewis.

They protested against election methods. As one of the early leaflets put it: "Pay-roll agents of the various administrations employ bribery with money and liquor, and the most brutal forms of intimidation, to accomplish their corruption of the ballot." A climax was reached in 1926 when Brophy, heading the progressive ticket as candidate for international president, was defeated by thousands of votes from non-existing members of dead or "blue sky" locals. Little by little the facts were brought to light, but no official analysis of that vote has ever been published.

All sorts of tactics were used against the militant leaders including expulsions, police persecution, and thuggery. When the first Left-Wing miners' relief committee was functioning in Pittsburgh in 1922-23, the police raided a meeting and the homes of active workers and arrested 23 persons. Later it came out that United Mine Workers' officials had been back of the attack. This was the first of several incidents of this kind.

Again and again thugs were brought into play. At Ziegler, Illinois, thugs started a fight and set the stage for the frame-up that sent Henry Corbishley and three other miners to the penitentiary. That such tactics led to murder in the anthracite has already been noted.

One after another militant leaders were expelled from the U. M. W. A.; in the spring of 1928 even mass expulsions of active locals were resorted to.

Frequent charges that the whole revolt was the work of Communists were backed by continuous false propaganda against Communism and the Soviet Union. The 1927 convention of the United Mine Workers—a body packed with delegates from the same dead locals that had reëlected Lewis —amended the constitution of the U. M. W. A. and in line with general A. F. of L. policy formally excluded all Communist miners from membership in the union.

Progressives and Left-Wing miners of all groups continued to work together until 1928 in the Save-the-Union Committee drive to oust the Lewis machine and compel the United Mine Workers to adopt a more militant organizing policy. The mass convention at Pittsburgh in April of that year brought together 1,000 rank and file miners from all parts of the country and marked a high point of enthusiasm. But differences in policy were growing sharper within the Save-the-Union movement, and a split among them was inevitable.

On one side was the group headed by Brophy and Hapgood, who believed that the miners were too discouraged and disillusioned for any tactics except a slow campaign of education and a gradual driving out of the crooked grafting officials. They thought the old union was still worth their support. They held to the United Mine Workers' official tradition that bargaining is better than fighting, though they knew that there would be struggles ahead for union recognition, for higher wages, and for fair working conditions.

On the other side were the Left-Wing leaders, who realized that the rank and file were ready for an immediate program of uncompromising struggle against the operators. Experience had proved that this could not be carried on within the framework of the United Mine Workers. The intensified crisis in the coal industry had sharpened the conflict of interest between the employers' drive for speed-up and profits and the workers' right to jobs and a living wage.

Now a clean sweep and a new fighting union were necessary.

In September, 1928, under Left-Wing leadership, rank and file miners from eleven states organized the National Miners Union, while the progressives withdrew to watch from the side lines.

THE SPRINGFIELD U. M. W. A.

Personal rivalries within the United Mine Workers led in 1929 to a break between the Lewis faction and the district officials of Illinois. Lewis, finding the national treasury in bad shape, removed the district officials on charges of corruption and set up a provisional government for the Illinois district. Fishwick appealed to the courts and prevented the provisional district officers from functioning. He wired to the American Federation of Labor convention at Toronto, offering to submit the district records for examination provided the international records at Indianapolis were also opened to impartial auditors. William Green, president of the A. F. of L., had been secretary-treasurer of the U. M. W. A. in the earlier years of the Lewis reign, and the Fishwick telegram was quietly ignored. Charges of corruption, together with an endless stream of epithets, are still being passed back and forth, but neither Lewis nor Fishwick has brought a libel suit against the other.

Fishwick, meantime, with other officials who are tired of Lewis' domination and want a freer hand for their own careers, has set up a rival "international" machine to carry on the U. M. W. A. A thin veil of progressivism was thrown over the project by having Brophy, who is out of the industry, and ex-progressives like Howat, Allan Haywood, and Loda, who were holding office under the Lewis machine, join in signing the call for a convention at Springfield, on March 10, 1930. Much was said about returning to the spirit of John Mitchell. Howat was elected national president, and Adolph Germer and John H. Walker, old-time

Socialists, were made vice-president and secretary-treasurer of the reorganized union. Fishwick and Nesbit continued as president and secretary of the Illinois district. Frank Farrington, who had been openly on the payroll of the Peabody Coal Company (at $25,000 a year), was not only seated as a convention delegate but has been a frequent and honored contributor to the columns of Fishwick's organ, *The Illinois Miner,* now the *American Miner.*

Ever since the convention a hot fight has been raging between the Lewis and Fishwick-Howat organizations for the allegiance—and the per capita—of such local unions and district organizations as remain in the bituminous fields. The Springfield union has not attempted to capture the anthracite districts.

Progressives who look to the Springfield union as the most hopeful sign on the miners' horizon have to admit that in Farrington, Fishwick, Nesbit, and others, they are playing with machine politicians with doubtful records, scarcely better than the record of John L. Lewis himself.

The union is keeping an eye to the welfare of the operators—including many in Illinois who have been steadily and aggressively non-union at their mines in other states. It approves the wage reduction of 1928 and blames Lewis for not having yielded sooner. Fishwick himself negotiated the clauses in the Illinois agreement which give the operators a clear road to drive for "stabilizing" the industry in that state at the expense of the workers. The Fishwick-Howat union repudiates the local struggles of miners who refuse to pay for that agreement with joblessness and speed-up. Like the Lewis machine it stands firmly with the operators in slandering and fighting the Left-Wing movement.

But the struggles continue and widen. The workers are awakening to the realities of their situation. More and more of them are turning from the Springfield union to throw all their fighting will and mass support with the Left-

Wing union. This union, unlike both branches of the U. M. W. A., considers only the needs of the workers and recognizes the miners' struggle as part of the world-wide irrepressible conflict between the capitalist class and the working class.

CHAPTER XII

THE REVOLUTIONARY UNION
AND THE FUTURE

A CALL to rank and file miners to organize a new fighting union independent of the United Mine Workers of America was issued by militant leaders in June, 1928. All summer they went up and down through the coal fields urging a definite break with the U. M. W. A. and finding everywhere groups of workers who were ready for fresh organized struggle.

When several hundred miners assembled at Pittsburgh in September, 1928, they came not only from Pennsylvania and Ohio, Indiana and Illinois, and from the anthracite, but from West Virginia and Kentucky, and from Kansas and the fields further west. They came from local unions; from little rebel groups within local unions; and from unorganized mines. They represented thousands of workers who were not only convinced of the corruption of the old machine but were ready to organize a new union for aggressive struggle against the operators.

The week before the convention, Frank Bonita, a local Left Wing leader in the anthracite, had been murdered. Two days before the convention, George Moran, leading the demand for election of Left Wing delegates from the local union at Bentleyville, near Pittsburgh, was so viciously attacked that he died of the injuries. Moran's assailant, Louis Carboni, had been a stool-pigeon among the Left Wingers; he was cleared by the grand jury.

At Pittsburgh the reactionary mine union officials and the police mobilized their forces to prevent the convention from meeting. Paid pickets, thugs, and United Mine Workers' pay-rollers marched up the street and attacked the delegates as they were entering the hall for the opening session. After delegates' heads had been cracked, the police dashed in and arrested the victims. Some 25 Left Wing leaders and delegates were taken from the hall and thrown into jail. Then the police raided the hotels where delegates were staying and gathered in over a hundred more. After twenty-four hours in jail without a hearing, the prisoners were discharged by the court.

The National Miners Union

Meanwhile most of the delegates had found their way to a hall outside the city limits, where the convention continued until it was located by detectives and broken up by the sheriff of Allegheny county just as the army of Lewis thugs were driving up to renew their vicious assault. But the National Miners Union had been organized and basic principles had been adopted, which were later incorporated in the preamble to the union constitution.

Our organization declares that the interests of the employers and those of the workers have nothing in common but are diametrically opposed to one another. The history of the coal miners, as well as all the workers of the country, is that of an incessant struggle between these two classes—the class struggle. . . . We will proceed on this basis to wage a militant struggle for our rights against the employers. Simultaneously we will strive to educate our members and the workers of other industries to recognize the need of independent working class political action as an additional weapon in this struggle. . . . We declare we will not only organize the Negro miners in every field but also draw them into full participation and leadership in our organization. . . . Our organization shall ever remain truly class-conscious. It will render support and show its solidarity with all workers in their struggles in other industries as well as with the working class internationally. . . . It shall by the use of all the power at its command, vigorously carry out its mission to secure for its members shorter hours, higher wages and better working conditions and proceed as an organization of the class struggle for the final abolition of capitalistic exploitation.

Salaries of officers and organizers are limited to "the average wage earned by the miners when fully employed." The last word in the calling of strikes is left not with the officials of the union but with the rank and file workers themselves.

Against this militant union based squarely on the class struggle and repudiating all agreements signed by the U. M. W. A. officials, both branches of the old bargaining union have lined up with operators and police.

In southern Illinois when some 10,000 mine workers struck under N. M. U. leadership in December, 1929, the Fishwick machine followed the same old Lewis tactics, sending thugs to attack the picket lines, welcoming the state militia, and helping the operators to bring the strikers back to the mines. The *Illinois Miner* has kept up with the *United Mine Workers Journal* in spreading slanderous stories against the National Miners Union.

In the anthracite where U. M. W. A. officials have been powerless to prevent mass walk-outs at some of the biggest collieries, the district officials, mine superintendents, and local authorities have pounced down on every N. M. U. organizer who attempts to hold a meeting.

In Ohio, where the Left Wing following is large, the criminal syndicalism law (like the sedition law in Pennsylvania) is dangled over the heads of Communists and other militant leaders.

In Alabama, organizers among miners and other workers have been arrested and convicted under the old "vagrancy" law and threatened with imprisonment and the chain gang. The demand for equality of white and Negro workers rouses specially vindictive hostility in southern fields.

Six months after its organization the National Miners Union, in accordance with its principles of international class struggle, affiliated with the Red International of Labor Unions. A strong delegation of white and Negro miners took part in the rousing convention which organized the Trade Union Unity League at Cleveland in September, 1929.

Several local strikes against unbearable wage cuts were successfully led by the N. M. U. in northern West Virginia, western Pennsylvania, Ohio, and Kentucky.

REORGANIZATION IN 1930

Organizers had also been sent among the metal miners, and at the second national convention of the National Miners Union at Pittsburgh, July 1930, the union was placed on a broader industrial basis and the name was changed to Mine, Oil and Smelter Workers Industrial Union. The constitution was amended to make even more emphatic the class struggle basis of the union:

This industrial union is organized to unite all workers in the mining, oil, smelting and refining and quarrying industry and to lead them in their struggles against the capitalists for better working and living conditions and for ultimate abolition of wage slavery. This industrial union is founded on the principle of the class struggle . . . which must continue until the working class has conquered political power and abolished capitalism as a system, replacing it by a socialist society. . . .

For this reason our industrial union does not limit itself to narrow craft or occupational interests, or even to the far wider interests of all the workers in our industry, but considers itself always as an integral part of the forces of the working class.

The new M. O. S. W. I. U. will fight for the day by day needs of the miners and for their interests as a section of the whole working class. The major immediate demands include the following:

1. A minimum wage of $35 per week.
2. Union checkweighman elected by the rank and file.

3. Extra pay for extra work.
4. Abolition of the check-off.
5. Five-day week, 6-hour day.
6. Workers Social Insurance Bill, including work or full wages for all unemployed mine workers.
7. Unconditional release of all class war prisoners.

The union also demands recognition of a mine committee elected by the rank and file to take the lead in local struggles over daily grievances. Local union committees are responsible to district and national committees, but at the same time responsibility of the central leadership to the will of the rank and file members is a basic principle.

Struggles of the mine workers affect the entire working class population of the mining centers and wives, daughters, and sisters of the miners have often shown their militancy. Their active participation in the union is indispensable. A woman's department is organized to bring the workers' families into the union on a basis of full equality with the mine workers.

A youth section is devoted to the special problems of the younger miners.

Formation of unemployed councils by the unemployed mine workers is stressed as a major task. "Since permanent mass unemployment is characteristic of present-day capitalism, the M. O. S. W. I. U. declares for the unity of employed and unemployed workers in all struggles."

Solidarity of white and Negro miners is a reality in the revolutionary union as it is not in the United Mine Workers of America. While the U. M. W. A. has been one of the few A. F. of L. unions admitting Negro workers to membership, no Negro has ever sat on a national committee nor held an important district office. Also the U. M. W. A. has accepted without a fight the grossest race discrimination by mine bosses, landlords, and shopkeepers at various places where the mines operated under union agreement.

The Perspective of Struggle

The new M. O. S. W. I. U. will oppose at every turn the policies of both branches of the United Mine Workers which are trying to help union operators to increase their profits, accepting speed-up practically on the operators' terms, and agreeing that thousands of workers must somehow find their living outside the mining industry.

All groups of U. M. W. A. officials talk about "remedies" for the coal industry under capitalism, such as regulation by a capitalist government, or amendments to the anti-trust laws to hasten consolidations and monopoly price-fixing by the operators. Liberals and Socialists offer plans for government regulation of production or for actual nationalization of the mines—with compensation to the mine owners which for years to come would drain off more millions for the capitalist class from the product of the mine workers' labor.

Militant union leaders approach the whole problem differently. They believe that all the "remedies" proposed for the operators' problems would make the crisis more serious and more unbearable for the workers. Nationalization under capitalism would intensify the speed-up and unemployment, while at the same time it would reduce the workers to a condition of strikeless servitude. They believe there is no permanent solution of the coal problem under capitalism. But they know that even in this period of worldwide crisis, the capitalist class is drawing off millions of dollars every year from the value created by the mine workers; therefore, the first and most immediate function of a strong aggressive union is to increase the workers' share in this value which the workers are creating.

By leading militant local strikes against wage cutting and

speed-up and for its immediate demands, the Mine, Oil and Smelter Workers Industrial Union is working toward a far wider basis, when workers in all mines and related industries will be organized in a nationwide union and ready to carry on a militant nationwide struggle in the interest of the whole working class.

Not only in the economic struggles of the miners but also in the political field the M. O. S. W. I. U. declares its principles. It states:

While striving constantly for the immediate improvement of all living and working conditions in our industry, our industrial union cannot and does not limit itself to the economic aims and struggles alone; but since in their economic struggles workers always come into conflict with the capitalist government, and economic struggles always become political struggles, our union also takes part in all political struggles led by the political party of the working class.

Declaring that the only political party of the working class is the Communist Party, the M. O. S. W. I. U. during October, 1930, went on record as endorsing and wholeheartedly supporting the election platform and candidates of the Communist Party in the elections of that year.

MINERS IN THE SOVIET UNION

Such floods of false propaganda have been poured forth against conditions in the Soviet coal mines that many American workers do not yet realize what the Russian Revolution has brought to Russian miners. For years the old-line union organs have been making false statements about miners' earnings in the Soviet Union. Now coal operators find a chance for rousing anti-red prejudice by claiming that the small importation of Russian anthracite is a menace to the American anthracite industry; they claim that it is produced by convict or forced labor and will therefore pull down the living standards of American miners.

The absurdity of these charges is plain. As far as the menace to the American anthracite industry is concerned, they know that the total imports from all countries are less than 1 per cent of the anthracite tonnage consumed in the United States and less than one-tenth of the anthracite exported yearly from American mines. They know that imported anthracite brings a higher price than American anthracite because of exceptional quality, meeting special industrial needs. And they know that a far larger tonnage of British than of Soviet anthracite is imported year by year.

The charge of forced labor is a direct and deliberate effort to misrepresent to the restless and exploited American workers the true condition of workers in the Soviet Union.

What are the facts?

Workers' Freedom

The mine worker in the Soviet Union has far greater freedom than the worker in any capitalist country. He has freedom to criticize his mine manager and his government. The personal attitude of the workers and the columns of the Soviet press testify to every traveler that the rank and file use this freedom with vigor and intelligence.

Practically all the mine workers are members of the labor union which negotiates with the coal trust as management the collective agreements fixing details of wages and working conditions for the industry as a whole and for the individual mine. But the management does not represent a separate class whose interests conflict with the interests of the workers, for all private profit has been eliminated. The state coal trusts function as part of the workers' state, and union representatives sit with technicians and administrators on the various bodies which plan and control production. Most of these executives are themselves men who were formerly rank and file workers in the industry. Taking the mineral industries as a whole, including oil works and metal mines, about 6,000 workers have been transferred to administrative positions. This figure does not include workers who are executives in the union.

The coal miner gets his job through the public labor exchange. After a brief trial period he is taken on as a permanent worker who cannot be discharged without due cause, although he is free to leave the job and seek another if he so desires. Strikes are few, not because they are forbidden but because conditions are well adjusted through the union, and the economic basis for the conflict of interest between operators and miners has been eliminated.

Miners through their labor union control general conditions of safety and share with other workers in administration of employment offices, social insurance funds, and hospitals.

The miner, like other Russian workers, is free from the three great haunting dreads of the working class under capitalism, for the Soviet Union has a complete system of social insurance, maintained by contributions from the industries, and providing for old age, sickness or injury, and possible unemployment.

The worker is free to enjoy labor-saving machinery. "Rationalization" in capitalist countries brings speed-up, more intense exploitation, and mass unemployment. In the Soviet Union, where industry functions in the interest of the working class, "rationalization" is shortening the hours of work and raising the level of life for all workers.

Day by Day Conditions

A miner works six hours a day underground, and the six hours are reckoned *from bank to bank,* including the traveling time from the mine mouth to the face of the coal and back again to the surface. Hours are even shorter when the working place is exceptionally wet or difficult. Thousands of surface workers already have the 7-hour day.

Under the Five-Year Plan, no worker in the coal industry will after 1931 have a day longer than 7 hours.

Miners like other industrial workers in the Soviet Union now have one day of rest after every four days of work. Every underground worker receives a month's vacation with full pay every year. The surface worker has a two weeks' vacation, also with full pay.

If a mine worker is so sick or so badly injured that he must go to the hospital, he is cared for free of charge and in addition receives 75 per cent of his regular wage if he is married and 50 per cent if he is single. If hospital care is unnecessary, he has free medical attention and *full pay* throughout the time of illness or disability.

Housing is free for workers in the Soviet coal fields, or the charge for rent is so small as to be merely a nominal payment. Electric light, fuel and other municipal services are entirely free. Working clothes, boots, tools, and lights, are supplied to miners by the industry. Restaurants, clubs, and schools are also supported by the administration. The Workers' Club at the Stalin Coal Mines in the Donetz Basin is a fine modern building far better in physical equipment than any "welfare club" provided by the most "progressive" private corporation in this country. Unlike the "welfare work" and the company towns of the United States, which are poisoned by despotism and anti-union espionage, all such activities are managed by the workers themselves. Clubs and libraries have spread throughout the coal fields in recent years. The workers having an active share in such cultural work are five times as many as they were in 1923.

While wages in every capitalist country are being pushed downward and mass unemployment has thrown millions of workers and their families into a destitution that borders on starvation, the Soviet Union alone is raising the level of wages and eliminating unemployment. Soviet miners are already earning more in a 6-hour day than they earned before the Revolution in a 10- to 12-hour day. Their daily wages, including insurance, housing and work clothes, are higher than the wages of miners in Great Britain or any European country.[1]

Carefully planned expansion of the coal industry is a basic feature in the Five-Year Plan for the upbuilding of Socialist industry in the Soviet Union.[2] This includes not only increased production but a systematic increase of wages. During the year 1929-30 coal mine wages rose by 12.5 per cent and a further increase of 15 per cent is planned for 1930-31.

Improved housing is also raising the miners' standard of living. Before the Revolution more than 40 per cent of the workers in the Donetz coal fields were crowded into badly built, unsanitary barracks maintained by the companies. Great progress has already been made toward housing all mine workers in modern dwellings of a substantial and convenient type. During the current year (1930-1931) about 250,000,000 roubles ($125,000,000) will be spent under the Five-Year Plan for additional dwellings in the coal fields. Housing construction is managed by the workers through their labor union.

The rising coal production has drawn tens of thousands of new workers into the industry. While one-fourth of the coal miners in the chief coal countries of the capitalist world have been thrown out of the industry, the number employed in Soviet coal mines has doubled. Not unemployment but a shortage of workers is the problem there.

With their regularity of employment, their steadily rising wages and standard of living, their social insurance, and their freedom in the workers' state, the Russian miners are already better off than the miners in any other country in the world. For them the future is full of hope.

Struggles Ahead in Capitalist Countries

In every other country, between a dark present and the hopeful future, lies a period of struggles which will grow steadily sharper. The capitalist class is making a last desperate stand to defend its "right" to exploit the workers.

Coal operators, like the masters in other industries, are trying to save themselves in the world crisis of capitalism by reducing the numbers of workers and compelling those whom they employ to produce more at lower wages. Social-Democratic unions in Germany, the Labor Government in Great Britain, "progressives" and reactionaries in control of the old-line American unions, are all serving the capitalist class and betraying the workers in this crisis. All the forces of the capitalist state are lined up to prevent resistance by the working class.

They will continue to spread poisonous lies about the Soviet Union in a vain effort to convince the workers who are still in subjection to capitalism that the workers' state is a failure. The capitalist class and its servants seek to blot out from the vision of workers in capitalist countries the great achievements of the Soviet Union which give these workers fresh hope and eagerness in their struggle.

It is already a worldwide conflict which may break at any moment into open war between the capitalist governments and the workers' state in the Soviet Union. The Left Wing union will lead the mine workers in the United States, already driven to revolt by the tactics of the operators, to see their struggles against this worldwide background of class conflict and to throw their great fighting power with the revolutionary forces of the working class.

REFERENCE NOTES

CHAPTER I

1. Aktien Gesellschaft Reichskohlenverband, *Jahresberichte,* 1924-25 and 1928-29.
2. *U. S. Census of Manufactures,* 1927. The 1927 "value added" is adjusted for comparison with 1919 "value added." See U. S. Bureau of Labor Statistics bulletin No. 521, page 72, for changes in wholesale purchasing power of the dollar, non-agricultural commodities.
3. Lloyd's Register of Shipping, *Annual Reports of the Society's Operations.*
4. Lubin and Everett, *The British Coal Dilemma,* p. 61.

CHAPTER II

1. *What the Coal Commission Found,* p. 92.
2. *Hearings under Sen. Resolution 105,* pp. 1143-47. For full title see documents in Bibliography, p. 250.
3. *U. S. Coal Commission Report,* p. 41.
4. Capital stock tax returns, in United States Internal Revenue Office report on *Statistics of Income for 1925,* showed for 3,793 companies (including coke and peat producers) a total of stock values, bonds and mortgages of approximately $2,500,000,000 in 1925-1926. Bonds and mortgages represented 22 per cent of this total.
5. Based on analysis of income tax data in *Preliminary Report on Depletion* filed with the Joint Committee on Internal Revenue Taxation, 1929 (pursuant to Section 1203 (b) (6), Revenue Act of 1926, Vol. I, Part 8).
6. United States Federal Trade Commission, *Investment and Profit in Soft Coal Mining,* 67th Congress, 2d session, Senate Document 207.
7. *Wall Street Journal,* April 27, 1929.
8. Pittsburgh Coal Company $20,000,000 bond issue, advertisement in *New York Times,* January 21, 1929.
9. Standard Corporation Records, Individual Reports Section, E 2, revision of January 8, 1929.
10. Standard Trade and Securities Service, Industries Section, October 11, 1928.
11. *Wall Street Journal,* August 27, 1928, and August 16, 1930.
12. Figures for 1924 to 1926 are based on analysis of income tax data in *Preliminary Report on Depletion.* (See note 11, 5, above.) Figures for 1927 were secured by correspondence with Internal Revenue Office.

CHAPTER III

1. Black Mountain Corporation, with 2 mines in Harlan County, Kentucky; American Eagle Colliery Co., with a mine in Raleigh County, W. Va.; and Superior Smokeless Coal and Mining Co., with a mine in Illinois and a mine in Oklahoma.
2. Seneca Coal and Coke, Tulsa County Coal, Leavell Coal, and Trojan Coal.
3. Koppers subsidiaries include Koppers Coal Co.; Elkhorn Piney Coal Mining Co. (W. Va. and Ky.); Houston Collieries Co., Houston Coal and Coke, Thacker Coal and Coke, Tidewater Coal and Coke, and Black Betsy Consolidated Coal Co., all in West Virginia; and Keystone Coal and Coke, and Melcroft Coal Co., in Pennsylvania and West Virginia.
4. Short Creek Coal, Penova Coal, Pawva Coal, Pittsburgh and Western Mining Co., and Four States Coal Co.
5. *What the Coal Commission Found*, p. 287.
6. The Berwind interests control not only the Berwind-White Coal Mining Company (with large mines in Somerset, Cambria and Clearfield counties, Pennsylvania), but also the New River and Pocahontas Consolidated Coal Co. (with six mines in Fayette and McDowell counties, W. Va.). E. J. Berwind is a director of Baker Whitely Coal Co., Somerset County, Penn. H. A. Berwind is a director of Jamison Coal and Coke in Westmoreland County, Penn., and Marion County, W. Va. The *Wall Street Journal*, October 1, 1929, announced that the Berwind-White Coal Mining Company had just purchased 18,000 acres of coal land in Wyoming and McDowell counties, W. Va., paying more than $1,000,000. For a special report on their labor conditions, see pamphlet published in 1922 by Mayor's Committee (New York City) to Investigate Labor Conditions at Berwind-White Companies' Coal Mines.
7. *Wall Street Journal*, August 3, 1929.

CHAPTER IV

1. Pennsylvania, West Virginia, and Kentucky state figures as to color and nativity of coal mine workers show slight decrease in percentage of foreign-born and a slight increase in percentage of Negro workers. The estimated totals are derived from the current numbers of mine workers in each state and the known distribution (as to race and nativity) for 1920, slightly modified according to this general trend.
2. Underground work is illegal for boys under 18 in Arizona, Michigan and New Mexico; under 17 in Texas. But these four states together employ barely one per cent of the coal miners in the country. Underground work is also included in the occupations forbidden under 18 in District of Columbia, New Jersey and Wisconsin, but these have no coal mines.
3. These statements refer to 1920. A special analysis of unpublished data from the census of 1920 was included in the report of the U. S. Coal Commission.

CHAPTER V

1. *U. S. Coal Commission Report*, p. 1431.
2. Blankenhorn, *The Strike for Union*, p. 198.
3. *Coal Age*, March, 1930, p. 148.
4. Blankenhorn, *The Strike for Union*, p. 73.

CHAPTER VI

1. *Daily Worker*, January 16, 1930.
2. *Coal Age* gave the May, 1930, number over to special articles on the Wildwood mine as the latest development in underground coal mining.
3. *New York Times*, May 25, 1928.
4. Laws forbid employment of underground workers in coal mines more than 8 hours a day in Alaska, Arizona, California, Colorado, Idaho, Missouri, Montana, North Dakota, Oklahoma, Oregon, Utah, Washington, Wyoming.

CHAPTER VII

1. Figures on workers' earnings are based on payroll studies by the United States Bureau of Labor Statistics unless otherwise stated. See Documents in Bibliography, p. 250.
2. *What the Coal Commission Found*, p. 311.
3. Earnings for 1928-29 are based on average daily earnings for first quarter of 1929 and average days of mine operation during 1928. Bituminous mines operated 16 more days on the average in 1929 than in 1928, but wages were generally cut after the period covered by the Bureau's study. Totals given are therefore roughly correct for 1929.
4. United States Women's Bureau Bulletin No. 45: *Home Environment and Employment Opportunities of Women in Coal-Mine Families.*

CHAPTER VIII

1. Estimate published on page 2 of United States Bureau of Mines Bulletin No. 319 is based on records of 68 coal mines taking part in National Safety Competition. They reported 54 non-fatal accidents for every death in bituminous mines and 81 non-fatal accidents for every death in anthracite mines. But these mines had had no disasters killing 5 or more men at a time, during the years studied, so the Bureau of Mines excludes deaths in major disasters from the total number of deaths used as a base for estimating the number of non-fatal accidents.

In Utah, where all lost-time accidents are supposed to be reported, the ratio (for two years, July 1, 1926, to June 30, 1928) was 74 non-fatal accidents to one death. Nearly half of these men lost less than 4 days away from work. In Illinois, where records do not pretend to include accidents involving less than 7 days of lost time (and therefore exclude at least half the non-fatal accidents) the ratio for three years (1926-1928) was 48 men

non-fatally injured to one man killed. This indicates a ratio
of about 100 injured to every one man killed.
2. D. Harrington and C. W. Owings, *Mine Explosions in the United
States During the Fiscal Year Ended June 30, 1929.* United
States Bureau of Mines, Information Circular, 6178.
3. United States Bureau of Mines, *Report of Investigations,* No.
2993, April, 1930.
4. D. Harrington and C. W. Owings, *op. cit.*
5. United States Bureau of Mines, *Report of Investigations,* No.
2993.
6. Alice Hamilton, *Industrial Poisons in the United States,* p. 382.

CHAPTER IX

1. Peter Roberts, *The Anthracite Coal Industry,* p. 251.
2. For contemporary accounts which reveal the bitter hostility of
the coal operators and the whole capitalist class against the mine
workers, see *The Molly Maguires,* by F. P. Dewees (1877), and
The Molly Maguires and the Detectives, by Allan Pinkerton
(1878).
3. Roy, *History of the Coal Miners,* p. 99.
4. Evans, *History of the U. M. W. A.,* Vol. 2, p. 610.
5. McNeill, *The Labor Movement,* p. 251.
6. McNeill, *op. cit.,* p. 260.
7. Evans, *op. cit.,* Vol. 1, p. 129.
8. McNeill, *op. cit.,* p. 262.

CHAPTER X

1. Commons and Associates, *History of Labour in the United States,*
Vol. 2, pp. 498-499.
2. Suffern, *Conciliation and Arbitration in the Coal Industry of
America,* p. 56.
3. Trachtenberg, *The Heritage of Gene Debs,* International Pamphlets, No. 10.
4. Glück, *John Mitchell, Miner,* p. 82.
5. *Bill Haywood's Book,* p. 135.
6. Quoted in *John Mitchell Exposed,* a pamphlet published by New
York Labor News Co. in 1905.
7. United Mine Workers of America, *Proceedings of the Twentieth
Annual Convention,* 1909, p. 66.
8. Suffern, *op. cit.,* pp. 68 and 77-79. This was not an injunction.
Under the *state laws* of West Virginia combination, picketing,
and lawful persuasion of men to leave their employment were
permitted. The action brought in 1903 and upheld by the West
Virginia Supreme Court in 1906 was based on the old *common
law* provision against those who "maliciously entice servants to
desert the service in which they are engaged."

CHAPTER XI

1. Manuscript report on *Civil Liberties in the Coal Fields,* filed
with United States Coal Commission by Zechariah Chafee, Jr.,

and others, pp. 31-32. Copy is in files of American Civil Liberties Union. A summary by Winthrop D. Lane was published in 1924 by Doran (in the Christianity and Industry pamphlet series) under the title *The Denial of Civil Liberties in the Coal Fields.*
2. Manuscript report by Chafee and others (as above), p. 18.
3. Don Brown, "So This Is America!" in *New Republic,* October 12, 1927.

CHAPTER XII

1. *Economic Review of the Soviet Union,* April 15, 1930. See also Price, *Labor Protection in Soviet Russia,* and Chase, Dunn, and Tugwell, *Soviet Russia in the Second Decade.*
2. G. T. Grinko, *The Five-Year Plan of the Soviet Union,* 1930.

APPENDICES

I. BITUMINOUS COAL MINING, U.S.A.

Totals	1929	1923	1918	1913
Production (million net tons).	535	565	579	478
Men employed	503,000	705,000	615,000	572,000
Averages				
Days of mine operation	219	179	249	232
Daily tonnage per man.......	4.85	4.47	3.78	3.61
Yearly tonnage per man	1,063	801	942	837

II. ANTHRACITE COAL MINING, U.S.A.

Totals	1929	1923	1918	1913
Production (million net tons).	74	93	99	92
Men employed	152,000	158,000	147,000	176,000
Averages				
Days of mine operation	225	268	293	257
Daily tonnage per man	2.17	2.21	2.29 *	2.02
Yearly tonnage per man	487	592	672 *	520

III. SHIFT OF BITUMINOUS PRODUCTION, U.S.A.
(Ch. IV)

	1929	1923	1913
Northern mines		*(millions of net tons)*	
Pennsylvania	144	172	174
Other states	103	147	116
Southern mines			
West Virginia and Kentucky	199	153	91
Other states	39	41	38
Western mines	50	52	59
Total bituminous	535	565	478
Northern mines		*(percentage)*	
Pennsylvania	26.9	30.4	36.4
Other states	19.3	26.0	24.3
Southern mines			
West Virginia and Kentucky ..	37.2	27.1	19.0
Other states	7.3	7.3	7.9
Western mines	9.3	9.2	12.4
	100.0	100.0	100.0

* Heavy washery output.

IV. BITUMINOUS COAL MINE WORKERS BY STATES
(Ch. IV)

Northern mines	1929	1923	1913
Pennsylvania	131,774	194,981	172,196
Illinois	56,725	99,714	79,529
Ohio	25,399	54,555	45,815
Indiana	15,250	35,408	22,235
Michigan	1,336	1,977	3,305
Northern total	230,484	386,635	323,080

Southern mines			
West Virginia	104,942	117,300	74,786
Kentucky	58,649	60,811	26,332
Alabama	25,208	30,035	24,552
Virginia	12,053	14,120	9,162
Tennessee	7,619	11,244	11,263
Maryland	3,289	3,725	5,645
North Carolina and Georgia	262	317	500
Southern total	212,022	237,552	152,240

Western mines			
Colorado	12,057	13,340	11,900
Iowa	7,295	11,448	15,757
Oklahoma	6,321	7,130	9,044
Missouri	5,618	6,952	10,418
Kansas	5,139	9,761	12,479
Wyoming	4,839	7,529	8,331
Arkansas	4,299	3,754	4,652
Utah	3,458	4,381	4,158
New Mexico	3,233	4,095	4,329
Washington	2,946	4,306	5,794
Montana	2,283	3,511	3,630
North Dakota	1,421	1,621	641
Texas	1,313	2,452	5,101
Other states and Alaska	265	326	255
Western total	60,487	80,606	96,489

| Total, U.S.A. bituminous | 502,993 | 704,793 | 571,809 |

V. 1929 BITUMINOUS OUTPUT U.S.A. (CH. VI)

Northern states	Net tons	Cut by machine under-ground	Loaded by machine under-ground	Mined in strip pits	Average daily tonnage per man
		Percentage			
Pennsylvania (bit.)	143,500,000	70	3	*	4.7
Illinois	60,700,000	76	30	9	6.1
Ohio	23,700,000	89	*	7	4.6
Indiana	18,300,000	55	18	31	7.0
Michigan	800,000	98	—	—	2.8
Southern states					
West Virginia	138,500,000	86	2	*	5.3
Kentucky	60,500,000	92	1	1	4.6
Alabama	17,900,000	66	5	2	3.1
Virginia	12,700,000	86	8	—	4.2
Tennessee	5,400,000	60	*	1	3.1
Maryland	2,600,000	24	*	—	3.1
Other states					
Colorado	9,900,000	56	*	—	4.4
Wyoming	6,700,000	70	45	1	6.0
Utah	5,200,000	79	18	—	7.1
Iowa	4,200,000	30	*	—	3.0
Missouri	4,000,000	28	*	49	3.9
Oklahoma	3,800,000	68	*	13	3.4
Montana	3,400,000	50	21	36	7.9
Kansas	3,000,000	9	—	34	3.6
New Mexico	2,600,000	22	*	—	3.8
Washington	2,500,000	28	*	—	3.8
North Dakota	1,900,000	38	—	46	6.8
Arkansas	1,700,000	49	*	5	2.7
Texas	1,100,000	2	—	28	3.9
All others	200,000	—	*	19**	†
Total	534,988,593	75	7	4	4.8

* Less than one-half of one per cent.

** Only in Georgia, where whole output is strip mined.

† Alaska 3.8; North Carolina 1.2; Georgia 1.7; South Dakota 3.2; California, Idaho, Nevada and Oregon 2.2; Arizona 1.9.

VI. WORLD PRODUCTION OF COAL, 1890 to 1929
(millions of metric tons)

Year	World Total*	U.S.A.	Great Britain
1890-1894 average	538	156	183
1895-1899 "	649	192	205
1900-1904 "	836	285	230
1905-1909 "	1,053	392	260
1910	1,166	455	269
1911	1,185	450	276
1912	1,248	485	265
1913	1,342	517	292
1914	1,207	466	270
1915	1,193	482	257
1916	1,291	535	260
1917	1,356	591	252
1918	1,333	615	231
1919	1,173	503	233
1920	1,319	597	233
1921	1,134	459	166
1922	1,228	433	254
1923	1,359	597	280
1924	1,357	519	271
1925	1,372	528	247
1926	1,365	597	128
1927	1,473	542	255
1928	1,450	523	241
1929	1,540	552	265

* World totals include lignite, of which Germany is the largest producer.

World Totals	1913	1928
Coal	1,213	1,233
Lignite ..	129	217

VII. COAL MINE DEATHS PER MILLION MAN-HOURS WORKED (Ch. VIII)

	Bituminous	Anthracite	Total U.S.A.
Underground workers			
1911-1915	2.007	1.941	2.012
1916-1920	1.839	2.032	1.868
1921-1925	2.235	1.874	2.137
1926	2.230	1.705	2.114
1927	2.091	1.987	2.054
1928	2.261	1.931	2.188
All workers			
1911-1915	1.829	1.618	1.800
1916-1920	1.626	2.153	1.637
1921-1925	2.011	1.545	1.894
1926	2.002	1.403	1.861
1927	1.899	1.644	1.830
1928	2.015	1.602	1.916

VIII. PHILADELPHIA AND READING COAL AND IRON COMPANY (Ch. II)

This company owning or controlling one-third of the un-mined anthracite in Pennsylvania, and second only to Glen Alden Coal Co. as a leading producer of anthracite, has never paid a dollar in dividends since it was organized in 1871. Until 1923, it was owned by the Reading Company, a holding company which owned also the Reading Railroad. The transportation of anthra-cite was made so enormously profitable that the stockholders in the holding company received high dividends in spite of the fact that the *mining* company contributed little or nothing to the treasury of the holding corporation. But during the war boom the mining company accumulated a surplus of over $25,-000,000. Since the "segregation" in 1923, the coal-mining com-pany has been distinct, tied to J. P. Morgan and Company who also control the Reading, but with the operations of the coal company technically separate from other interests.

Each of the six years of separate operation, the company has shown a wide margin between "sales and other earnings" and the "cost of sales, etc." Even in the strike year, 1925, this margin was close to a million dollars. The other years it has ranged from the $10,513,000 reported for 1923 to the $2,175,000 reported for 1927. In 1928, the reported margin was $7,041,000. But the amounts reported both for "sales and other earnings" and for "cost of sales, etc." vary without apparent relation to the changes in tonnage mined and the changes in anthracite prices. The published figures leave much to be explained. Each year the company reports also "other income" in varying amounts,—since 1925 less than half a million a year.

Taxes, high because of huge undeveloped reserves; interest, mainly on funded debt of over $30,000,000; and depletion and depreciation charges, together consumed in 1928 some $7,227,000. But thanks to "other income" the company reported a "profit" of $33,771. By subtracting "adjustments" and federal taxes and then adding "profit and loss credits" this sum was finally transformed into a "current surplus" of $221,562.

With such figures before us we cannot take too seriously the "deficits" of about $4,000,000 in 1925 and $6,000,000 in 1927! We note also that in spite of excessive fixed charges the company admitted a profit of about half a million in 1926 and over a million in 1924. In the boom of 1923, the profit rose to more than $4,000,000.

But there have been no dividends for stockholders, and the policy of the company is now being shaped to satisfy the stockholders' demand.

The first step is a program of expensive technical improvements by which the engineering firm of Stone and Webster, Inc., estimates that the cost of producing coal will be cut by nearly 50 cents a ton. This means a serious reduction in the numbers of workers and increased exploitation of those who are employed, while it will greatly increase the amounts drawn off by the capitalist class. For apart from the dividends which the company confidently expects to pay when the technical reconstruction is completed, the interest paid on funded debt has already been doubled by the sale of a new $30,800,000 bond issue in the spring of 1929.

VIII. SOME BITUMINOUS COMPANIES MAKING PROFITS SINCE 1923. (See pages 50 to 53.)

Not all of these companies have paid dividends every year up to 1929. Several have paid dividends on preferred stock but not on common. Two or three reported a small loss instead of a profit in 1928 and paid preferred dividends from surplus accumulated in previous years. For others no statement of recent profits is available beyond the fact of a dividend payment.

This roughly grouped list, supplementing the statements on

profits in Chapter 2, does not attempt to cover all the bituminous mining operations which have reported a profit in spite of low coal prices or which have continued part at least of their dividend payments from previous surplus.

American Coal Company of Allegany County, an Atwater company, tied up also with the Taplin interests and operating in West Virginia and Maryland. From 1916 to 1920 it paid dividends ranging from 24 to 48 per cent a year. Since 1921 it has paid dividends of 16 per cent. It has no funded debt.

Chicago, Wilmington and Franklin Coal Company, owners of largest mine in the world at West Frankfort, Illinois. Linked through Boston directors with companies in West Virginia and Kentucky.

Clinchfield Coal Company, in Virginia, whose officers are close to the Rockefeller interests.

Cosgrove-Meehan Coal Corporation, a Pennsylvania company, with operations also in Illinois and West Virginia.

Davis Coal and Coke Company, a Rockefeller company mining West Virginia coal lands leased from the Western Maryland Railway.

Hecla Coal and Coke Company, of the Hillman group in Pennsylvania.

Jamison Coal and Coke Company, a company close to the Berwind interests and operating in Somerset County, Pennsylvania, and northern West Virginia.

Kingston Pocahontas Coal Company, a West Virginia company with Insull connections and also tied up with Allied Chemical and Dye Corporation interests.

Massachusetts Gas Companies' subsidiaries, the *C.C.B. Smokeless Coal Company* and the *New England Fuel and Transportation Company,* both operating large properties in West Virginia, return at least $1,500,000 income each year to the parent company. At hearings of Senate sub-committee on coal in spring of 1928, George A. G. Wood, vice-president and trustee of New England Fuel and Transportation Company, objected to questions on organization of the company or their holdings and refused information on prices paid for coal by related companies. (Hearings on S. Res. 105, pp. 1889 and following.)

New River Company, representing a group of Boston interests and operating through 15 subsidiaries in southern West Virginia.

Peabody Coal Company, the big Insull company in Illinois and elsewhere.

Pocahontas Fuel Company, one of several mining companies in West Virginia having at least one director in common with the Norfolk and Western Railway. Paid dividends of 10 per cent to 32 per cent a year from 1916 to 1919, and a 300 per cent stock dividend in 1922.

St. Louis, Rocky Mountain and Pacific Company, operating in New Mexico.

Sunday Creek Coal Company, in Ohio, paid a 10 per cent dividend in 1927. It had no funded debt.

Truax-Traer Coal Company, after operating in the lignite fields of North Dakota spread into Illinois, and in 1929 took over the Cabin Creek Consolidated Coal Company in West Virginia.

Virginia Coal and Iron Company, controlling Stonega Coal and Coke, and closely related to Westmoreland Coal Company and to the Markle and Wentz interests in the anthracite.

Westmoreland Coal Company, operating in Pennsylvania and owning properties also in West Virginia, has no funded debt and pays dividends regularly. Since 1929 these reach the stockholders through the new holding company, Westmoreland, Inc.

A SELECTED BIBLIOGRAPHY

Some additional titles are given in the Reference Notes, pp. 235 to 239.

Bimba, Anthony, *History of the American Working Class,* International Publishers, 1927.

Blankenhorn, Heber, *The Strike for Union,* a study of the Somerset Strike, 1922-23, H. W. Wilson Co., for Bureau of Industrial Research, 1924.

Coal Crisis, The: facts from the Samuel Commission, 1925-26, Labour Research Department, London, 1926.

Commons, John R., and others, *History of Labour in the United States,* Macmillan, 1918.

Eastman, Mack, "A Brief Survey of Coal-Crisis Literature," in *International Labour Review,* May, 1926; "The European Coal Crisis, 1926-1927," *ibid.,* February, 1928.

Evans, Chris, *History of the United Mine Workers of America from 1860 to 1900,* United Mine Workers of America, Indianapolis, 1920.

Foster, William Z., *Misleaders of Labor,* Trade Union Educational League, New York, 1927.

Frankfurter, Felix, and Greene, Nathaniel, *The Labor Injunction,* Macmillan, 1930.

Gandy, Harry L., "Some Trends in the Bituminous Coal Industry," in *The Annals of the American Academy of Political and Social Science,* January, 1930.

Glück, Elsie, *John Mitchell, Miner: Labor's Bargain with the Gilded Age,* John Day Co., 1929.

Goodrich, Carter, *The Miner's Freedom,* Marshall Jones Co., 1925.

Greer, Guy, *The Ruhr-Lorraine Industrial Problem,* Macmillan, for Institute of Economics, 1925.

Guyer, John P., *Pennsylvania's Cossacks and the State's Police,* People's Publishing Co., Reading, 1924.

Hamilton, Walton H., and Wright, Helen R., *The Case of Bituminous Coal,* Macmillan, for Institute of Economics, 1925.

Hapgood, Powers, *In Non-Union Mines,* Bureau of Industrial Research, New York, 1922.

Hardman, J. B. S., editor, *American Labor Dynamics,* Harcourt, Brace, 1928. Chapters on coal by Walter N. Polakov, Corwin D. Edwards, John Brophy.

Harrington, Daniel, "Safety in Coal Mining," *The Annals of the American Academy of Political and Social Science,* January, 1926.

Hinrichs, A. F., *The United Mine Workers of America and the Non-*

Union Coal Fields, Longmans, Green, for Columbia University Studies in History, Economics and Public Law, 1923.

Horner, Arthur, and Hutt, G. A., *Communism and Coal,* Communist Party of Great Britain, London, 1928.

Hunt, Tryon, and Willits, editors, *What the Coal Commission Found,* Williams and Wilkins Co., 1925.

Kober, George M., and Hayhurst, Emery R., *Industrial Health,* P. Blakiston's Sons, 1924.

Lane, Winthrop D., *Civil War in West Virginia,* B. W. Huebsch, Inc., 1921.

Lauck, W. Jett, *Combination in the Anthracite Industry,* report presented by United Mine Workers of America to U. S. Anthracite Coal Commission, 1920.

Lubin, Isador, *Miners' Wages and the Cost of Coal* (bituminous), McGraw-Hill, for Institute of Economics, 1924.

Price, George M., *Labor Protection in Soviet Russia,* International Publishers, 1928.

Raushenbush, Hilmar Stephen, *The Anthracite Question,* H. W. Wilson Co., for Bureau of Industrial Research, 1924.

Roy, Andrew, *History of the Coal Miners of the United States,* Columbus, 1907.

Selekman, Ben, and VanKleeck, Mary, *Employees' Representation in Coal Mines:* a study of industrial representation plan of Colorado Fuel and Iron Co., Russell Sage Foundation, 1924.

Sinclair, Upton, *King Coal,* 1917.

Suffern, Arthur E., *The Coal Miners' Struggle for Industrial Status,* Macmillan, for Institute of Economics, 1926.

Suffern, Arthur E., *Conciliation and Arbitration in the Coal Industry,* Houghton Mifflin, 1915.

Ware, Norman J., *The Labor Movement in the United States, 1860-1895,* Appleton, 1929.

West, George P., *Report on the Colorado Strike,* U. S. Commission on Industrial Relations, Washington, 1915.

Zola, Emile, *Germinal.* A novel of miners' life in France in the nineteenth century.

Periodicals

The American Miner, see *Illinois Miner.*

The Annals of the American Academy of Political and Social Science. Special coal number, January, 1924.

Anthracite Miner, Hazleton, Pa. Weekly.

The Coal Age, New York. Monthly.

The Coal Digger, Pittsburgh. Published from February, 1928, to March, 1930.

The Coal Miner, Springfield. Three issues: November-December, 1926.

Daily Worker, New York.

Economic Review of the Soviet Union, New York.

The Illinois Miner, Springfield. Weekly. Name changed in September, 1930, to *The American Miner.*

International Press Correspondence, Berlin. Weekly.

Joint Conference of Coal Operators and Coal Miners, *Proceedings,* 1898 to 1924.
Labor Defender, New York. Monthly.
Labor's News, New York. Weekly. Also daily mimeographed releases of Federated Press.
Labor Unity, New York. Weekly.
The Labour Monthly, London. Special articles on strike of 1926 in June, 1926.
The Miner, London. Weekly.
Monthly Labor Review, Washington.
The Red International of Labour Unions, London. Monthly.
Der Rote Bergarbeiter, Berlin.
United Mine Workers Journal, Indianapolis. Twice a month.
United Mine Workers of America, *Proceedings* of annual and biennial conventions.
For financial reports of coal companies: Moody's *Manuals* (annual); Poor's annual volumes; Standard Statistics Co., Inc., current publications; and *Wall Street Journal* (daily).

Public Documents

League of Nations, Economic and Financial Section: International Economic Conference, Memorandum on Coal (C.E.I. 18), Geneva, 1927.
United States Bureau of Labor Statistics. Hours and Earnings in Anthracite and Bituminous Coal Mining: Bulletins 279 (1921); 316 (1922); 416 (1926). Hours and Earnings in Bituminous Coal Mining: Bulletins 454 (1927); 516 (1930).
United States Bureau of Mines.
Coal Mine Fatalities in the United States. Annual report, and monthly mimeographed statements, "series C.M.F."
Mineral Resources of the United States. (Until 1923 this annual volume was published by U. S. Geological Survey.) The coal section is also published separately. It is supplemented by weekly mimeographed statements, "series W.C.R."
Sundry printed and mimeographed reports on safety.
United States Children's Bureau. The Welfare of Children in Bituminous Coal Mining Communities in West Virginia, 1923. Child Labor and the Welfare of Children in an Anthracite Coal-Mining District, 1922.
United States Coal Commission, Report, 1925.
United States Senate, 70th Congress, 1st session, Interstate Commerce Committee, Hearings under S. Res. 105: Conditions in the Coal Fields of Pennsylvania, West Virginia, and Ohio, March-April, 1928.
—— 70th Congress, 2d session, same committee, Hearings on S. 4490 (Watson bill), December, 1928, and January, 1929.
For earlier hearings and commission reports on coal see list in *The Annals of the American Academy of Political and Social Science,* January, 1924.

INDEX

A

Accidents, 143-162, 244.
Agreements, anthracite, 131-133, 185, 188, 203, 216; central competitive, 180 ff., 201, 203, 204 ff.; other, 134, 137-138, 175, 177, 179, 193, 198, 212-214.
Alabama, 67, 80, 85, 86, 90, 94, 125, 179, 180, 203, 204, 225; strikes, 186, 191 ff.; unemployment, 119; wages, 128, 133, 135, 139, 140, 142.
Alan Wood Iron and Steel Co., 61.
Amalgamated Ass'n of Miners, 175.
American Coal Co. of Allegany County (Atwater), 66, 246.
American Eagle Colliery Co., 60, 236.
American Federation of Labor, 161, 175 ff., 182, 219, 220, 227.
American Miners' Association, 163.
Ancient Order of Hibernians, 165 ff.
Anthracite, 35 ff., 43 ff., 47 ff., 59, 64, 65, 69 ff., 80 ff., 87, 92, 108, 110, 111, 116 ff., 141, 163, 214 ff.; strikes, 164 ff., 184 ff., 201, 203, 214, 225; unemployment, 120, 124; wages, 129 ff., 141.
Arbitration, 172, 177, 185, 187 ff., 191, 193, 200, 213, 215, 217.
Arkansas, 81, 161, 205.

B

Baker-Whitely Coal Co., 71, 236.
Bankers, 66, 69-74.
Barkoski, John, 211.
Bellwood Coal Co., 60.
Bertha Consumers Co., 72.
Berwind interests, 52, 71, 72, 236, 246.
Bethlehem Steel Corp., 65, 203, 204.
Black Betsey Consolidated Coal Co., 61, 236.
Black Mountain Corp., 60, 236.
Brady-Warner Corp., 101.
Brophy, John, 218 ff.
Budgets, workers', 128, 141-142.
Butler Consolidated Coal Co., 114-115.

C

C.C.B. Smokeless Coal Co., 246.
Cabin Creek, 195.
Cabin Creek Consolidated Coal Co., 247.
Captive mines, 53, 62, 65, 67-68.
Central Competitive Field, 180 ff., 201, 204 ff.
Check-off, 181, 193, 216, 227.
Checkweighman, 106, 169, 180, 185, 188, 193, 226.
Chesapeake & Ohio R'y, 36.

Cheswick, 210-211.
Child labor, 78, 107.
Chicago, Wilmington & Franklin Coal Co., 246.
Clearfield Bituminous Co., 65.
Cliftonville march, 202.
Clinchfield Coal Co., 64, 65, 246.
Clover Splint Coal Co., Inc., 62.
Coal, changing demand for, 20-25; fields, 79-88, 119-120; tonnage produced, 17-20, 118-121, 240, 242, 243; undeveloped reserves, 38, 41-43, 245.
Coal and iron police, 97-98, 186, 209-212.
Coal industry, crisis of, 25-32, 219, 228, 234.
Colorado, 81, 86, 88, 118, 171, 188 ff., 204.
Colorado Fuel and Iron Co., 52, 64, 65, 68, 189, 191.
Comago Smokeless Fuel Co., 62.
Communist Party, 229.
Communists, activities of, 217.
Company houses, 81-86, 89-102. See also Evictions.
Company men, 103, 106 ff., 113-114, 130 ff., 138, 141, 177.
Company police, 97-98, 180-181, 184, 191, 194.
Company stores, 94-97, 193.
Company unions, 98.
Consolidated Connellsville Coke Co., 72.
Consolidation Coal Co., 38, 42, 46 56, 59, 63 ff., 71, 98, 121, 203-204.
Consolidations, 59-74, 228.
Conveyors, 109-112.
Convict labor, 178 ff.
Cosgrove-Meehan Coal Corp., 246.
Country banks, 17.
Courts, 36, 102, 167, 170, 174, 181, 184, 191, 194, 200, 202, 207 ff., 215, 218, 223, 225, 227.
Coxe Bros. & Co., Inc., 16.
Crisis, 1929-1930, 31, 124, 234.
Crozer Coal & Coke Co., 72.
Crozer Land Ass'n, 36, 72.
Crucible Steel Co., 62.
Cutler, Bertram, 65.

D

Davis Coal & Coke Co., 64, 65, 203, 246.
Dead work, 105-106, 110, 132, 137, 141, 149, 213.
Deaths, 143-146, 148-157, 244.
Debs, Eugene, 182.
Delaware & Hudson Co., 43 ff., 65.
Delaware, Lackawanna & Western R.R., 16, 47.

251

MAN TRIP COMING OUT FROM A PENNSYLVANIA MINE

—Photo by Ewing Galloway